D1624141

Praise for *The Humorless Ladies of Border Control*

"A truly remarkable book. On the surface, it's a tour diary of shows around the wilder reaches of Eastern Europe and Russia. In actual fact, however, Franz has written a profound and perceptive travelogue in the vein of Paul Theroux or Rebecca West; like them, he teaches you about the places he visits, about the people he meets, about a forgotten but fascinating corner of world culture, and ultimately, about himself." —Frank Turner, author of *The Road Beneath My Feet*

"In this amazing road tale, Nicolay captures how it feels for a wandering artist, scrounging in the underground punk scenes of Russia and the Balkans—sleepless nights and shaky trains, strong beer and unsavory companions— watching history turn inside out." —Rob Sheffield, author of *Love Is a Mix Tape*

"If there isn't already a shelf for Classic Punk Literature, we need to build it and stock it with Franz Nicolay. Part low-budget tour diary and part Slavic history lesson, this book is a love letter to the punk *vie bohème*." —Amanda Palmer, author of *The Art of Asking*

"Funny and wistful, *The Humorless Ladies of Border Control* is an engrossing romp that casts fresh eyes on Old World cultures rich in paradox. Nicolay taps into the current cultural zeitgeist in the best travelogue tradition, with vivid scenes capturing the absurdities of daily life in the context of history and a deft reading of some of the most important cultural figures." —Gregory Feifer, author of *Russians*

THE HUMORLESS LADIES OF BORDER CONTROL

Touring the Punk Underground from Belgrade to Ulaanbaatar

Franz Nicolay

THE NEW PRESS

NEW YORK
LONDON

Some material contained in this book first appeared in *Vice* (www.vice.com), *Noisey* (noisey .vice.com), *The Ruckus* (www.whatstheruckus.com), the chapbook *Complicated Gardening Techniques* (Julius Singer Press), and the essay collection *The Road Most Traveled* (Milner Crest).

Map by Ariana Nicolay

Many thanks to Emily Meg Weinstein for early readings, edits, and suggestions.

Requests for permission to reproduce selections from this book should be mailed to: Permissions Department, The New Press, 120 Wall Street, 31st floor, New York, NY 10005.

Published in the United States by The New Press, New York, 2016
Distributed by Perseus Distribution

LIBRARY OF CONGRESS CATALOGING-IN-PUBLICATION DATA

Names: Nicolay, Franz.
Title: The humorless ladies of border control : touring the punk underground
    from Belgrade to Ulaanbaatar / Franz Nicolay.
Description: New York : New Press, 2016. | Includes bibliographical
    references.
Identifiers: LCCN 2016014069 (print) | LCCN 2016014551 (ebook) | ISBN
    9781620971796 (hc) | ISBN 9781620971802 (e-book)
Subjects: LCSH: Nicolay, Franz—Travel—Europe, Eastern. | Nicolay,
    Franz—Travel—Russia (Federation) | Nicolay, Franz—Travel—Mongolia. |
    Europe, Eastern—Description and travel. | Russia
    (Federation)—Description and travel. | Mongolia—Description and travel.
Classification: LCC ML410.N615 A3 2016 (print) | LCC ML410.N615 (ebook) | DDC
    781.66092—dc23
LC record available at http://lccn.loc.gov/2016014069

The New Press publishes books that promote and enrich public discussion and understanding of the issues vital to our democracy and to a more equitable world. These books are made possible by the enthusiasm of our readers; the support of a committed group of donors, large and small; the collaboration of our many partners in the independent media and the not-for-profit sector; booksellers, who often hand-sell New Press books; librarians; and above all by our authors.

www.thenewpress.com

Book design and composition by Bookbright Media
This book was set in Minion Pro and Gloucester

Printed in the United States of America

10 9 8 7 6 5 4 3 2 1

For Maria: traveling companion, musical compatriot, translator, friend, trusted first reader, and beloved wife, without whom none of this would have been possible.

Contents

Part II

Part III

"Were I in the place of the emperor, I should not be content with forbidding my subjects to complain; I should also forbid them to sing, which is a disguised mode of complaining. These accents of lament are avowals, and may become accusations." —The Marquis de Custine

"The gentle reader cannot know what a consummate ass he can become until he goes abroad." —Mark Twain

RUSSIA

• Yekaterinburg

Tomsk
•

Krasnoyarsk
•

Barnaul
•

Olkhon Island

Irkutsk •

Ulaanbaatar
•

MONGOLIA

Introduction

I became a professional traveler. It said "musician" on my tax returns, but if you drew a bar graph illustrating how I spent my years, "music" would be a matchbox, and "travel" and "waiting" twin towers. I stopped having real friends. My old friends still saw one another, met for drinks, fell in and out of love—they just did it without me. And my new friends were either friends of necessity—we were trapped in the same rolling boxes—or of transience, necessarily shallow relationships since I wouldn't see them until their own orbit blipped through mine again. "I understood what it was like to be dead," wrote Paul Theroux of the itinerant life. "People might miss you, but their lives go on without you."

To those of an unsettled, anxious, or fretful temperament, a life of perpetual travel is a convenient Gordian solution. The insistent flicker of unease, the failing fluorescent bulb holding back despair, is at home a problem, even a sickness, crying for a solution: a new job, a new love, a new new, the unanswerable. But in travel, acknowledged to be at best uncomfortable and disorienting and at worst dangerous, one finds a convenient and all-encompassing skeleton key to the existential lock: "There is always gain," said Montaigne, "in changing a bad condition for an uncertain one." Out of sorts? Blame the jet lag. Tired? Blame the bunk on last night's train. Lashing out at those around you? Those around you are strangers and don't understand a word you've said anyway.

Having dispensed with the existential questions, we travelers are free to indulge nearly any pursuit that doesn't require possessions. Many of us settle on voyeurism, the flip side of solipsism. We adopt a God's-eye view, lordly in our solitude. We spend an afternoon—by necessity or accident—in a strange city, passing snap judgment on a society based on its customer service, road maintenance, the fashion sense of thirty minutes' worth of passersby at a café, manners of queueing and bargaining, pornography, or street-sign graphic design. We generalize from particulars and approach individuals armed with preprogrammed stereotypes. Confident in our conclusions, we claim an intuitive gift. "It is true that I have not fully seen," wrote the Marquis de Custine in his Russian travelogue, "but I have fully divined."[1] We claim the privilege of the inquisitive foreigner, the dignified heritage of Herodotus and Alexis de Tocqueville. We may get some details utterly wrong but still capture something of the larger truth—or, conversely, misrepresent the larger story but preserve some quotidian or piquant details. We ask leading questions of innocents, then spend a suspiciously long time in

---

1. Custine wrote eight hundred pages on Russia after a three-month trip, Rebecca West twelve hundred on Yugoslavia after a mere six weeks.

the bathroom scribbling out their answers or pecking them into a phone. We are sketching what V.S. Pritchett called the "human architecture," gathering basketfuls of Ford Madox Ford's "little bits of uncompleted lives," trying to patch the holes we've torn in our own lives by our leaving with rags we've picked from those of the people we pass. But let the last word on wanderlust go to Melville's Ishmael:

> Whenever I find myself growing grim about the mouth; whenever it is a damp, drizzly November in my soul; whenever I find myself involuntarily pausing before coffin warehouses, and bringing up the rear of every funeral I meet; and especially whenever my hypos get such an upper hand of me, that it requires a strong moral principle to prevent me from deliberately stepping into the street, and methodically knocking people's hats off—then, I account it high time to get to sea as soon as I can.

There is another way to travel, of course, and that is with a companion. My wife, Maria—a musician and an ethnomusicologist from a family of postwar refugees from western Ukraine—and I had long planned to ride the Trans-Siberian Railroad. In late spring of 2011, we met Dima, a young Russian from Saint Petersburg, in Kyiv. Dima had booked and was managing a month-long tour in Russia and the Russian-speaking eastern regions of Ukraine for Jeff Rowe, a singer-songwriter from Boston I'd recently met in London. When the tour reached Kyiv, I happened to be there, taking a few weeks off after finishing my UK tour, and I opened the show. Afterward I laid out my plan to Dima:

could he book me and Maria from Saint Petersburg to Lake Baikal, playing shows along the way?

He agreed, and the first leg of what became a six-month tour,
from March to September 2012, was in place: we would start in
Kyiv, tour down the industrial cities of eastern Ukraine, cross
into Russia, head north to Saint Petersburg, south to Moscow,
and then board the Trans-Siberian proper east to Irkutsk and
Lake Baikal.

From there, we reasoned, there were two options: we could
continue the three days' journey to Vladivostok on Russia's
Pacific coast, but there was nowhere of interest to stop on
that route. Alternately, we could turn south, on the Trans-
Mongolian line, through Ulaanbaatar to Beijing. I set myself
on the project of finding gigs in Beijing (where at least I had
a lead—New Jersey punk band the Bouncing Souls had played
there and put me in touch with their contact) and Ulaanbaatar
(where the best I could do was post on expat messageboards and
hope for a reply).

Tours have a way, like gas leaks or bread dough, of expanding to fill the space available. We sublet our Brooklyn apartment
in March 2012 and didn't return until September: six months,
twenty-one countries, 104 shows, and more than fifty thousand
miles later.

This story will focus in Part I on my travels with Maria in the
former Eastern Bloc countries Ukraine, Russia, and Mongolia
(May through July 2012); in Part II on my trip alone the next
year to the former Yugoslavia and farther south into the Balkan
Peninsula, Romania, and Bulgaria (March and April 2013); and
in Part III on our return the following summer, in July 2014, now
with a young daughter, to a postrevolutionary Ukraine that had

become international news in the wake of a confusing Russian invasion. (In a few places—parts of Serbia, Croatia, Hungary, and Poland—I combine and conflate two visits, one with Maria and one without, for the sake of narrative clarity.)

I concentrated on this part of the world not only because DIY punk touring in the United States, Western Europe, and the British Isles is, both literally and metaphorically, well-trod ground. First, I had a personal motive. A Slavophile since a high school Russian literature class and an enthusiast of Balkan music since an encounter with a bootleg cassette of the Bulgarian clarinetist Ivo Papasov, I wanted to visit the countries I'd spent years imagining, to put myself in the paths of past traveloguers and literary portraiteers and to compare their impressions, sometimes a century or more old, to mine in the present day.

Second, I wanted to hone in on what I think is an interesting dual story about the past and future of underground punk and rock in formerly Communist states. On one hand, it is a backward-looking story, in which a surprising number of aging rebels, from scenes and bands that had defined themselves in opposition to authoritarian communism in the 1970s and 1980s, took an unexpected (or perhaps not, like grouchy old American punks who discover a misanthropic taste for guns and libertarianism) turn toward reactionary nationalism in the 1990s and 2000s.

On the other hand, it is a forward-looking series of portraits, in their own words, of a young and Internet-enabled generation with a utopian idea of American punk, DIY, progressive politics, and communitarian ethics not unlike the romantic idea of the "Imaginary West" that anthropologist Alexei Yurchak described taking hold in their parents' Soviet generation. Despite

having little real analogue in the actual distracted and fickle
punk scene in the United States, this idea of punk provides this
generation with the moral fortitude to carve out a fragile, tenu-
ous, but extensive and resilient autonomous zone for themselves,
and to defend it against the actual physical threat from police
and right-wing gangs and the psychological battering of cynicism and disillusionment of life in societies that must often seem
to be existing, in the words of Rebecca West, in "a permanent
state of simultaneous anarchy and absolutism."

When I began writing, Russia, despite its best efforts to re-
assert itself on the world stage, remained a geopolitical cipher,
apparently impotent and certainly aggrieved. By the time I finished, Ukraine had undertaken a second popular revolution,
and Russia had responded with a passive-aggressive invasion
premised on a wink-nudge implausible deniability. It became an
international crisis when Malaysia Airlines Flight 17 was shot
down by rebels in eastern Ukraine. Overnight, the foundations
of the postwar European peace seemed a little less secure and the
resolutions of the Cold War a little less resolved.

I thought of West's *Black Lamb and Grey Falcon*, a book that
arose from her compulsion to trace how another violent act in a
distant corner of Europe—the assassination of Archduke Franz
Ferdinand in Sarajevo—led to the catastrophe of the Great War
and that tracks, almost meteorologically, the growing pressures
that led to the next war. In her epilogue, written in the midst of
that second war, she said, "If a Roman woman had, some years
before the sack of Rome, realized why it was going to be sacked
and what motives inspired the barbarians and what the Romans,
and had written down all she knew and felt about it, the record

would have been of value to historians. . . . Without doubt it was my duty to keep a record of it."

One of the people I met in Ukraine said, "It's like I'm reading a book of history, and I don't know how it ends." In my travels up until then, my engagement with the history of every place was with its past, both literary and political, but always transitory and always in a rush. Now I found myself in the midst of a story as it was written. There is nothing like West's sense of inevitable disaster in this book: several postcommunist countries, such as Poland and Croatia, seem likely to be secure and successful in the long term. Mongolia will probably remain a country on the periphery of world events, half-engulfed in the romance of its name. But Ukraine, despite an engaged and empowered polity with a liberal and European-looking vision for its future, remains unstable and vulnerable. An unpredictable and bellicose Russia is keen to exercise a renewed ambition for international influence. The story of history unfolds fast enough that the telling of it cannot hope to keep pace, and parts of this book may read like old newspapers by the time of its publication—but there is a value in capturing how people felt in the transient moment. Perhaps none of the people in this book are destined to be the men and women in the headlines, but their lives, whether they want to be a part of shaping their countries' future or just to drink cheap beer by the dam and listen to punk rock, will be parts of that story, and this book a marker of their small claim.

PART I

I.

The Humorless Ladies of Border Control *(Ukraine)*

Our roommate on the sleeper train from L'viv to Kyiv was a stocky, ham-fisted forty-five-year-old veterinarian. A friend of his, he told us, had a visa to America in the 1980s, but he got caught stealing from the grain quota and now can't go to America ever. He had conspiracy theories and opinions he was eager to share: they didn't kill bin Laden, it could have been "any tall guy with a beard"—for that matter, I, Franz, look a little like bin Laden, don't I? And we haven't seen that much of Michelle Obama recently, have we? If there's not a trumpet, it's not jazz. Vitamin C doesn't work, all you need is raspberry tea with lemon and the love of a good woman. Everyone's been there—first beer, first guitar, first girl.

He stripped down to what would once have been called his BVDs, nearly obscured by his hairless belly, and snored all night.

When we awoke, he was gone, replaced by an older man with a lined face and Clint Eastwood stolidity. "He has the saddest face I've ever seen," Maria said. He slept first, facedown and fully clothed; then, when I returned from the bathroom, he was sitting upright, bag beside him, staring out the window. He never said a word.

I was a musician then, often traveling alone, sometimes with my new wife, Maria. I hadn't always traveled alone: for years I had been a member of the kind of bands who traveled in marauding, roving packs, like "Kerouac and Genghis Khan," as the songwriter Loudon Wainwright once put it. First there was the nine-piece circus-punk orchestra World/Inferno Friendship Society, a monument to pyrrhic, self-defeating romanticism and preemptive nostalgia that still haunts me like a family lost in a war. But I had ambitions, and World/Inferno had "underground phenomenon" baked into the concept. So I jumped to a rising neo–classic rock band called the Hold Steady, which became, for a few years, one of the biggest bands in what is, for lack of a term of representation rather than marketing, called "indie rock." We opened for the Rolling Stones and played the big festivals and bigger television shows. Our victory-lap touring constituted an almost audible sigh of relief that we'd finally arrived—we'd never have to work a day job again.

But I couldn't, it turned out, take "yes" for an answer, and it seemed to me that I was still too young to settle into that comfortable chair. Amid the usual dull stew of misaligned personalities and creative sensibilities, I shrugged off (or threw aside) this rare sinecure for a keyboardist in a rock band. Compare it to the gamble of the ambitious young lawyer or financier who knows he'll never make partner at the firm. When you're on the train, one friend said, and you realize it's not going where you wanted to go, you have no choice but to jump off. You'll get bumped and bruised, and you don't know where you'll stop rolling, but you do know the train's not swerving from its track.

I enjoyed a brief palate cleanser in Against Me!, who shared the dual title of most influential punk band of their generation and most controversial soap opera of their scene. It was a brief interregnum. I wanted to test myself as an entertainer, without the crutch of volume. I wanted to see if I could walk into a room full of strangers, who might not even speak my language, and keep them, at bare minimum, from walking out of the room. I aspired to the tradesman's charisma and practical craft of the old vaudevillian, the one who may not be the best dancer or singer but knows a few jokes, can do some soft-shoe, whatever it takes to get over that night.

There is a great deal of similarity between touring life and military life: small groups of men (and it is still, almost always, men) of disparate backgrounds, bonded by close quarters, foreign places, and meager rations, engaged in activities of dubious purpose but governed by vague and powerful ideals—patriotism, punk rock, machismo. The rules are the same: Do your job. Pack light. Defend your gang, don't get off the boat, beware of strangers. Sleep stacked three-deep in bus bunks like submariners or curled in hard foxhole corners. Release your tensions in promiscuity, alcoholism, and violence. Keep your mouth shut. Keep your feet dry. Above all, don't complain.

And, like army men, when we finish our tours of duty, even if we remain in the touring world, we lose our taste for adventure: we return, like World War II veterans creating the Eisenhower suburbs, and quickly domesticate. We pair off, leave the cities for places like the Hudson Valley, Northern California, or Oxford, Mississippi, places within driving distance of an airport and a music scene but far from chance encounters with tour acquaintances. We drink quietly and alone, avoid loud bars and rock shows as places of entertainment and possibility. We tell and retell, buff and hone, our debauched and criminal war stories with those who were there when we see them, in a mutual, fictionalizing reassurance that what we did had some meaning, that we fought for the right side and maybe even won a small skirmish here and there. To outsiders, we no longer brag: we're no longer sure we were noble.

Now I lived like a pack mule, a dumb and anonymous brute whose only purpose was to carry weight from one place to another. Accordion in a backpack on my shoulders; a day bag slung from my neck over my chest; a banjo in my left hand, my right dragging a suitcase full of CDs, vinyl records, and T-shirts with my name on them. From Brooklyn by subway to Manhattan, by train to Newark, by air to Frankfurt or Kraków or London, by cab to some club or another, dragging bumping bags across cobblestones to a kebab-and-pizza storefront to wait out a winter downpour. Often it was cold—I should have brought my overcoat, I would think, but that would have meant too much excess weight and bulk. You don't travel for comfort; you travel to justify the daily discomfort, what in the last century would have been called existential neurosis. It's a kind of therapy: the nagging doubt, sadness, weariness, the sense of being a stranger in a world viewed at an oblique angle suddenly, miraculously, all has a reason—you've been traveling. It's not your past, your guilt, your family. It's just the road: you *are* tired and sore, you *are* a stranger.

I lived like a pack mule, but I had to exude the appearance of ease and confidence. I packed carefully. I traveled alone out of thrift. The shows were rarely large, but I never lost money. It was a point of pride but also a necessity and a justification. I lived like a wealthy man, though I spent as little as possible; I had little to spend. I sometimes traveled with musicians whom hundreds of people paid to see and who were provided with bread, cheese, beer, fruit, hot food, orange juice. I scavenged like a beggar or a half-forgotten houseguest. I nibbled trail mix by the handful, like a rodent. I crushed single-serving bottles of water in my fist, as if my thirst might expose me if it, itself, was exposed.

I chipped my front tooth on the rubber cork of a bottle of wine. I had pushed it in too deeply, and taken it in my teeth and twisted the bottle to squeak it loose. A true cork might have torn or bruised, but the stubborn rubber ripped the tip of the tooth before popping free. Just a flake, a grain of sand on a pristine bedsheet, but, like the princess, my tongue grew restless in its sleep, probing, rubbing, aware.

Be inconspicuous all day, I learned, except for the thirty minutes onstage, when you must be the most conspicuous thing in the room. Your livelihood depends on being unable to ignore. Artistry has nothing to do with it: anyone can ignore a good song, but few can ignore someone singing even a terrible one in their face. They want to be entertained, but they don't want it actively; you must both convince them of their need and fulfill it. You are the bottle and the wine, the vessel and the salve; they are the stubborn cork to which you put your jaw, in a grin that is both welcome and a challenge, like strange dogs meeting in an alley. Whose will is stronger? Is your wheedle wilier than their indifference? Can you bully or seduce them or turn their curiosity into interest, and then to attention? And for what? The restless tongue probes the tooth.

I marked my aging by renunciations: first I traveled with a band of nine, then with five, then with none. I sloughed off concentric circles of friends: my college friends and then my band friends stopped noticing I was away and filled my empty chair with others. Then instead of friends I had passing acquaintances with fake names whom I saw once a year when I came back through their town, if I ever saw them again. Time passed, and my body began to set its own contracting boundaries: first I couldn't sleep on floors anymore, then I couldn't sleep on couches, finally I couldn't sleep in shared rooms.

But that changed again, and I could too: I married Maria, and she joined me in this world of transience and assumed names. Two years later, we were three months into a six-month tour, playing together on our way from Poland to Ukraine. The previous months had included six weeks around the United States, followed by a counterclockwise spiral through Central and Eastern Europe. It was time, then, to abandon the car for the train and slim down for Russia and Asia, mailing or abandoning anything we couldn't carry. We repacked our remaining things in the parking lot of a rest stop: one acoustic guitar in a hard case, one banjo in a soft case, one accordion in a backpack case. Six audio cables, one tuning pedal. One hiking backpack filled with day clothes—for me, one pair of pants, one shirt, three undershirts, six pairs of socks, six pairs of boxer briefs. I had learned the army style of folding one's clothes, first in halves and then rolled into themselves, tight and elastic like hot dogs or police batons. One rolling suitcase, mostly merchandise: one dozen large white T-shirts, one dozen each black and white mediums, one dozen large black, one dozen small white; two ladies' tank tops; two dozen LPs, fifteen vinyl EPs; some stray one-inch pins. Two boxes of CDs met us in Kraków; we had sold enough to fit more in the suitcase and hoped we could restock before we crossed into Russia. Only one stage suit—two would be better, but space and airline baggage charges didn't permit the luxury. No room for regular shoes, so I wore my dress shoes onstage and off: the uniform comes first.

We returned our rental car without incident. We changed forints, crowns, and euros into złoty and back into euros, then tried to spend the change on gewgaws and water bottles. "Every traveler experiences," says Gogol in *Dead Souls*, "when scraps of paper, pieces of string, and such rubbish is all that remains strewn on the floor, when he no longer belongs to a place and yet hasn't regained the road either." We had to downshift from libertarian car touring, in which we could control our route, stop for lunch, and air-dry our dirty laundry across the backseat, but also were responsible for our pace and parking and gas and the logistics of the journey, to the contained social-democratic leisure of train travel, for which you have to pack tight and efficient and mobile, but once you're on board and give yourself over to a power greater than yourself, your time is your own. On travel days you're in an Internet-free bubble with a window and a bed and nothing to do but read, nap, snack, and think.

From Poland into Ukraine we rode a new generation of sleeper trains, an upgrade from the clunky metal midcentury model: molded plastic and triple-decker bunks with private sinks and en-suite bathrooms that don't stink of the filth of decades. Our roommate was an elderly and cranky Pole. Who could blame him for his mood as we clattered and tripped and, sweating, hoisted a camping backpack, a suitcase full of merch, a guitar, a banjo, and assorted day bags above our heads and onto the shelf? We finished a half-bottle of Italian frizzante and tried to get a few hours' sleep before we had to reckon with Ukrainian customs agents. Time to get our story straight: we're not playing any official gigs. We have some friends with whom maybe we'll play a few songs. We're giving away the CDs. We don't have any concrete plans. Just a couple of slacker Americans.

Three youngsters, two guys and a girl named Larisa, picked us up at the Kyiv station. They had moved from Kharkov and other more provincial centers to the big city and were sharing an apartment in one of the beige Soviet housing projects on the far side of the river. A couple of people had driven their cars down into the shallows and were bathing them with soap and soft sponges. Along the public beaches people sunned themselves. Russians and Ukrainians like to sunbathe vertically: stripped to their Speedos, they stand, hands on hips and arms akimbo, sans headphones or other distractions, dignified, bellies oiled, like little Easter Island statues lined up facing the water.

We showered and changed while our hosts watched roller-blading stunt videos scored to "Gonna Fly Now" and Lil Wayne. The blades had the middle two wheels removed and a reinforced bridge for sliding on railings. Larisa asked if we skated.

"No," I said. "I used to ski, though—downhill racing."

"Really? Respect." She gave me a high five.

We offered them a hard-boiled egg. "We're vegan," she said. "But can I have it for the dog?"

I didn't know dogs liked hard-boiled eggs, and anyway this

seemed conceptually inconsistent for a vegan house—but never mind. The dog wolfed down the egg.

"The country is like it's dying," said a different Larissa, a rare American of Ukrainian heritage who had repatriated. "I come home tired and depressed and I realize it's not me, it's that I was walking all day among people who are tired and depressed and it just rubs off."

"Why do you stay?" I asked.

"Well—it's just, like, I live here now. I've built a place for myself. And I can't just leave"—*like a tourist can* was the implication—"because, well, I come from an easier country, and good luck to the rest of you."

"It is not a civilized country" was the judgment of a Pole I'd met a few days before, eating with Maria's aunt and her posse of aging hipster friends at a Brazilian steakhouse in Łódź. I struck up a conversation with an owl-eyed, mustachioed man who winced when he heard we were bound for Ukraine. He had tried to set up a renewable energy program there. "Everyone warned me that it was corrupt and impossible to do business there, and I never will again. I lost 50,000 euros." He shook his head. "The people are wonderful—it is just the system is impossible."

The show was in Malaya Opera, a pink-and-white neoclassical theater that had been a cultural center for transportation workers. It was now a dilapidated hulk with dance studios and old socialist realist murals of Ukrainian peasants along the staircase. We were in the musty basement, where a kid (whose beard almost covered the "24" tattooed on his neck) ran a studio and a rehearsal room, and, apparently, lived: he dragged a twin mattress and pillow out of the show room when we arrived for soundcheck. The show was with local heroes Maloi—who would be flat-capped, anthemic punk stars if they lived in the United States or England—and was packed and sweaty.

The rhythm of train touring is not unlike that of bus tours. You are delivered to the station after the show, at midnight or one, get in your bunk, and let yourself be rocked to sleep by the sway of the car and the white noise of strangers' snores. You'll be picked up in the morning by the next town's promoter, drive to their— or, more often, their parents' or grandparents'—flat, shower, eat breakfast, nap if necessary, and try to see some of the town.

That's how it's supposed to work. In this case, when we rolled into Dnipropetrovs'k around six a.m., there was no one to greet us but a few sad pigeons. We called Vlod, our contact, twice before he answered, obviously still asleep, grunted, and hung up. We settled in at the station cafeteria for what promised to be a wait.

When he arrived, Vlod proved to be tall, slouchy, hungover, and dour. Maria tried some small talk, gesturing around the station and saying, "These buildings are pretty."

"There is nothing pretty in this town."

Off to his grandmother's apartment (his mother also lived there) on the sixth floor of a crumbling housing project, a gray skeletal torso with rotting balcony ribs. Vlod had been a journalism student and worked at a newspaper "singing songs of praise to the rich people and politicians." Now he was a technical writer, making more money, he said, but without as much fun and travel.

We wanted to go downtown to see the museum, or maybe a fortress. Vlod was unenthused: "Maybe you want to see something more . . . unconventional? There is a huge abandoned building ten minutes' walk from here. It is a monument to Soviet stupidity."

We walked to another disintegrating apartment tower, this one beyond habitation. It had been built on the side of a hill and almost immediately started sliding down into the valley. It was about twenty yards from the elementary school Vlod had attended. When the floors and walls of the building started cracking, the students didn't worry too much about a collapse: "We were just happy school was canceled." After the tower was abandoned for good, the money to tear it down never materialized. Eventually the school, which had closed to keep the kids out of the way of the demolition, simply reopened in the shadow of the gap-toothed hulk.

We scrambled over the piles of rubble, clumps of weeds, and blooms of broken bottles, up the urine-scented remains of the stairs to the soggy roof. The whole city was ringed with identical "monuments to Soviet stupidity"—a miles-wide Stonehenge of graffiti-splashed white concrete, separated by the green blooms of trees. Dnipropetrovs'k is, according to the UN, the world's fastest-shrinking city, forecast to shed 17 percent of its population in the next ten years. Vlod and his friends did "rope jumping" from the top of the ruin—a kind of amateur ziplining in which you just freefall and wind up hanging in the middle of the slack rope like abandoned laundry until your friends haul you back to the roof.

Vlod had been to the United States twice on summer work/travel visas. It is common for Ukrainian and Russian teenagers to be given a temporary visa arranged through a U.S. business looking for cheap summer labor. Nearly universal is the complaint that this often means, in practice, working grueling hours at someplace like a Carvel in a rest stop in middle-of-nowhere New Jersey. The more resourceful quit and hit the road while the visa is still good.

Vlod was sent first to Connecticut, where he finished his job and then took a Greyhound across the country. "It was the trip of a lifetime," he said. "I prefer traveling on bus. In Ukraine, on a train the view is always the same—station, factory, trees, station, factory, trees." When he signed up for a second go-around, though, they sent him to Pennsylvania, where "they treated us like slaves. I said they couldn't do that. They said I'd be fired, and the next day I was and they put me on a bus to New York and a plane home."

There was an unusual culture clash at the show, and I wondered how Vlod came to organize it at this particular venue. We usually ended up in dank, graffiti-covered "youth centers," but this was a spotless white gallery and cultural center, funded by a single rich benefactor. The theater's director, Olya, was from Kazan' in Russian Tatarstan but had just returned from a failed marriage in California. The staff were ironic, urban, cosmopolitan. They and Vlod—who usually booked punk and metal at a bar on the other side of town—regarded each other warily, if at all. Sophisticate or no, Olya was rubber-legged drunk at the end of the night. We bunked up in the attic and hit the train station in the morning bound for Kharkov.

Stations upon stations indeed, as Vlod had complained: some piled with rusted debris, some graffiti-splashed concrete, one home to a dark-green old train car emblazoned with a red star, as if from a Cold War newsreel—what Proust called "peculiar places, railway stations, which do not . . . constitute a part of the surrounding town but contain the essence of its personality."

Families parked their old Ladas next to the tracks and spread out picnics, the coming and goings of trains enough entertainment for the day. Young men in stonewashed jeans and ponytails, or with shaved heads and black Adidas track pants, watched an endless array of thin, busty blondes in vertiginous patent-leather heels. Next to the tracks wiggled a dual carriageway of bicycle-wheel ruts. A wall of trees shaded a shrubbery moat. Then miles of fields.

Nearly every ex-Hapsburg town in Eastern and Central Europe will tell you they have the biggest clock or bell tower and the biggest central square in Europe. In Ukraine, they will add that they have the biggest remaining statue of Lenin. Kharkov's claim is the largest square in Europe, depending on whether you count Red Square or something (Kharkov native son Eduard Limonov says in his 1990 book *Memoir of a Russian Punk*, "'Only Tiananmen Square in Beijing is bigger than our own Dzerzhinsky Square'—Eddie-baby knows that first commandment of Kharkov patriotism well"). Writer and musician Alina Simone wrote of the city, from which her parents had emigrated, "Invariably, the two words people used to describe Kharkov were either industrial or big. Occasionally big and industrial were helpfully combined to yield the illuminating phrase 'a big industrial city.'" I saw many more Soviet remnants in Kharkov than anywhere else I'd been: hammer and sickle facades, shiny red Lenin medallions on sides of buildings, the odd "Glory to Work" mural over a gray housing project. The apartment towers were missing the pastel-wash veil they get in Eastern Europe.

The Kharkov show was abruptly canceled, if in fact there ever was a show. The status reports went from TBA to "open-air picnic" to "I don't know, it says rain" to "You must have known the show could get canceled." We couldn't find our hotel, which was supposed to be near the train station. It was pouring rain. We took shelter under a liquor store awning and asked for directions from a kiosk operator, then a cabdriver, then some young dudes on the sidewalk—no one seemed to be able to agree where the street our hotel was supposed to be on was. We mule-trained up a hill that seemed right only to find a dirt road. This couldn't be it—the station hotel, within sight of the McDonald's, on a dirt path? I ran up the hill and back. Sure enough, that was it, and in fact it was a perfectly nice little place with a *banya* (steam bath) in the basement. After a pilgrimage for Georgian food (it was getting on six, we still hadn't eaten yet, and I was now sick as the proverbial dog), it was a circuitous walk home past the Constructivist gigantoliths overlooking that second-biggest-square-after-Red-Square and, for good measure, "the second-biggest Lenin." Lenin gestured in approval of the tents that crowded the square, advertising the upcoming Euro 2012 soccer tournament. The rain had stopped.

We had a message from booking agent Dima: "You have a show tomorrow in Donetsk, no guarantee, but they'll pay your ticket to Rostov-on-Don." We stopped at the bus station to see how painful it would be to get to Donetsk by tomorrow. There was a bus at noon, but "they don't sell that ticket in Ukraine."

They don't sell in Ukraine a ticket for a bus . . . in Ukraine?

No. "Six a.m. or eight a.m."

Eight a.m. it would have to be, and we hit the banya to sweat out the bad news.

The morning's cabdriver quoted us a price of fifty, Maria said forty, he hemmed for a minute, and, thinking she was my guide, said in Russian, "How about forty-five? Tell him fifty, and you can keep the rest for yourself." When he dropped us at the station, a man was loading boxes of live chickens into the storage bins beneath the bus. The fact that there was a space under the bus was actually a pleasant surprise, since it meant we were in a modern bus, not an old Soviet Ikarus, an exhaust-stinking, shock-free diesel monster. We asked to put our bags in the bays. "Not now," said the driver. "There are cameras on me. You will have to pay extra." The bus swung around the corner of the building and parked a hundred yards away. We threw the bags underneath and boarded without incident or extra charge.

The bus stopped for a bathroom break in a village (Izyum, meaning "raisin") about halfway between Kharkov and Donetsk. A statue of a woman in a flowing dress strode confidently into the future. A dog slept in the sun in front of an ice cream cart, whose attendant yelled at me for leaving the freezer door open while I counted my cash. A young boy fingered a Rubik's Cube faster than I'd ever seen, first with both hands and then with just one. He was the "Tommy" of Rubik's Cube. Two tall, bullet-headed Georgians with sleepy eyes made gentle fun of the etchings of Georgian tourist attractions printed in their passports. My health had started to crumple under the effects of the short, sleepless nights, and there's not much worse than having a cold in the dusty summer heat. Primary-color Ladas scattered across the streets like M&M's.

Halfway through the six-hour sauna of a bus ride, we got another text from Dima: "The Rostov venue"—this was the first show in Russia, supposedly two days hence—"gave me the wrong date! It's tomorrow. Oh, by the way, there are no trains to Russia either. Please buy a bus ticket at the station when you arrive."

Andrey, who was supposed to pick us up in Donetsk, called Maria, who'd been sleeping, for a status report. "I think . . . the bus broke down, we're still in Slovyansk." That's what she'd heard the guy behind us saying to his friend on his phone. The guy tapped her on the shoulder and explained that he'd been lying to his friends because he was late. "Oh, we're in Donetsk!" she corrected. "Almost there."

We pulled in. "Where's our guy?" She scanned the parking lot. "Not the hippie!"

A gangly ostrich of a man strutted across the gravel, juggling, woven bag over his shoulder, a couple of halfhearted dreadlocks, zipper pull in one earlobe, a curl of bone in the other, apron tied over corduroy cutoff shorts. He grinned, gathered his juggling balls, waved.

"Yup, it's the hippie," I told Maria. "Are you Andrey?"

"Nope, they sent the waiter. I'm Anton!"

Anton was a cheery fellow, as are most hippies at first. He took Maria to the ticket counter to explore our options for crossing the Russian border.

"You got a ticket?" I asked when they returned.

"Yeah, but you're not gonna like it!" Anton grinned. "Leaving tonight at midnight, arrive seven a.m."

Donetsk seemed less weighted by physical history than other eastern Ukrainian or Eastern European cities. It was founded only in 1869—by John Hughes, a Welsh mining magnate—and destroyed in World War II. It had, to me, the faint scent of Texas: new mineral wealth showing off, fresh construction, unstained pavement, a pink Hummer parked outside a coffee shop. Donetsk is home to Ukraine's richest man, the steel and coal tycoon Rinat Akhmetov, who operates the region nearly as a personal fiefdom (when fighting broke out two years later and ground the local economy to a halt, thousands of workers stayed solvent because his factories stayed open and continued to pay their salaries). Anton came to our table in the club with plates of pasta.

"Dinner for my capitalist friends!" he announced.

"Did he just call us his capitalist friends?" I asked Maria.

"Is a joke!"

We asked promoter Andrey if he thought that the bottle of wine he had given us would be an issue at the border. "In this part of the country, it's barely a border," he said.

(Two years later, it barely was. In the wake of the annexation of Crimea by Russia, separatist provocateurs began referring to the southeastern provinces of Ukraine as Novorossiya—"New Russia"—and declared a "Donetsk People's Republic." Unacknowledged Russian arms, tanks, and soldiers poured across the border from the Rostov region. Bombing destroyed the Donetsk airport and much of the city, including the hospital. The train station closed. Heat and water were scarce. Those who could leave the region fled: 1.5 million of the region's prewar population of 4.5 million are said to have gone either to Russia or to western Ukraine, depending on their political sympathies. The Russian government both represented the separatists at peace negotiations and denied any control over them. The American government considered sending arms to the Ukrainians.)

"I don't like U.S.A., but I like you!" said an audience member after the show. The cab we were supposed to take to the bus station sped away in a huff because his trunk was full and we had too many bags. We packed into the next one, and a drunk jumped in the front seat. I thought he was with the driver until he got out at an intersection, gave us a double thumbs-up to confirm that we had the money, and split.

We passed the new stadium, built to hold Euro 2012 matches. The old one had been tiny and on the outskirts of town. The new one was lit up in blue like Giants Stadium and was almost as big. A massive statue of Winged Victory, also lit, stood out front. The cabdriver gestured to the hotel across the way: "That, too, has been there forever. And now in the last month they're calling it a four-star hotel." (The stadium was damaged by artillery shelling in 2014, and the Donetsk team now plays on the other side of the country, in L'viv.)

The station was dark, but the security guard, smoking cigs and drinking beer, assured us that the bus to Rostov was coming. He told the driver that it was a four *hryvnia* charge to continue into the parking lot. We got out on the curb instead. The bus pulled up some time later.

It was an hour's wait to board, and a two-year-old girl had the best idea of anyone for making use of her time: jump on the curb, jump off the curb, shake your ass, kick the aluminum wall, get daddy to swing you around like an airplane. Cabdrivers offered to take us the six hours straight to Rostov-on-Don. We all boarded, crammed into every seat. Truly, as Dr. Pangloss never said, this was the worst of all possible worlds.

It was three a.m. when we reached the border crossing. The horizon brightened even as the near-full moon was still in the sky. The Russian authorities filed on, tight-lipped and tight-haired, and I had an idea for a worst-selling pinup calendar: "The Humorless Ladies of Border Control." A guard mumbled his way through some boilerplate. As he left, someone said, "Use your street voice!" The guy sitting next to us joked, "He was asking 'Everyone all right? Need a drink? Not too cold?'"

We sat for three hours at the border, from three a.m. to six a.m. Legions of pigeons were nesting and hatching in the eaves under the tin roof of the Ukrainian exit station, and the cacophony of coos, chirps, and warbles was maddening. We were given two cigarette breaks. A dozen giggling women ran into the field and hoisted their skirts to pee.

Of nineteenth-century Russian customs and border agents, the Marquis de Custine wrote, "The sight of these voluntary automata inspires me with a kind of fear . . . every stranger is treated as culpable upon arriving on the Russian frontier."

The paranoia and vindictively selective enforcement had begun thousands of miles to the west, at the Russian consulate on the Upper East Side of Manhattan. We'd expected some procedural difficulty getting an entry visa at the Chinese embassy, located in the shadow of the USS *Intrepid* on the desolate West Side, but had sailed through the lines, frictionless. We simply dropped off our passports, photos, and a check for two hundred bucks and a week later picked up the passports with our photos laminated onto a visa page.

The Russians, though, were a different story. Mark Twain, writing over a hundred years earlier, complained that Russians "are usually so suspicious of strangers that they worry them excessively with the delays and aggravations incident to a complicated passport system." We were required to fill out the PDF application in advance and show up at the consulate building between nine thirty a.m. and twelve thirty p.m. to apply in person.

The first day, we arrived at ten thirty a.m. and joined the line on the sidewalk, about twenty people deep.

"Well, this shouldn't take too long," I thought.

Two hours later, only five people had entered the building.

"Come back tomorrow," said the burly security guard in a thick Russian accent and slammed the iron cage around the door shut.

We looked at our linemates, none of whom seemed shocked. All of them, besides ourselves, were professional line-standers, paid by visa applicants with more money and less free time—or more sense—than we had. They brought books, lined up before the doors opened, and hoped for the best (or, if they were paid by the hour, the worst).

We returned the next day, at nine a.m. this time, and waited a mere hour and a half outside before being ushered through the glass doors into a waiting room, then to a Plexiglas window like a bank teller's. A blonde stereotype of a sadistic Slavic bureaucrat didn't look up from her desk.

"Papers!" she barked, of course. "Passports!"

She read unhurriedly through the applications, marking them with a red pen, first mine, then Maria's.

"Twenty-six!" she said, circling that box forcefully. "It is wrong." She shoved the papers back through the slot beneath the window.

Item number 11 took one's passport number, issuing country, and dates of validity. Item 26 asked, "List all countries which have ever issued you a passport." Since she had already entered her passport information, Maria had left it blank instead of entering "United States."

"Obviously this was just an oversight," she said to the lady. "Can't I just write it in?"

"No! Reprint it and come back tomorrow." If she'd had a shutter to slam shut, she would have.

"We've been here two days in a row!"

She muttered to herself, scribbled something in Russian on a Post-it note, slid it to us, and got up from her chair. The interview was over.

"What does the note say?" I asked Maria.

"It says, 'Can skip line.'"

"We're supposed to show armed guards a Post-it note?"

"Russia is the land of useless formalities," complained Custine, who was himself detained in customs for twenty-four hours while trying to enter Saint Petersburg. "Much trouble is taken to attain unimportant ends, and those employed believe they can never show enough zeal . . . having passed through one formality does not secure the stranger from another."

Yet societies that insist on procedure and red tape can be simultaneously riddled with informal, ad hoc loopholes. We arrived early on the third day, not a little dispirited. We knocked on the cage and showed the guard the note. He waved us in.

I should properly introduce my other traveling companion on the Russian leg of our journey: a Frenchman, the Marquis Astolphe de Custine, author of the 1839 book *Empire of the Czar: A Journey Through Eternal Russia*. He served the same role for me in Russia that Rebecca West would in the Balkans: a perceptive, acid perspective from a different era against which to measure my own impressions. Born in 1790, Custine lost both his father and grandfather to the guillotine at an early age. He became an object of scandal when in 1824 he was found unconscious, stripped, and beaten, the result of a misplaced sexual advance toward another man. He became one of the most notorious homosexuals of his conservative day—"a problem for everyone," as a contemporary put it—and he grew snide, bitter, and scandalous. He had literary ambitions, but his writing was ignored during his lifetime; Heine called him "a half-man of letters." But his discomfort in his homeland, and seemingly in his own skin, made him an ideal traveler. "The real travelers," said his countryman Baudelaire, "are those who leave for the sake of leaving." Custine was a connoisseur of places, he said, that were "more singular than pretty or convenient; but singularity suffices to amuse a stranger: what we seek in traveling are proofs that we are not at home." He first wrote a travel book about Spain, which garnered him a complimentary letter from Balzac, who suggested he write about another "semi-European country"—Italy, or perhaps Russia.

Emboldened by Balzac's suggestion and envious of Tocqueville's example, he traveled to Russia in 1839—a short trip, mostly confined to Russia's northwest, but as George F. Kennan, the American Russia hand and Cold Warrior, wrote, Custine "read countries, he claimed, as other people read books." Custine arrived in Russia a born elitist and returned (despite his personal respect for then Tsar Nicholas I) a confirmed democrat, sickened by what he saw as the debasing effect of authoritarianism on the population. "When [Russian nobles] arrive in Europe," his German hotelier tells him on his way to Saint Petersburg, "They have a gay, easy, contented air, like horses set free, or birds let loose from their cages. . . . The same persons when they return have long faces and gloomy looks; their words are few and abrupt; their countenances full of care. I conclude from this, that a country which they quitted with so much joy, and to which they return with so much regret, is a bad country." The Russian customs agents themselves questioned his motives:

"What is your object in Russia?'"

"To see the country."

"That is not here a motive for traveling!"

His ensuing judgment of the country was severe, perhaps unfair, certainly condescending, and somehow persistent: perhaps because his pessimism echoes the "curiosity, sarcasm, and carping criticism" he—and I, and many other observers—found among Russians themselves. It is in his role as critic, and as the personification of the opinion of a Europe toward which Russia has historically looked with a mixture of envy, self-deprecation, and defensiveness, that he served his most recent turn in the public eye. In Alexander Sokurov's 2002 film *Russian Ark*, filmed in one ninety-six-minute shot, Custine and an unnamed narrator stroll through the Hermitage and thus through scenes from Russian history, from Peter the Great to World War II, still trying to identify the soul, or the narrative, or the fate, of the nation.

II.

Party for Everybody *(Rostov-on-Don to Saint Petersburg)*

This was my first vision of Russia: miles of rolling hills, not a house or tree to be seen, the Don steppe, and vast farms. "All this region," said Herodotus two and a half millennia earlier, "is entirely bare of trees, wild or cultivated . . . the land consisting of a rich and well-watered plain, with excellent pasture, and the rivers being almost as numerous as the canals are in Egypt." The treelessness, he points out, has an additional complication: "Because there is no wood in Scythia to make a fire with, the method the natives adopt after skinning the animal [for sacrifice] is to strip the flesh from the bones and put it into a cauldron . . . and then make a fire of the bones underneath it. In the absence of a cauldron, they put all the flesh in the animal's paunch . . . and boil it like that. . . . In this way an ox, or any other sacrificial beast, is ingeniously made to boil itself."

Our first Russian show was in Rostov-on-Don, in the far south-west. Rachel Polonsky devotes a chapter of her book *Molotov's Magic Lantern* to the city—the site of the decisive battles of the Russian Civil War ("Take Rostov at all costs, for otherwise disaster threatens," Lenin warned his armies)—and its prostitutes. The pre-1917 Rostov was the home of a cosmopolitan, industrial nouveau riche: "The river was fouled with factory waste . . . and the water stank, but the main streets were paved, and electric trams ran along the Garden Ring, past banks, fashionable shops, clubs, insurance companies, cinemas and *belle-epoque* private residences," Polonsky writes. The budding bourgeoisie was crushed and scattered by the Bolshevik cavalry army (which included the Jewish writer Isaac Babel, who wrote his *Red Cavalry* stories about his experiences); then the city itself was left in ruins for a decade after the German occupation in World War II. Rostov-on-Don now has the mix of genuine danger and scruffy sense of irony I associate with cities isolated, troubled, but not without a certain municipal patriotism, like Baltimore or Newark. Three years later, the city would be the main staging area for the Russian incursion into Ukraine: young Russian soldiers understood that "going to exercises in Rostov" meant deployment to eastern Ukraine.

The bar we were playing was called Nemets Perets Kolbasa, which means "German Pepper Sausage." It's the first line of a teasing playground rhyme dating back to World War II:

Немец, перец, колбаса,
Кислая капуста.
Съел мышонка без хвоста
И сказал, что вкусно.

German, pepper, sausage,
Sauerkraut.
Ate a mouse without a tail
And he said, "Eat that."[1]

The wall outside the club indeed had a mural of a red pepper, a sausage, and a fat, mustachioed man in a Tyrolean cap.

The mistress of the house was Ksusia, who was sweet but odd, with a quality of noncommittal disengagement. When asked a question she didn't know how to or didn't care to answer, she laughed loudly and quickly, then stared into the middle distance until the subject was changed. She had moved to town a year earlier, working at an office with "strange ugly bad people" before taking over management of this little bar (now with adjoining tattoo shop) owned by a handsome, silver-haired fortysomething named Sergey.

After an afternoon nap of jet-lagged, disorienting intensity (I had been awake for thirty solid hours by that point), there was a soundcheck and an interview with a local journalist that was not so much about music—not at all about music, really—as it was an interrogation, of the "Russians are like this/Americans are like this" variety.[2]

"Here the average Russian makes $600 a month," he said.

---

1. The phrase also appears in the Soviet satiric singer-songwriter Timur Shaov's song "строим новую страну" (Building a New Country), a mix of defensiveness, criticism, and pride one friend described to me as not unlike the sentiment of Bruce Springsteen's "Born in the U.S.A."

2. Which, per Custine, is an old anxiety: "I am much struck by the extreme susceptibility of the Russians as regards the judgment which strangers may form respecting them. The impression which their country may make on the minds of travelers occupies their thoughts constantly."

"How much does the average American make? Russians have the idea that every American loves fast food. Is that true? What is your stereotype of Russia?"

I mentioned corruption, and he agreed, but "surely there is also corruption in America?"

"Yes, but I think it happens on higher levels of power and money, and more secretively, not on the level of police and small bureaucrats. You don't get shaken down by traffic cops."

"Ah—more professionals!"

We laughed. Many Russians, and citizens of other countries in which corruption and repression are the norm, find it frankly unbelievable that the rest of the world doesn't operate in the same fashion.[3] No country is entirely free of corruption, of course, but all exist on a sliding scale between the systemic and the episodic incidences—the difference between countries where it is endemic and considered part of the normal order of things and those where it is infrequent, considered aberrant, and condemned.

"Have you been on public transportation yet?" the journalist continued. "No? Are you scared?"

---

3. Custine:

> Those who pretend to judge our country, say to me, that they do not really believe our king abstains from punishing the writers who daily abuse him in Paris.
>
> "Nevertheless," I answer them, "the fact is there to convince you."
>
> "Yes, yes, you talk of toleration," they reply, with a knowing air, "it is all very well for the multitude and for foreigners: but your government punishes secretly the too-audacious journalists."
>
> When I repeat that everything is public in France, they laugh sneeringly, politely check themselves; but they do not believe me.

"No, I've only been here five hours, and I spent four of that dead asleep."

"They say Russian women are the most beautiful—do you agree?"

"You're going to ask me that in front of my Ukrainian wife?"

The show was fine, if intermittently interrupted by a hulking, friendly drunk everyone called "Mongol." Ksusia said the neighborhood's main trouble is a couple dozen roving drunks. "Sergey has too big a heart. He thinks if they can come here and hear music and poetry they will be cured."

She, for her part, finally called the cops on Mongol. ("Actually," she laughed, "it is just the police academy"—that is, cadets in training, assigned to the drunk patrol.)

Maria and I had the idea of going to Taganrog on the Sea of Azov, the birthplace of Chekhov (and the supposed site of Tsar Alexander I's self-exile among the conspiracists who believe he faked his own death), on our day off but were discouraged by the dismissive laughter of everyone we asked about beaches in Taganrog. Guess it's not that kind of waterfront.

Back at the club that night, a French jazz pianist was leading a trio with two Russians and an American lady sitting in on vocals through an improv set. We met a guy from "the most popular band in Rostov," whose hit was called "Kill the Niggers." When we looked shocked, we were reassured that it was some kind of joke, though one that went unexplained.

After a few rounds of vodka shots with Sergey, we were delivered to the station. We had twelve hours of sleeper car that night, heading due north to the small city of Voronezh, and the compartment to ourselves. It felt like some kind of reward.

Osip Mandelstam, after the disclosure of his poem "The Stalin Epigram" ("His fat fingers, slimy as worms . . . the huge laughing cockroaches on his upper lip") in 1933, was arrested and tortured but eventually allowed to choose his place of exile—excluding what were then the twelve major Russian cities. He chose Voronezh, once the center of the People's Will terrorist movement that had led to the assassination of Tsar Alexander II and at the time of Mandelstam's exile "a chaotic deposit of poor, small houses, wildly scattered over the ravines and hillsides," according to the poet Victor Krivulin.

Mandelstam may have chosen Voronezh as a kind of "macabre pun," a black joke on his situation: *Voron* means "raven"— "the vans in which the arrested were transported were called by the people 'black ravens' . . . or 'little ravens' (*voronki*)," Krivulin explained—and a *nosh* is a homicidal robber's knife. Mandelstam ended one of his first poems in exile: "*Voronezh—blazh', Voronezh—voron, nosh*" (Voronezh—you are a whim, Voronezh —you are a raven and a knife).

Mandelstam lived in "the sleepy, sleight-tracked town/Half-town, half-mounted-shore" for three years of poverty and isolation with his wife, Nadezhda. (At one point, his translators Richard and Elizabeth McKane relate, he "resorted . . . to reading his latest poems on the telephone to his NKVD . . . surveillance person.") He was visited by fellow poet Anna Akhmatova, who wrote about the encounter in her poem "Voronezh": "In the room of the exiled poet/Fear and the Muse stand duty in turn." A collection of poems, *The Voronezh Notebooks*, was published only decades after Mandelstam's death, reconstituted by Nadezhda, Akhmatova, and others from poor copies, scraps, and memory.

He was allowed to return from exile in 1937, only to be rearrested the following year. "Happy poverty. . . . Those winter days [in Voronezh] with all their troubles were the greatest and last happiness to be granted us in life," Nadezhda remembered in her last known letter to her husband. Mandelstam died in December 1938, on a train bound for a Siberian labor camp.

We were picked up in Voronezh by a young punk who worked in market research at an orthopedics company. The talk turned immediately to politics: "Anyone who can think hates Putin. He is just like Lukashenko," the anachronistic Belarusian dictator.

We were caught in the choking traffic that we would come to find is the hallmark of second-tier Russian cities. "I have old car. 1985 Lada. Don't be afraid!" He pulled a heart-stopping maneuver and gestured to the car in front of him: "A new Lada!"

"Are the new Ladas better?"

"I think no." As if on cue, the driver in the new Lada killed his engine in the middle of the street, got out, and opened the hood with a frown.

Our host and his dozen friends took us past a bronze statue of the "Russian Bob Dylan," Vladimir Vysotsky[4]—shirtless with a vest!—and to dinner in a mall at a cavernous establishment that resembled a Medieval Times, with wood-hewn communal

---

4. Vysotsky was probably the best known of the *bardy* ("bards"), an explosion of singer-songwriters in the 1970s who considered themselves poets and spokesmen for a life of individuality, camaraderie, and authenticity. Their unpolished performances of *avtorskaya pesnya* (a term musicologist J. Martin Daughtry translates as "author's songs" or "auteur songs") were widely bootlegged on homemade LPs scratched into x-ray plates—at the time, the most convenient source of hard plastic. These were colloquially called "rock on bones" (*rok na kostiakh*) or "rock on ribs" (*rok na rebrakh*).

tables and heavy benches. Its incoherent decor included taxidermied bears, a mural of wolves playing cards, servers dressed in medieval bodices and jerkins, Brazilian carnival footage playing on TV screens in every corner, and pizza. It was called something that roughly, and roughly accurately, translated as "Confusion Pub."

The show was in a basement indie cinema with theater seating. It was sweaty as a banya and there was no booze for the crowd, so, despite the show being sold out, the mood was subdued. One of the openers was named Roman, from Belgorod, across the border from Kharkov. Maria misheard this as "a Roma from Belgrade," which would have been a more substantial trek. He was a slight fellow in glasses and a NOFX T-shirt who sang, of all things, a cover of a song by the obscure Midwestern band Two Cow Garage.

Is it possible to write four hundred pages about touring and never describe a show? I'm tempted. I'm a mid-career musician who's played thousands of shows. For me, they're the least interesting part of the story. The reader will already have noticed that there is a certain repetitive rhythm to the days as they pass. "If it be necessary that I should offer excuses for repetition and monotony, it is equally necessary that I should apologize for traveling at all," says Custine. "The frequent recurrence of the same impressions is inevitable in all conscientious books of travels." All the more so for a musician, whose days are organized around a predictable routine—get to show, play show—punctuated by logistical snafus and unreliable strangers. It's why the details of those strangers and the slow, or sudden, changes in scenery are what I focus on. The bones of the day are indistinguishable.

People ask, "Do you get nervous before shows?" The answer is not really, not at this point. I get nervous each time I play a show that's at a new level—the first show for five hundred people, the first for a thousand, the first time on television, the first with a new band, the first on my own. Then once I've breached that level, I snap back into equilibrium. Some I'm more excited to play, some I dread, some are clock-punchers. But they all have the same arc. I'll describe it once, then you can mentally copy and paste this into the hole I gloss over toward the end of each day.

I usually arrive at the venue around five. We go through a charade of "advancing" the show, which means contacting the promoter a few days before and clarifying arrival times, soundcheck times, and set times. But unless something is unusual, arrival is always at five or six, soundcheck to follow (assuming the soundman is on time, which is a big assumption), doors at seven or eight, show around ten or eleven.

I pull up to the club and try to park. There's parking, or there isn't, or there's metered parking until six. In some European cities, the club is in a central pedestrian zone, which I don't realize until some cops run at me, waving their hands and yelling. The club should be open, but it isn't, so I bang on the black iron doors and the windows covered with posters for upcoming shows. Hopefully one of them has my face on it. After a few minutes someone opens a different door around the corner and says, "Can I help you?"

"Hi, I'm Franz, I'm playing tonight?"

"Oh yes, come in," they say (I hope). "I'm doing your sound tonight. The promoter will be here shortly."

"Nice to meet you. My setup is pretty simple: three DI boxes at the front of the stage—guitar, accordion, banjo—and a center vocal mic." (Two vocals, if Maria is playing.)

"OK, no problem."

As he sets up the stage, I bother him with the Four Basic Questions: Where should I set up merch? Do you know the Wi-Fi password? Is there a backstage area? Can I get a beer? Then I load our bags in, put the instruments on the stage, and take them from their bags and cases. I uncoil the cables, plug one into an instrument on one end and a tuning pedal on the other, then another cable out of the pedal into the direct box that leads to the sound system. I tune the guitar and the banjo. I change the guitar strings if necessary—once a week at least. I strap on the accordion and see what's broken today. Accordions have hundreds of small moving pieces—they look like a typewriter inside—and are not optimized for hard travel. I have a spreadsheet of accordion repairmen around the world, lonely grouches in their sixties with garage workshops an hour out of town: the sad old men of accordion repair. Between these pilgrimages I do my best with superglue, duct tape, needle-nose pliers, and a soldering iron.

I pick up the guitar and start playing and singing. The same song each night for the whole tour, usually—that way I've got a constant. The sound guy will get the idea and start turning the channels up. If he hasn't already decided he hates me from the moment I pull out the accordion or banjo, I can move through the other instruments. When we're both satisfied, I pack up the instruments and re-coil the cables so the opening acts can have the stage.

Now is my downtime. I've usually got about three hours. Sometimes they've made dinner for me—as cheaply and easily as possible, but free food is free food. In Scotland it's often chili. In England, pasta. In Germany, what we simply call "vegan slop" over rice. (In America you won't get fed. Pizza if you're lucky.) Anything you can stick in a big pot, turn on a flame, and feed two to ten people.

Otherwise, I head out and wander around the neighborhood. It's my last chance for some peace and quiet. Sushi or noodle soup and some hot sake is the ideal preshow dinner: filling but not sleep-inducing, with a little warmth. Mexican or Indian food is absolutely off-limits—too heavy (the only time I've vomited onstage, a burrito was the culprit). If I'm overseas, my phone's on airplane mode, so I can spend some time with a book. Treat yourself.

If I time it right, I'm back at the club about an hour before set time. I've missed the first opening act or two. There are a decent number of people milling around. Mostly people won't buy merch until after the show—who wants to carry around an LP for another two hours?—but I go lurk by the merch table for a few minutes anyway. Now it's time to get dressed.

Country star Porter Wagoner was once asked why he wore sequined Nudie suits. "I don't know what business you're in, but I'm in show business," he replied. I've always dressed up for shows. They're a special occasion, and you dress up for a special occasion. And it's a way of making the psychological break between the daylight introvert and the effusive nighttime persona, a way of getting in character. Like Superman putting on the cape. For this tour, I'd brought just one black suit with a white French-cuffed shirt, which I wore with an open collar and a maroon pocket square. I had a pair of pewter cufflinks with the head of a Spanish conquistador on them. They had belonged to my great-grandfather, a clotheshorse in his time. I had a round black-brimmed hat and a pair of $30 black shoes from Target I wore until they fell apart. With luck, there is a back room or a kitchen or at least a storage closet to change in. Without luck, the men's room. Maria has a couple of dresses (they pack smaller than suits) and a pair of short heels, and she puts on bright red lipstick and liquid eyeliner.

Now it's showtime. There are usually a decent number of people in the room, not a lot, but maybe the promoter won't lose money. They're young, mostly. Outside of the UK, people over forty don't really go to bars to see live music. The young men tend to wear black cutoff shorts, a black band T-shirt with white print, slip-on skater shoes, a scruffy beard, and earlobe plugs. The women are usually in tight black jeans, Converse, black tank tops, Bettie Page black bobs and bangs or bleached and chopped and dyed hair. Neither, for some reason, wear socks. Everyone has a can of cheap beer. Some of them sit cross-legged on the sides of the floor, most stand. Sometimes they clap in time.

"Hello," I say, "hi there," loud enough to get their attention, "I'm Franz Nicolay, from Brooklyn, New York, it's great to be here!"

I open with an accordion song: "The Hearts of Boston," usually, a new song, on the record that's not quite out yet. It's rousing, with an Irish-sounding riff and a foot-stomping tempo. Maria plays banjo. It makes the point: I'm not just another guy with an acoustic guitar. On the first three songs of the set I play accordion, guitar, and banjo, to set the parameters of the night. I stop in the middle of songs to comment on the action. I tell stories. Like a standup comedian, I only have one or two set stories for each song, but I can play with the length and eliminate beats if I feel like the crowd isn't in the mood or their English isn't strong enough. I try not to repeat the stories in towns I've been to recently, but that's not a problem in Russia.

> I recently befriended a five-year-old kid with the unlikely name of Jasper Christmas. Well, I say befriended—this was two years ago, which is a long time in the life of a five-year-old. He may not even remember me by now. Jasper had discovered that if you use the construction "Do the [blank]" that that's a dance craze, and he set himself to the task of coming up with dance crazes. He had one called the Snail, in which you get down on your knees and pull yourself forward with your hands. He had one called the Pillow, in which you curl up in the fetal position on the floor and you don't move at all. Very popular dance. Anyone can do it, and most people do. And he has one called the Struggle, in which you take a chair, and you put it up against the wall, and you take the top of your head and you put it against the back of the chair, and you run your feet as fast as you can and try to push the chair through the wall. I heard that and I said, "Jasper, you're a fucking genius," and then I thought, "Shit, I shouldn't say 'fuck' in front of a five-year-old," and then I thought, "Fuck it, he's going to have to learn from somebody." Jasper, you're a fucking genius. That reminds me of all my friends who are activists, and touring musicians, and spend their lives trying to push chairs through walls. This one's for them, it's called "Do the Struggle," and it goes like this . . .

I try to play about an hour. Twelve songs, give or take. More if the crowd is with me, less if they're not. End with a rousing crowd-pleaser, usually "Jeff Penalty," a semi-novelty song about the replacement singer of the Dead Kennedys, with a "whoa-oh" sing-along chorus. I drop to my knees with mock guitar heroics in the bridge. Then I use my instincts: end it there, on the high-energy note, or unplug the banjo and sing a sentimental ballad in the middle of the floor. That can be a magical moment. I've got a couple sad banjo ballads—"This Is Not a Pipe" or "Cease-Fire"—but the longtime winner is the Jimmy Durante song "Hi-Lili, Hi-Lo." If there are tables or a bench, I'll get up on them. End on a showbiz major sixth, doff the cap, and skedaddle.

Exit to the backstage, or the bathroom, for a polite minute or two, then reappear behind the merch table and sell some CDs, LPs, and T-shirts, pose for a few pictures, sign some things (keep a Sharpie in the suit pocket), and try to pack up the stage before the club staff are all packed up themselves. I change back into my street clothes and hang the suit on hangers so I don't have to put it away sweaty and wet. Mostly I don't have that luxury, though, and at the end of this six-month tour the suit will be unsalvage-able, crusty with white salt, the hat bent and ripped, the knees of the pants patched and patched again. I promise Maria we'll have a ritual fire and feed the suit to the flames.[5]

Then it's off either to the stranger's house where we're sleeping—the last great suspense of the day: will it be a bed, an air mattress, a couch, or a floor, and how many cats?—or to the

5. We made a video of the immolation for the song "The Hearts of Boston."

train station, to pile as quietly as possible into the coupe with all our bags without waking our new roommates.

There is a ritualistic quality to boarding a sleeper train, and a liturgy of grunted courtesies. You slide open the walk-in cooler door and nod to the strangers who got there first, and perhaps claimed the lower bunks. Personally, I prefer the foldaway upper shelves, both for privacy and for the dismount: at least then you're the one stepping on someone else's bed, not the stepped-on. You stash your luggage in the metal storage box under the lower bunks and the deceptively spacious cubby over the door. You unwrap the cellophaned and starchy sheets and the scratchy wool blanket and make, of the plastic-padded bunk, your bed. The attendant checks your ticket and offers tea or instant coffee. You prepare your supplies for the night: water bottle tucked against the wall, book and headphones and earplugs handy in the net pocket on the wall. The passengers separate into two tribes: the men in track pants and shower shoes, traveling alone, who stand in the corridor staring at passing fields, and the women and families who share the small tables that jut from below the curtained compartment windows.

One of the great treats of train touring is those times when the ride to the next show is long enough to spend a night, the whole next day, and another night on the train before disembarking. You snack, snooze, scribble, read, have a beer, nap again, wander to the dining car, get some fresh air at a provincial station, and try not to get left behind. It was a twenty-four-hour journey from Voronezh to Saint Petersburg. Through the window coquettish beech leaves flashed their silver undersides in the breeze. It was the kind of manicured forest you see from eastern

Germany through Poland: tall thin pine or birch on a lawn of low grass and shrub or middling oak, the sign of a land that has been logged and resown again and again. Every few kilometers, a small village huddled its hovels shank by haunch: amid an endless expanse of land, they shared waved-tin fences between their small gardens, brick walls, and moldering plaster. Then a few miles of marsh, the trucks on the Don highway visible just to the east. Then a sort of plain, where the shacks by the tracks showed their peaks over squat fruit trees.

We asked the *provodnitsa* (the iconic uniformed carriage attendant who brings linens and dispenses tea) if anyone else will be in our coupe. "For a thousand rubles," she said, "I can make sure there isn't."

We passed a train labeled HOBOTPAHC, which is pronounced "Novotrans" but which I couldn't help but read as "Hobo Trains." Finally, they've got their own! Separate but equal.

Before one truly awakens in a moving vehicle, one is subject to synaesthetic misfire; you peer out the window, bleary, and echolocate. This forest tastes like California, this thigh cramp smells of camping. I always have a cycle of night sweats when sleeping on a train bunk. No matter the temperature, I go to sleep uncovered, awake upon a soggy pillow, turn it over, pull up the comforter against the chill; then, in the morning, I dress, clammy and hunched. I awoke four hours from Saint Petersburg in a new landscape: thick birch and conifers of military bearing punctuating patches of swamp. Here were no villages at all. When they appeared, they were a new breed, wood houses instead of brick, weathered to a dark brown or painted a shocking aquamarine, or yellow with maroon trim, or bright royal blue. They were startling and unnatural hues, and probably that was the point. Instead of communities set in relief on the edge of acres of flat farmland, we were now passing woodland riverbank logging towns. Railcars stacked with ruler-straight pine logs waited for deployment. There were more than the usual number of burnt-out houses, skeletons with double-chimney spines. Some houses shared their airspace with birdhouses set at an extraordinary height, twice that of the house itself. I caught glimpses of a sprawling graveyard engulfed in the forest, each plot popping with bright ribbons and flowers around the silver, pressed-aluminum crosses.

The pace of the stations accelerated, coming every minute or two now. Old men and women carried sacks alongside the tracks. More trains rumbled past station houses and cargo holds. The petite green cabooses with red stars on the front trundled back and forth, dragging a car here and another back there. A city is a matter of pace as much as population, and we accelerated into Saint Petersburg.

Saint Petersburg's Moskovsky station set the imperial stage with triumphant orchestral music made somehow more martial by the tinny public-address system. A wild-eyed bust of Peter the Great faced a stylized map of the entire Soviet train system, from Berlin and Moscow in the west to Almaty in the east. We were finally meeting up with Dima, the architect of our itinerary and linchpin of this Russian DIY touring family. He was slim and Scandinavian-looking, with quick-crinkle eyes. The city did not quite possess the European affect of its reputation and intention (Tsar Nicholas I told Custine, "Petersburg is Russian, but it is not Russia"); the upwardly mobile vulgarity of the new Russia resisted the staid gravity of the imperial architecture. The canals might recall Venice, until a pair of dudes on jet skis came tearing up past the garish Swarovski domes of the Church of Our Savior on the Spilled Blood (which marks the spot of the assassination of Tsar Alexander II). The bars offered sushi and mojitos (or virgin mojitos—that is, Sprite cocktails). The opportunistic nightclub Barakobamabar used the current U.S. president's signature for a logo. In the stained, damp, overrun skeleton of Venice itself, what once was a living city had become a kind of corpse that sustained only parasite colonies of tourists and merchants. Meanwhile Petersburg, built by slave labor, now stood as an outpost of muted, aspirational Western liberalism in a revanchist state.

There was another outpost of Westernness here: the global youth culture of punk rock. Dima had arranged for us to stay with two elfin blondes, Anna and Sveta, who wore black jeans and Converse sneakers, translated lyrics by the politically outspoken Florida band RVIVR, and talked longingly about traveling to Gainesville for the annual international punk gathering The Fest.

Sveta barely ate—her breakfast was one slice of homemade seitan—though, perhaps unsurprisingly, she loved to watch us eat. They shared a bed so we could use the other, but it was the White Nights, when the sun hardly sets and the sky never darkens ("summer nights," says Custine, "consist of no more than two twilights"), so they were out almost all night anyway. Maria and I were not quite ten years older than they, but when it came to staying up late, these months of sleep-short touring made the difference feel like decades. We met them at the local—and upscale—punk bar, where the DJ was spinning vinyl of my song "Jeff Penalty" as we entered, followed by the Bouncing Souls and the Gaslight Anthem. They sold croissants at the bar. Drinks were surprisingly expensive—except for vodka, which was as cheap as juice—and the prices and the cigarette smoke quickly chased us from the premises. We tried to buy wine at the supermarket, but the staff had pulled down beer ads like window-shades over the liquor shelves. Stores stop selling alcohol, by law, at eleven p.m.

"Try the *magazin* (deli) across the street," advised the clerk. "He will sell."

The *magazin* across the street had the beer ads pulled down as well, but as we debated our options two loud Russian girls in high heels and tight jeans negotiated over a bottle of cognac with the man behind the counter. We took this as a cue that the beer ads were just for show, and sure enough, the cashier ducked behind them and sold us a bottle of wine.

We had a week in the city before our show and two practical tasks to accomplish in addition to sightseeing. We were sold out of my album *Luck and Courage*. I'd tried to arrange to have a case shipped to Saint Petersburg from the label in London, but the distributor's message was unequivocal: there was no point. The shipping was astronomical and the customs agents unreliable. The box might arrive in time, or weeks late, or never. We would have to bootleg my own record. We spent all day trying to find a copy center, blank CDs, plastic sleeves, and glue sticks, and then spent all night at handicraft (which included cutting up a half-dozen unsalable American XXL T-shirts and refashioning them as more Russian-appropriate smalls).

Secondly, I had to record a song—a Noël Coward cover, for a split seven-inch with the British singer-songwriter Frank Turner—and it had to be done while we were on the road in order to make the October release date. Dima had engaged for us, at a shockingly low rate, two hours at Petersburg Recording

Studio. Dima's friend Yegor, a well-traveled, dour, and cynical photographer, was our chaperone for the day. On the bus to the studio, I asked him about some of the more obscure post-Soviet regions he'd visited.

"You'd never know [in Belarus] by being there what's going on"—he meant politically. "It's not like a Soviet state. There's no border, it's like Europe, you just drive in. But the police will stop you for no reason and you had better have your papers. In Transnistria it is more like a Soviet time capsule. You can't use a Ukrainian phone or a Moldavian phone because [the governments] are fighting, you have to go there and buy a whole new phone. So I couldn't call [ahead] and make a hotel reservation. So I walked to this place and there was a drunk passed out in a pool of—well, some kind of liquid—in front of the reception desk.

"I think Ukrainians are more relaxed than Russians," he continued. "In L'viv, I saw a group of drunk guys who the police were trying to arrest. They were saying to the police, 'No, we don't want to go,' and eventually the police just let them go. This would never happen in Russia! They would hit them with rifle butts and drag them off to jail."

"A work . . . entitled *The Russians Judged by Themselves*," wrote Custine, "would be severe." It had been just a few months prior that large antigovernment protests in the wake of Vladimir Putin's reelection had foundered, and demonstrations were planned for the next day, Russia Day. Dima and his friends were buzzing with rumors that nationalist gangs would cause trouble. I asked Yegor if he planned on attending.

"I am not so interested. I talked to some of the guys who would know, and they said this one will be a mixture of people, including very right-wing groups. A lot of people just come to get their aggression out. All of these protests, they are only middle-class people from Saint Petersburg and Moscow. It will be impossible to really make any change without the people in the rural areas, the religious and conservative people." He dismissed the blogger Alexei Navalny, who had been portrayed in the Western press as a driving force behind the election protests, as operating more in the service of his own ambition than of true political change.

Young Russians were markedly more cynical about the possibility of political change than their counterparts even in culturally similar countries. "In Ukraine," wrote William Dobson in his book *The Dictator's Learning Curve*, "people younger than thirty were three times more likely to join the Orange Revolution [in 2004] than any other age-group. Meanwhile, in Russia, a large majority of young people accepted Putin's explanation of the revolution as a Western conspiracy directed at weakening the motherland. The same 2007 poll indicated that 87 percent of young people did not want an Orange Revolution in Russia." They had reason to be suspicious, even of supposed "opposition" leaders: many headed movements, called "systemic opposition," that had been quietly created and funded by the government (which also controlled over 90 percent of the media) to be an outlet for frustration "while never pushing their criticism beyond the boundaries set by the Kremlin." Anyone—the educated class, children of either the perestroika era or the post-Yeltsin era—who showed an inclination toward forming a liberal intellectual elite was encouraged to emigrate as a matter of unofficial government policy. The result, said the French intellectual Bernard-Henri Lévy, was a Russia "whose most discouraging side . . . was its amorphousness and its passivity."

The studio had a majestic, yellow-lit live room, housed in an eighteenth-century Lutheran church with a pipe organ, a full-size Steinway grand piano, and a harpsichord. Opened in 1959, it had been the studio for the Soviet state record label Melodiya for twenty-five years, and a severe reserve still chilled the atmosphere. A thick-bearded piano tuner finished his work. An unsmiling woman with a tight ponytail introduced herself as Kira, our engineer, and led us up to the control room two floors above. Vintage Soviet guitar amps and framed, faded photographs of house engineers of the 1970s and 1980s ringed what looked like a rec room. A five-foot bass balalaika stood propped beneath a picture of Beethoven. Efficiency was the rule of the day, and we were finished and out the door in three takes and two hours, with a faint smile from Kira at the end as our reward.

Maria had noticed posters for a concert that week by the Buranovskiye Babushki, and much to the consternation and disdain of Dima and his crowd, we bought tickets. The Babushki—their name translates to "Grannies from Buranovo"—were a novelty act of septua- and octogenarians from a small town in the Ural Mountains who had unexpectedly risen to be the Russian representatives in the kitsch-pop Eurovision Song Contest. (They eventually finished second to the Swedes.) The Svengali of the group was a decades-younger woman who had taken these shrunken-apple gnomes and set their village-style a capella harmonies to Eurodance beats, filling out the records with covers of "Let It Be" and "Smoke on the Water." Their hit was a pile of English-language nonsense called "Party for Everybody" ("Party for everybody/Come on and dance/Come on and boom-boom-boom-boom").

Of course, you want to see what kind of crowd turns up for that show: mainly middle-aged mothers with their daughters (and the rare husband), plus a strong showing of barely prepubescent boys likely to discover they were gay in fairly short order. One wore a T-shirt reading "I ♥ My Sister," another a full velour tracksuit in the blue and yellow of the Ukrainian flag. A droopy man in a blue polo shirt sat behind a laptop at the back of the stage, cheek in the palm of his hand, the most despondent or bored DJ imaginable. A terrifying woman in a tight leopard-print dress was the leather-lunged host, handing off to a local radio presenter. He came out into the crowd—there was plenty of room to move—and made straight for Maria and me, asking where we were from.

"Look! These people have come all the way from New York just to see the Babushki!" he exaggerated.

The opening act took the stage: two young men flanking three young female dancers in dresses very loosely based on folk costumes. The men wore knockoff Converse sneakers and baggy, light blue velour tracksuits with some folk-ish embroidery on the shoulders. Their matched, loose-limbed choreography and TV preacher grins indicated that they were pretty clearly lip-synching to the folk/dance track—the club kind of folk dance, not the clogging kind. The unplugged balalaika held by one, and the glittering, very probably hollow, *bayan*—a button accordion—carried by the other, confirmed it.

The Babushki themselves were lovable and clearly thrilled to be there. They had the homey charisma of sun-shriveled Hummel figurines in red patchwork dresses, multicolored headscarves, and silver-coin necklaces. Although under the schoolmarm eye of their younger ringleader, they drifted off-mic, shuffled through their turn-to-the-right, turn-to-the-left dance steps, and belted out "Party for Everybody" in their high, creaky harmonies with the enthusiasm and good humor of the amateurs on a lark they were.

It was a spectacle of low-end show business, and it wasn't without surprise that I turned and found Maria teary.

"I know it's ridiculous," she said, wiping her eyes. "But think about what these women have been through in their lives: Lenin, World War II, Stalin, famine, the Cold War, communism, probably tons of children and grandchildren. And now, in their eighties, can you imagine—they get to be pop stars!"

Custine believed that Tsar Peter, the megalomaniacal Europeanizer from whose imagination Saint Petersburg sprung whole, was wrongly lionized, and that his single-minded project of education and Westernization of his people both underscored and cemented their inferiority complex regarding Europe, crippling them with the cult of a strongman. Like the suicidal modernization of Mao's Great Leap Forward and the Stalinist collectivizations, Peter's reforms were the manifestations of a tyrannical will imposed on a dehumanized population. The productive results that many saw in Peter's upheaval, Custine thought, were secondary to ensuring a sullen and submissive culture of half-fulfilled command from above, rather than fecund innovation from below.

One of the remnants of Peter's reign is his Kunstkamera, an ethnographic museum of sorts in the manner of a rich dilettante's cabinet of curiosities. The floor *de résistance* is a collection of fetal deformities, human and animal, stored in formaldehyde and displayed for the edification of his people and the debunking of superstition. There are two-headed cats, hydrocephalics, fetal cyclopses, and fetuses with cephalic hernias (in other words, with brains spilling out of their heads). It shows a portrait of the tsar as ringmaster and barker of his own personal chamber of freaks—and of a man whose sense of the humanity of his fellows was something less than full and empathetic.

Such is the nature of aristocracy, I thought, as we toured Peterhof, the Summer Palace of its namesake and his Romanov heirs. It's sometimes called the Russian Versailles, and it's redolent with the same Olympian self-regard as that icon of elitist indulgence. "The rich would rather choke," wrote Rebecca West, "than not have their mouths full." I am not normally given to revolutionary class rage, but all I could think the whole day was: I would've overthrown the crass fuckers too.

That night I dreamed that I was given a key, and in a hallway at a school there was a keyhole like that of a safe-deposit box, except that where a normal keyhole might be oriented in halves, with a 180-degree range of motion, this was divided into sixty-fourths. I turned it to the first sixty-fourth mark and pulled out a small box, six inches wide and two inches high, made of thick metal, with eyeholes at one end like binoculars. I held it to my eyes and inside saw a vision of a green and watery paradise—it was so beautiful I cried and was moved to improve my ways of living, so that I might match this vision. I turned the key another sixty-fourth turn before looking inside again, and this time I was in a boat in a flooded landscape and spoke to a fisherman in another boat in an unfamiliar language. I turned the key again, and again, until I came to the last turn, which revealed simply a small room, and myself within, dressed simply in a white button-down shirt and khaki pants, sitting in a chair and staring back at myself with eyes that were all black with dilated irises. This was death, and I awoke with gooseflesh that would not abate.

Fantasies of murder and dreams of death. The next morning, I made a brief and solitary pilgrimage to Dostoyevsky's spartan apartment, and we boarded the train for Moscow.

III.

A Real Lenin of Our Time
(Moscow)

Much of classical Moscow, the "inland Byzantium," the third Rome,[1] was destroyed in the auto-immolation of the Napoleonic War, and again in Soviet modernizations and developments. No more, as in Custine's time, the "thousands of pointed steeples, star-spangled belfries, airy turrets, strangely-shaped towers, palaces, and old convents . . . a phalanx of phantoms hovering over the city . . . a series of phantasmagoria, in broad day, which reminds one of the reflected brilliance of lamps in the shop of a lapidary." In their place was a skyline dominated

---

1. In the wake of the fifteenth-century fall of Constantinople to the Ottoman Turks, Russian nationalists saw Russian Orthodoxy, centered in Moscow, as the natural inheritor of the mantle of the true church from Rome and Byzantium. Many considered the recapture and incorporation of Constantinople, which they called Tsargrad, to be a natural culmination of Russian imperial expansion.

by the neon-topped high-rises of the past twenty years and the Gothic, even Gotham-ic, Stalinist hulks known as the "Seven Sisters." It was in one of these manila-tan elephants that our host rented an apartment. Błażej was an avuncular Pole, Maria's cousin, in the employ of a multinational advertising agency and primarily tasked with marketing the candies of the Mars corporation in the former Soviet Bloc. It was his determined dream when exiling himself to Moscow that he would live in one of these iconic buildings—from which, it is said, the secret police still spy on the U.S. Embassy from hidden rooms in the basement.

The inside of Błażej's building was no less grand, forbidding, and monolithic than its exterior. Marble columns and tiles lined the lobby, and the elevators could fit dozens comfortably. The hallways and doors were twelve or more feet high, the latter equipped with brass knockers and carved handles of six-inch circumference.[2]

Błażej's lease was arranged under the table with a family whose matriarch had acquired the apartment decades before. They were nominally prohibited from renting it, a prohibition both common and commonly circumvented. The family made it a habit of coming en masse to collect rent.

Belying the authoritarian majesty of the structure, though, was a casino—until recently, owned by Chuck Norris—on the

---

2. Custine, to whom it often seems architecture is destiny, wrote of the thickness and massiveness of official Moscow, its watchtowers and walls, that "everything betrays the constant surveillance necessary. . . . To inhabit a place like the Kremlin is not to reside, it is to defend oneself. Oppression creates revolt, revolt obliges precautions, precautions increase dangers, and this long series of actions and reactions engenders a monster; that monster is despotism, which has built itself a house in Moscow."

first floor, to the right of the main entrance, serving a cheap and filling cafeteria-style buffet. In the basement was a bar, the Real McCoy, where older American men could meet young Russian women, "both," Błażej noted, "there for the same purposes."

The bar was open twenty-four hours. There was a mania for twenty-four-hour service in Moscow and Saint Petersburg. (Anya in Saint Petersburg had just started a new job at a twenty-four-hour Apple Store, working the ten p.m. to ten a.m. shift. The first night someone came in to use the bathroom, she told us. The second night no one came at all.) "Before," Błażej said, gesturing around the hookah-and-shashlik restaurant where we went for lunch, "they would have a belly dancer as the special attraction. Now there are no more belly dancers and everything is twenty-four hours. Even the flower shops! In case you are coming home late and drunk, you can buy flowers and say, 'Hey, I'm sorry I'm home late, but here!' Or you wake up at two in the morning thinking, 'Hey, if only I could buy something.' Good news! You go out and get five tulips and now you can sleep happy."

Probably this was an extension of the city's long-prevalent enthusiasm for conspicuous consumption. In Moscow, as in Kyiv and Saint Petersburg, there were functionally two economies and two pricing schemes: one for normal people, and one for oligarchs and those with ambitions to the oligarch class. No doubt, round-the-clock availability of whim fulfillment was catnip to the ambitious parvenu. The, yes, twenty-four-hour karaoke bar Błażej frequented offered live-band karaoke (no extra charge) in addition to the DJ.

Custine despaired of the morals of a Russian people degraded by an autocracy that shunted individual responsibility upstairs from superior to superior and rewarded the underhanded, the black marketeer, and the hustler: "The principle which chiefly actuates their conduct through life is cunning," he wrote, and a kind of social Darwinism. Błażej had recently attended an advertising awards ceremony, a glittering, upwardly mobile affair, and struck up a conversation with a well-dressed young woman at his table. They exchanged business cards, and he noticed, first, that her card was from Mercedes, and second, that it had a man's name on it.

"It's not my card," she said. "It's just the car I'm borrowing." She scribbled a phone number on it.

They turned to watch a speech, and when he turned back she was gone, and so was the iPhone he'd left on the table. He borrowed a phone and called her cell.

"Hello—I just thought maybe you had accidentally grabbed the wrong phone on your way out."

There was a pause. "If I had taken it," she asked, "what would you do about it?"

"So what did you do?" I asked.

"Just as she predicted, I did nothing. I bought a new phone."

At the entrance to Red Square, a brass disc was set in the cobblestones marking the theoretical center of Moscow, the "zero point" for measuring distances. Tourists stood on the center of the disc, their backs to the square's gate, and tossed coins over their shoulders for luck. Just outside the circle's bounds, a handful of old drunks and hunched women waited, then scurried in to pick up the thrown coins, eyes fixed on the ground, careful not to make eye contact. Their sacks of small change jingled. A pair of men dressed as Lenin and Stalin posed for pictures on the sidewalk.

Russians have contradictory ideas about propriety. Maria had to wrap a cloth around her waist to cover her shorts, which were considered immodest, in the Kremlin cathedral. In front of me, as we climbed the narrow stairs to the steeple, was a slim woman with a young son. She wore a white mesh bathing suit cover, hemmed high in the back, just long enough to cover a thong and a maxi pad the size of a baguette. But it was, theoretically, a dress, and thus appropriate to the reverential setting.

We went to see dead Lenin in his still-futuristic mausoleum, a squat ziggurat hunched, sleek and gleaming, in the shadow of the Kremlin walls, a mummified alien in a bubble—discordant with both the medieval baroque of the old keep and the deluxe arcade mall opposite. "Like the bones of certain gigantic animals," said Custine, "the Kremlin proves to us the history of a world which we might doubt until after seeing the remains." We filed past the graves and busts of all the Soviet leaders and heroes, save the disowned Khrushchev, in the midst of a crowd of Chinese tourists (and there is no crowd like a crowd of Chinese tourists). Inside the bunker was cold and silent but for the shuffle of feet and umbrellas as the guards hustled us along. No pictures allowed, but I didn't feel cheated. I would only have gotten a picture of something that looked like a wax figure, and which for all I knew may well be. "Our grandfather Lenin/Has withered away/He's decayed into mold and wild honey," goes Yegor Letov and Grazhdanskaya Oborona's classic anti-Soviet song "Everything Is Going According to Plan." A pair of Chinese tourists stopped and bowed to the bier.

"Lenin!" cried Błażej, a gleeful connoisseur of irony and Strongbow cider, later that night. "I had a friend in university, a real Lenin of our time. He said he'd organize a New Year's party for everyone, asked us for a hundred złoty each. He bought the cheapest vodka, the cheapest beer, the cheapest food, but everyone was having a good time. At some point someone broke something or vomited and I went downstairs to his girlfriend's flat to find him, and I realized they had a whole other party—a VIP party!—with fancy food and so on, all paid for by the cheap party. A real Lenin!"

He ordered another round of drinks. "He was the only true Communist I knew, by the way. He still votes for them."

We played at an outdoor festival, organized in the parking lot around an old factory building that now housed a collection of boutique clothing stores. The event was nominally in honor of the queen of England's jubilee. A two-story banner with the queen's image hung across the front of the building, and the flyers were in English. Nevertheless, the crowd was entirely Russian, and all were dressed in the international hipster style commonly associated with *Vice* magazine. A small group loosed paper balloons with lit candles inside aloft into the gray drizzle. An American in "the only bluegrass band in Russia" invited us to their weekly jam session, which they hold in a Starbucks.

The Moscow subway was a real triumph. Each station was a spotless museum hall of marble, chandeliers, and socialist realist ceramic murals of jet planes and grain harvests. More important, the trains run every ninety seconds. New York City MTA, I thought, this is your Sputnik moment. I looked at our fellow passengers: A pregnant, leashless dachshund squatted at the feet of its owner, who was focused on a crossword. A man accessorized his black velour tracksuit with a red plastic gym whistle on a lanyard.

We were on our way to the so-called Fallen Monument Park, where statues of Stalin, Dzerzhinsky, Molotov, Brezhnev, and the others came to rest after 1992. To which one might say, "Look upon my works, ye mighty," etc., but looming over the park was an exponentially taller and more decadent monument combining the deification of the will of a single man with the gaudy baroque of the corrupt. It was a hundred-foot steel column studded with the prows, sterns, and flags of various embedded ships and topped by a full ship with a mast twice its length. An outsize statue of Peter the Great, taller than the largest ship was long, grasped the uppermost ship's wheel in one hand and flourished a rolled parchment in the other. The whole thing sat on an artificial island in the middle of the Moscow River and was three hundred feet tall if it was an inch. It was designed by the Georgian sculptor Zurab Tsereteli, infamous flatterer and megalomaniac gigantophile, who has made a career of designing and building huge monuments and offering them to cities around the world—for example, a forty-foot teardrop titled "To the Struggle Against World Terrorism" for the harbor of Bayonne, New Jersey.

Although Tsereteli has successfully placed such projects in various locations around the world, more often they are rejected for barely disguised reasons of good taste. The Peter statue was conceived and built for the Christopher Columbus quincentennial and offered to the United States, which politely demurred, then to Puerto Rico, which begged off, citing financial problems.

Yuri Lezhkov, the corrupt Moscow mayor and boss, stepped in and offered to buy the statue on one condition: that Tsereteli remove the head of Columbus, add a mustache, and call it Peter the Great. (The now-unnamed *Niña*, the *Pinta*, and the *Santa Maria* remained in situ.) Tsereteli duly complied, and the towering monstrosity was installed in the river and soon voted one of the ten ugliest statues in the world.

We had big plans to go see the Mayakovsky museum (a ramped maze of cartoon propaganda), or the Bulgakov museum (two competing museums, actually, one private and one public, the latter his old apartment, with giant cat graffiti curling up the stairs and an actual obese, fluffy black feline roaming the halls), or the Treasury. Błażej had bigger plans, though, to get drunk in the sun with his colleagues, and steered us to a rooftop patio. When we ordered Bloody Marys, they came in pieces: a tray with tomato mix, a shot glass of vodka, and greens laid out next to each other. Self-assembly drinks, an Ikea of booze. Thus passed the remainder of the long afternoon. We stumbled home past a monumental classical pile of columns and caps. I asked what the building was.

"It looks like the Moscow Opera," said Błażej, "so, knowing Russia, it must be a supermarket."

In a globalized and franchised world, the only things left unfamiliar are food and language. Everything else you've seen in pictures. We were to take the Moscow–Almaty train southbound to Samara, boarding in the evening for an overnight ride. We went for Armenian food. The restaurant was, naturally, right next to the Azerbaijani place. On the patio outside, a violinist played along to karaoke tapes. Inside two synths and a singer did the same alongside cages of songbirds. We picked at rolled egg-plant stuffed with spinach and garlic, drank wine, and didn't re-alize that the train was leaving in forty-five minutes. We hadn't packed.

Panic: Maria ran ahead to Błażej's apartment to stuff every-thing in the bags. We tried to corner the Armenians to pay, but their credit card machine wouldn't work. We raced home; grabbed the backpacks, the rolling merch suitcase, the guitar, the banjo, and the accordion backpack; and ran across the un-crosswalked street, then down the endless escalators. Moscow's underground is the third deepest in the world, and it takes sev-eral minutes to reach the platforms. We hiked up more escala-tors, elbowing other riders, to the transfers, breath burning in our lungs. I ran ahead, then stopped, panting and soaked. We got to the train platform with two minutes to spare, the train already starting to roll, a dozen other procrastinators clamor-ing to get through the nearest door, the amused conductor half-blocking the entrance and mocking the scrum shoving and pushing our way on. We squeezed through as the train picked up speed. Jogging to keep up, Błażej threw the accordion over the crowd's heads onto the train, and then chucked the white plastic bag of bread and vegetables we'd bought for the ride. It hit the conductor in the back and exploded. A middle-aged man disap-peared in a blur down the gap between the train and the plat-form. People looked at each other for what seemed like minutes until the young conductor yanked the emergency brake. Pande-monium took hold on the platform, and I said, "We better get out of here." Maria nodded, and, dripping, we pushed through the corridors, car after car, until we reached our compartment. We stashed our bags under the bunks and over the sliding door, then stood in the hallway, staring out the windows, as the sweat started to dry and we started to shiver.

"The man was seriously injured," texted Błażej. "Not dead," said the *provodnitsa*. "He was drunk."

"I feel rotten," said Maria, and I nodded.[3]

---

3. "Evidently something unusual had happened. The people who had left the train were running back to it.

   "'What? ... What? ... Where? ... Run over ...' shouted the passers-by."
   —*Anna Karenina*

   "'He was an alcoholic. Can't you understand?' [A] woman began to wail. The passengers were asked to go back to their seats, the guard blew his whistle, and the train started on."—*Dr. Zhivago*

IV.

God-Forget-It House
(Trans-Siberian)

"'No doubt it is beautiful. It is the great road to Siberia.' These words chilled me through. It is for my pleasure, I said to myself, that I travel this road: but what have been the thoughts and feelings of the many unfortunate beings who have traveled it before me? . . . That Russian hell is, with all its phantoms, incessantly before me. It has upon me the effect that the eye of the basilisk has upon the fascinated bird." —The Marquis de Custine

With blood on the wheels, the train rolled toward Siberia. Geographically speaking, Siberia proper wouldn't begin until Tyumen' (or maybe Yekaterinburg), but it was appropriate that our entrance onto the Trans-Siberian Railroad itself be accompanied by an anonymous, maybe fatal, accident, uncommented on and unnoticed by all except those at that door.

The great railroad combines in itself not just the allure of long-distance rail travel, long vanished from the United States, but also the chill of centuries of associations with the massive region itself—something between the wild heart of the Russian nation and the black stain on its moral soul. To Americans, the idea of the vast (in our case Western) frontier is an idea of freedom and a clean slate. The Kerouacian literature of Route 66 and the great westbound highways tell tales of arterial outflowings of optimism and possibility. The romance of the Russian frontier is a darker one, and its eastbound vein—the old Sibirskii Trakt cart road and the railroad that replaced it—is deeply scored with the dusk of punitive journeys and the impossibility of redemption.[1] To go west in America was to go beyond the reach of Washington, but the trains to Siberia, covering twice the distance, run on Moscow time.

"There's no way this will end well," I thought when I saw the little plastic potty on the floor of the train compartment and the wild-eyed child for whom it was intended. A hyperactive, malevolent tempest in a neon-green tank top, he cackled in my face, made a grab for my phone, and raced out the door and down the hall. His mother and grandmother gave weary half-chuckles and opened up glossy magazines.

We were headed directly south toward Samara, an old Volga River pirates' den by the Kazakh border. Previously called

---

1. Dostoyevsky, though, in an essay supporting the Russian imperialist move into Central Asia, saw refuge and possibility in such terra incognita: "When we turn to Asia . . . there may occur something akin to what happened in Europe when America was discovered . . . our spirit and forces will be regenerated."

Kuybyshev, it was to have been the fallback capital of the Soviet Union during World War II and still boasts a never-used bunker built for Stalin. Most of our fellow passengers were Kazakhs headed home, as was the *provodnitsa*—though we discovered she was born in L'viv in western Ukraine, Maria's ancestral homeland. Having made that connection, she was friendlier to us. A pair of plainclothes policemen demanded our passports, while half a dozen children terrorized the hallway. "*Bandity, ne dity*" (bandits, not children), muttered the conductress to Maria. Two men with trays hung around their necks hawked toys—spinning, glowing toys, furry cube-shaped plush toys, battery-powered personal fans—and the gang of feral children screamed louder. The little demon sharing our room made a grab for one of the trays of toys. The dining car was full of Kazakhs who had seen us trudge through, sweating, with our instruments a few hours before, and they asked if we would play. We demurred and, exhausted, went to sleep. When we awoke, Maria's shoes were filled with little puddles of urine.

The approach to Samara was a massive Volga River crossing at least two kilometers across, over swamp and runoff, before we pulled into a futuristic blue-glass phallus-*cum*-shuttle-launcher that was the new train station. We saw for the first time the slouching, two-story wood houses with painted eaves, a distinctive village style that would become more familiar the farther east we went.[2] The Samaran examples were near-destitute

---

2. Custine, describing similar houses in villages outside Saint Petersburg: "[The] roofs are loaded with ornaments which might be considered rather ostentatious, if a comparison were made between the exterior luxury and the internal lack of conveniences. . . . Both peasants and lords take more pleasure in ornamenting the road than in beautifying the interior of their dwellings. . . .

shacks; not until Tomsk and Irkutsk would we see them restored and—up to a point—protected, like the balconied bagatelles of New Orleans.

The other thing that Samara is known for is its brewery, and the town punks, having taken full advantage of its wares, were in high spirits when they greeted us. It was Ruslan the promoter's birthday, and while it was clear that before too long he wouldn't be much help, he was able to organize a ride to the apartment where we would be staying so Maria could shower. Meanwhile his friends took me to the brewery.

It was a brick building by the sandy beach of the Volga. Framed black-and-white photographs showed it in its nineteenth-century heyday, with barrels loaded onto horse-drawn sledges lined up in the mud. These days it was easier: you queued with empty plastic jugs or soda bottles outside a corrugated aluminum shack, next to the salted and dried whitefish. It was nobody's idea of balmy, but if you squinted you could just about imagine you were on a Jersey Shore boardwalk, and the neon beer taps looked like the swirling frozen-drink extruders of any good trashy beachfront. The actual beer was green with spirulina but not undrinkable.

The club was in a basement on the main drag. The walls were covered with intricate Sharpied murals: Stalin in hot pants and a belly-baring top, brandishing a sickle and riding a terrified Hitler, who was himself wearing a KISS T-shirt. It was a drunken and sweaty mess and one of the best shows of the entire tour.

Before and after this tour, Westerners often skeptically asked

---

A nation of decorators." In his condescending fashion, he puts this down to a preference for exciting envy, but it is just as likely a human impulse to break up the monotony of the taiga with colors other than the brown and green of the summer and the white-on-white of the winter.

me, "Do people there know your music?" And the answer was, somehow, yes. The punks of today have an infinitely more comprehensive music-sharing network than their predecessors: the Facebook-aping social network VKontakte. A Western reader is invited to imagine a combination of Facebook, Napster, and Pirate Bay, on which users can stream, share, or download a functionally universal library of popular media with the tacit approval, or benign disinterest, of the authorities. Kids on this circuit had as comprehensive a knowledge of RVIVR, Hot Water Music, and more obscure acts like Bridge & Tunnel and Good Luck as any Gainesville bike punk. And they had the enthusiasm that greets anyone who visits places located off the conventional touring routes—if no one goes there, but *you* go there, people are happy you came and at least curious to come see. Since they had universal access to my music on VKontakte, however, few were interested in buying CDs, preferring the T-shirts and vinyl records, which are prohibitively expensive to import. My already small stock of both was quickly exhausted.

Throughout the entire show the kids clapped aggressively, and polyrhythmically, and a good chunk of the crowd came back to the apartment where we were staying. This was unfortunate. Because of the short travel time to Orenburg the next day, we were getting on a train at four in the morning, and no one was in the mood to let us nap. People packed into the kitchen, laughing and smoking, and we tuned them out as best we could while lying on air mattresses in the next room. When my alarm went off at three thirty, we stepped carefully over the kids passed out around us, bought grapefruit juice at the station, and got on the train for another couple hours of not-quite-sleep.

When the train pulled into Orenburg—"famous," said the

novelist Viktor Sorokin, "for its fine, intricate shawls and its narrow-eyed Russian-Chinese beauties"—at nine a.m., we went straight to the club. It was on the third floor of an office building, and a downright classy second-floor restaurant served us omelets before it was time to go to a hotel and get some real sleep. Said hotel, a thirty-minute drive out of town, past the statue of the cosmonaut Gagarin with upraised hands, in the middle of a dusty field, was an absurd nugget called the Hotel Jamaica. On the outside it was painted bright yellow with red polka dots, and decorated inside with a picture of a hula girl and a school of tropical fish. But the room was sunny and airy, and there was a little green praying mantis in the room and a banya in the basement. We ordered up a steam bath for after the show and took another nap. Maybe three three-hour stretches of sleep would somehow add up to a full night.

The major attraction in Orenburg was a white pedestrian bridge over the rather small Ural River that claimed to be the geographic border between Europe and Asia. Like the largest Lenin or the largest central square, though, this is a distinction promiscuously claimed. No matter: we photographed the column saying "Asia" and the colorful locks left by lovers on the bridge, and then treated ourselves to ice cream.

To the evident dismay of that day's show promoter, who was serving as our local host, we asked to go to the Museum of Orenburg Town History, which Maria had read contained a display about Pugachev's Rebellion. Pugachev was a Cossack ex-soldier who found himself at the head of a motley serf rebellion against Catherine the Great and passed himself off as the tsarina's late husband Peter III (whose murder Catherine had if not directed, certainly sanctioned). Pugachev was inevitably beaten, brought in a metal cage from Orenburg to Saint Petersburg, beheaded, and drawn and quartered, and the rebellion caused Catherine to abandon her progressive plans toward emancipation. Pushkin wrote about him in *The History of Pugachev* and *The Captain's Daughter* (there is a statue of Pushkin outside the Orenburg museum), and Soviet history adopted him as an anti-imperialist martyr.

Our host couldn't have been less interested in this dusty local historical society, but the dowdy woman working the desk was thrilled to air her specialty. Despite our protestations that we didn't need a formal guided tour, she insisted on reciting a well-rehearsed presentation on Pugachev. They had devoted a whole room to him, though none of the artifacts were authentic: a rifle much like his rebels would have used, a replica of the metal cage in which he was dragged to his execution, a diorama.

The show was early, so we were backlit by the midsummer sun shining through the floor-to-ceiling glass windows while we played to an audience of timidly clapping young girls. Afterward we hid in a booth around which we could draw a red velvet curtain, ate pizza and coughed on cigarette smoke, went home early, and steamed in the banya.

The next day we rode a hulking old Volvo bus to Ufa in the July heat. It had a cracked windshield, a dignified Tatar driver with a white crew cut, and an interior decorated with warning signs in Swedish and a poster of Kim Kardashian. The radio played Russian pop that sounded like a continuous series of variations on "I Saw the Sign." Each town we passed was announced by a thirty-foot stele, a 1960s-era attempt to express the full essence of a map-speck village in concrete, paint, and tin. We stopped for a bathroom break, and I ordered a coffee. The ubiquitous instant brand is MacCoffee, which comes in a tearable foil packet decorated, for some reason, with eagles and stars-and-stripes. It reminded me of a passage in novelist Viktor Pelevin's *Babylon* in which a Russian advertising executive advises a client to litter his business card with eagles, dollar signs, and sequoias "because they'll assume you have American investors." For convenient literary contrast, a group of young men in mismatched military outfits boarded the bus, their berets still sporting the hammer and sickle.

We arrived in Ufa, and I called our contact. Maria had been making the phone calls, since she speaks passable Russian, but in this case we were surprised to find it wouldn't make a difference. Dave was an American: balding, sideburns, a blue John Deere T-shirt, a toddler, and a beautiful Tatar wife—the picture of a happily aging hardcore kid in one of the most unlikely places. Ufa was the capital of the autonomous region of Bashkortostan, the Bashkirs being a Turkic Muslim ethnicity with an alphabet just dissimilar enough from Cyrillic to require bilingual signs.

Dave came here from Columbus, Ohio, in 1998 on a whim and simply stayed, solving his middle-American Gen-X malaise by removing himself to a place so unknown to the wider world that his very existence as an American there guaranteed his uniqueness. He sang in a local hardcore band, booked shows, and toured the same circuit we'd been traveling.

From the moment we had arrived in Russia, people asked about our itinerary, and as soon as they heard we were going to Ufa, they all had the same reaction: "You have to see the horse with the giant balls." "They have a statue of a horse there with the biggest balls you can imagine." "I was drunk there once when I was in the army, and we saw the horse with the huge balls."

As promised, so delivered. At the highest point in the city, on an anvil of concrete blocks overlooking the smog and the fork of the Ufa and Belaya Rivers, was a massive green statue of Bashkir national hero Salawat Yulayev atop a horse with, indeed, a scrotal sac of larger-than-average proportion relative to the horse. Until the town posted special security, local ne'er-do-wells had a tradition of sneaking up the hill and painting the balls every Easter.

Souvenir kiosk yurts framed the walkway leading to the overlook. You could buy a magnet of Russian prime minister Dmitry Medvedev dressed in Bashkir national costume, blue with gold trim and a kind of matching fez (Putin magnets were sold out). You could buy Batman T-shirts. You could buy cheap champagne and flowers for your skinny girlfriend in heels. Two men with mangled or missing legs had set up begging stations. The public bathroom cost eight rubles. A sign warned of a hundred-ruble fine for washing shoes in the bathroom sinks. There was a skateboard ramp in front of a brand-new statue of Lenin.

We passed a white Hummer limo with a bachelorette party hanging out of the windows. There was a lot of oil money in town, Dave said. The old two-story wooden houses were in better shape here than in Samara, though the locals told me that these were just facades and that they had been completely renovated inside. Once again, I had the feeling that between the sagging clapboard houses and the lugubrious humidity, I'd been transported to a dusty version of a French colonial outpost, a Dakar or a New Orleans.

—∞∞∞—

If someone came to me the next morning and said, "For $100, you can have three more hours of sleep," I would have said, "That sounds like a very fair price and I will take that deal." Misha had driven down from Perm' the day before to open the show, and we would head back and play with his band the following night. It was an eight-hour drive, with the merch suitcase on my lap. "Like Gagarin said," said Misha, "let's go!"

Misha's stoic and good-humored record-store coworker Alexei drove a Singaporean Hyundai. We asked Misha how his night had gone.

"We had an alcohol fight"—a drinking contest. He sighed. "I was the winner."

Aside from the usual birch and pine, the distinguishing flora of this slow climb up the misting foothills of the southern Urals was a kind of ten-foot Queen Anne's lace that fills the meadows. Misha claimed that this strain was genetically engineered to feed cows but had gone rogue and invasive, leaving welts if you touched it—an example of the kind of conspiracy theory rampant in this part of the world. (A botanist friend identified the plant as giant hogweed. Its sap does cause something called phytophotodermatitis: if you get it on your skin, nothing happens until it's exposed to sunlight, at which point you break out in horrifying blisters.)

We passed a town called Kukushtan, elephantine hay bales that shadowed stooped babas harvesting *sunitsi* (a kind of snub-nosed blueberry), nodding brass-knuckle derricks, socialist realist roadside sculptures emerging from rough-hewn stone, and the best-dressed nuclear cooling towers in the east, painted blue-and-gray stripes with triangular white trim. I had headphones on, listening to Future of the Left while watching the remnants of its past.

Driving in Russia was a challenge at best. The passing conventions were anarchic, the lawlessness of great stretches of the country bred a variety of scams and blackmail, and the cops tended to be on the take. If you were pulled over and didn't want to, as the local idiom has it, "feed the paw," your only recourse was to play dumb and engage the cop in a stalemate. You won when your tolerance for sitting around ignoring his hints surpassed his frustrated realization that every minute he was wasting on you was keeping him from drivers who would simply slip twenty rubles under their license and be done with it.[3] As the porter says in *Dr. Zhivago*, "Wheels don't run without oil."

Many Russians had taken to mounting a video camera on their dashboard, for protection in case of accidents and/or to have their interactions with the police on record. (This practice has led to a profusion of websites where proud drivers post their most hair-raising maneuvers.) "Professional" drivers were no great improvement. Misha told us a story about hailing a taxi in Perm' and opening the door to find a fiftyish driver with a beer in his hand, his teenage girlfriend sprawled in the passenger seat, and a cat sleeping on the dash.

"Like Gogol said, Russia has two problems, roads and fools," Misha said. We pulled off onto a muddy dirt track, a farm road with bluebells and conifers to the left, fields to the right, and clods of dirt scraping the undercarriage. "Russian autobahn. That's how we roll."

It was meant to be a shortcut, but it was several miles before

---

3. Maria suspected that the latter strategy works only if you're foreign, though.

the paving recovered, and then the road dead-ended against a fenced-in Lukoil holding facility. Alexei pulled off the road and laughed guiltily. "We thought this road would be better than the one we knew," said Misha. "I see now it was a mistake."

At length we passed Kyeda, the next town, producing general cheering and self-satisfaction. Misha explained that the town has a "fancy" name—half each of the Russian words for "dick" and "cunt." It was time for a lunch break at a roadside cafeteria, which confirmed my impression that Russian food tastes better than it looks.

Perm' looms large in the literary and political history of Siberia as the quintessential "provincial capital" where ambitious young officers from Moscow or Saint Petersburg could either make their name or wither with frustrated malaise. It features pseudonymously as Yuriatin, where Dr. Zhivago flees ahead of the Bolsheviks, a town that "clung to the summit of the hill in tiers, house by house and street by street, with a big church in the middle on the top, as in a cheap color print of a desert monastery or of Mount Athos." The premise of Chekhov's *Three Sisters* is the titular characters' terminal dissatisfaction with their life in the "provincial capital," generally accepted to be based on Perm' ("which is of course," as one character says, "backward and crude"), after their father is sent there. Dostoyevsky described the kind of family who wound up in Perm': "A post in Siberia is usually a snug berth in spite of the cold. . . . The officials, who may fairly be said to be the aristocracy of Siberia, are . . . men who have come from Russia, usually from Petersburg or Moscow, attracted by the extra pay, the double traveling expenses and alluring hopes for the future. . . . [Those] of more levity and no capacity for solving the problems of existence soon weary of Siberia, and wonder regretfully why they came." There is no lack of regret, and disdain for Perm', in Chekhov:

CHEBUTYKIN: But what a wide, splendid river you have here! A wonderful river!

OLGA: Yes, only it's cold. It's cold here and there are mosquitoes.

. . .

ANDREY: Our town has existed now for two hundred years, it has a hundred thousand inhabitants—and not one of them who isn't exactly like the others, not one hero, not one scholar, not one artist, not one who stands out in the slightest bit, who might inspire envy or a passionate desire to emulate him.

It's not literary history, though, that has shaped most people's first associations with Perm', but its status as one of the premier centers and way stations of the gulag. One of only two camp complexes for political prisoners still open in the 1970s, it was where the dissidents of post-Stalinist thaw built furniture and sewed gloves and uniforms. In her book *Gulag*, Anne Applebaum reports that by the 1970s there were as few as ten thousand political prisoners in the camps, "low by the standards of Stalin's Soviet Union." The Perm' camps became a center of rebellion and hunger strikes from then on, claiming one of the last Soviet-era dissident martyrs, the Ukrainian poet Vasyl Stus, in 1985. In part this was because information had begun to flow more freely from the camps to the newspapers, radio, and samizdat of the outside world, so camp uprisings and abuses in the remaining political prisons were much more widely publicized in human rights circles and the Western press. The Perm' camps closed only in February 1992—outliving the Soviet Union itself, as Applebaum notes. The Russian historical society Memorial has reconstructed the Perm-36 camp in its entirety as a museum and monument to the gulag experience. Its neighbor, these days, is the local asylum.

Misha's grandfather was, in fact, an exile from Saint Petersburg who had been sent to the gulag for being too lenient with disgraced old Bolsheviks in the Stalinist purges. Yet Misha and his girlfriend lived in an unusually spacious and sunlit apartment (by the standards of DIY show promoters), decorated with sketches of beavers with captions like "Ginger Master."

"Here we have Perm'. On one side"—Misha gestured out the car window at a ramshackle structure—"God-forget-it house. On the other side"—pointing to a nouveau-riche mansion—"lions and Jacuzzi." A monumental abandoned military academy on the waterfront was adorned with building-size neoclassical graffiti: Ionic columns, mopey toga wearers, a massive QR code in a wreath, and a small crowd of business-suited silhouettes.

We arrived at a labyrinthine and metallic club that looked like a fashionable meat cooler. Misha's band opened for us, and afterward he had a DJ gig until four a.m., so he dropped us off at his apartment. His girlfriend had left dinner for us (pasta and bread with black cumin seeds), and we slept on a pullout couch.

Perm', a place where cathedrals were used as prisons, became in the literary imagination a place to leave or dream about leaving. At the end of *Three Sisters*, the army battalion that has been stationed there is shipped east:

CHEBUTYKIN [*getting up*]: I, my friend, am going away tomorrow, maybe we shall never meet again, so this is my advice to you. Just put on your hat, take your stick in your hand, and leave . . . leave and start walking, walk and don't look round. And the further you walk, the better.

We had a half-coupe—two bunks—on the same-day train to Yekaterinburg, a short trip. On the way out of town we spotted a fifty-foot, four-sided squared arch made of logs, meant to depict the Cyrillic Π for Perm' (Пермь) from every angle. Nearby was a hundred-foot concrete spire—a sundial shadowing a garden of flowery hours—topped with the inevitable Lenin. Blots of dark ash spilled from the cottage gardens toward the tracks, where households burned their trash. Babas on the platforms sold strings of long, dried, half-skinned fish, the flesh cubed for easy removal.

Compared with the other Siberian cities, Yekaterinburg was a boomtown. There was a wide waterfront with Sunday rowers and a tall, unfinished TV tower ("one of the tallest incomplete architectural structures in the world," per Wikipedia) popular with rock climbers and the suicidal. Best known as the execution site of the Romanovs, Yekaterinburg is also the hometown and early stomping ground of Boris Yeltsin. As party secretary in the 1970s and early 1980s, Robert Service has written, Yeltsin "ranted and threatened . . . used charm and guile . . . [and] turned public ceremonies into carnivals." Once, Service continues, after crashing his car in a ditch outside the city on the way to the October Revolution anniversary parade in the square, Yeltsin "bounded over the fields to the nearest village and commandeered a tractor and a drunken tractor-driver to get to the morning parade on time." Yekaterinburg briefly declared itself capital of an independent "Urals Republic" in the post-Soviet 1990s, but reintegrated quickly and with prosperous results.

We were playing in a hipster café four floors up, with couches and bearded baristas. I was offered a sandwich of stale white bread, a slice of cheese, and a pickle drowning in a swamp of mayonnaise. We retreated to the sushi restaurant on a lower floor. They didn't have most of the items on the menu, but I managed to fill the despairing hunger hole left by the sad sandwich with some soup.

One of the logistical traps I'd laid for myself in planning this tour was that I had a new record, *Do the Struggle*, coming out on a London-based label, and I was thousands of miles away, without a laptop and functionally unavailable by phone. I had a friend and a small gang of puppeteers working on a music video back in New York, and the director asked if I could shoot an intro for it. Down in the dusty parking lot, where a local taxi company had, by way of guerrilla advertising, spray-painted silhouettes of Lenin's head above its phone number, I punched out the bottom of a tin coffee can with a screwdriver. Maria held one phone, filming up through the can to literalize the song's "tin can" vocal effect, while I sang along to the track playing on a second phone. Showbiz! Also, modernity.

We were moving quickly across the country now and got back on the train after the show, for a final tally of some twelve hours in Yekaterinburg. A short sleep and we were awake in time to get a lungful of fresh air on the platform in Tyumen', the wartime home of the now-embalmed Lenin, encapsulated in the Lonely

Planet guidebook with the evocative phrase "nothing much to
see around the station," an assessment I can confirm.

More to the psychological point, though, Tyumen' is regularly cited as the "official" entry point to Siberia. Siberia is one
of those names, like Timbuktu or Samarqand, whose geographi-
cal specificity is dwarfed by its romantic and infamous aura.
Proust observes that a romantic personality "accumulate[s]" in
place-names "a store of dreams." The dangerous ground here is
what Alina Simone describes as "this mythic idea that Siberia
was where you went to experience the real Russia," that it was
"only here, among the descendants of Cossack warriors, political prisoners, and religious dissenters, in these gray and cosseted
cities, that I would become one with the True Slavic Soul." I try
to do my best to avoid a sentimentalizing or fantastic impulse in
prose recollected in leisure, but even the vaguest of border crossings can give me the vertiginous thrill, in both three and four
dimensions, of looking and saying to myself, "Here is Bosnia,"
or "Here is Siberia," or "Here is Mongolia," all implying "Here
is a place where things happened that still resonate in human
imagination."

After the frantic pace of the last few weeks, a few unhurried
days on the train were more than welcome, and I was happy to
stare out the window for hours at a time. As the explorer George
Kennan wrote of riverboat travel, "One has all the advantages
of variety, and change of incident and scenery, without any ex-
ertion: all the lazy pleasures." The endless, martial conifer forests had given way to birch and oak, unpredictable and fecund
meadows, and swampy immobile rivers with an algae glaze. Re-
stricted to cities and trains, we were spared the Siberian sum-

mer plague of mosquitos. The greatest hazard of the climate was merely the heat, somehow both humid and dusty.

"Monotony is the divinity of Russia," wrote Custine, "yet even this monotony has a certain charm for minds capable of enjoying solitude." Wood, wood, always wood: rough Lincoln-log cabins of bisected trunks, more refined houses of plank and carved filigree with cords of four-foot firewood stacked up the north sides and shiny tin roofs. The occasional burned-out shell with a pyrrhic chimney stood as warning and inevitable consequence. Birch-and-pine, birch-and-pine—the landscape held a rhythm in time with the train's wheels.

Eventually a new topography emerged: marsh with a thicket— more than a thicket, a forest, of beheaded and beleafed birch drowned in the thaw but still pristine white, a choir of flagpoles in a vast marching ground of scrub.

We retired to the dining car for toothsome fried potatoes and buckwheat kasha with mushrooms. Hours of grass and short trees passed. The only signs of animal life were one or two white birds, like seagulls, though we were far from any sea; a more prosaic duck; and a couple of goats and cows in a village an hour and a half from Omsk. Twice in twenty hours I saw what you might call a highway. "Distances! These are the curse of Russia," said Tsar Nicholas I to Custine. The Frenchman replied, "Do not, sire, regret them: They form the canvas of pictures that are to be filled up." He was an accomplished flatterer; later in the book, he shared his true impatience: "There are no distances in Russia—so say the Russians, and all the travelers have agreed to repeat the saying . . . unpleasant experience obliges me to maintain precisely the contrary. There is nothing but distance in Russia, nothing but empty plains extending farther than the eye can reach."

Omsk appeared, a little Lego city of industry and housing complexes. One tower produced a miles-long charcoal effluent. Here Gorbachev was punched by an unemployed drunk at a campaign stop in 1996. Here, too, Dostoyevsky was imprisoned for anti-tsarist activity from 1850 to 1854, and the Irtysh River that bisects the city loomed in his imagination ever after. In *House of the Dead*, his fictionalized memoir of prison camp life, he reminisced about the coming of summer and the restlessness it induced in the prisoners: "One suddenly notices dreamy eyes fixed on the blue distance, where far away beyond the Irtysh stretch the free Kirghiz steppes, a boundless plain for a thousand miles." The riverbank was the location of the brickyard where some of the prisoners worked, the only "free [and] open" view, an opportunity "to see something not the regulation prison surroundings. . . . I speak of the riverbank so often because it was only from there one had a view of God's world, of the pure clear distance, of the free solitary steppes, the emptiness of which made a strange impression on me. It was only on the bank of the Irtysh that one could stand with one's back to the fortress and not see it."[4]

For our part, we had just about twenty minutes to run out onto the platform and across the pedestrian bridge over the tracks to a snack kiosk. There we queued impatiently behind a

4. In the epilogue to *Crime and Punishment*, Raskolnikov also works in the prison brickyard on the Irtysh. The prostitute Sofya Marmeladova has followed him to Siberia and lives in what must be Omsk; it is here they have their religious epiphany of love and redemption: "Raskolnikov went out of the shed onto the bank, sat down on a pile of logs and looked at the wide, solitary river. . . . There, in the immensity of the steppe, flooded with sunlight, the black tents

chatty drunk to stock up on chips, ice cream, and beer for the night. I glanced at the time and then at the train, imagining being stranded in this unappealing factory city, and was not reassured by the inspirational banner "V.V. Putin Guarantees Development for Russia."

of the nomads were barely visible dots. Freedom was there, there other people lived, so utterly unlike those on this side of the river that it seemed as though with them time had stood still, and the age of Abraham and his flocks was still the present."

V.

The Knout and the Pierogi *(Tomsk to Baikal)*

W e were awoken at five a.m. for the approach to Novo-sibirsk. As I assembled our bags, I caught a glimpse of an otherworldly, serpentine fog hovering inches off a riverbed, winding through the field to the horizon. It had been a twenty-four-hour trip, during which our cabinmate spoke twice: "Hello" at the beginning and "Good luck" as we loaded off.

Novosibirsk station has a deservedly high reputation. It's a green-and-white neoclassical palace with an arched and chandeliered main hall—one of those "vast, glass-roofed sheds," Proust wrote, "beneath which could be accomplished only some solemn and tremendous act, such as a departure by train or the Elevation of the Cross." The town is, as its name implies, a recent (founded in 1893) and successful (the third-biggest city in Russia) development, a by-product of the construction of the railway itself. It has the wide boulevards and half-empty look of a Western boomtown—Denver or Calgary. And, like a Western town, everywhere there were remnants of 1950s and early 1960s décor—in this case, the Art Deco genericisms of Soviet storefront signage: "BREAD," "CLOTHES."

We were picked up by another Andrei—nearly every promoter on this tour seemed to be a Dima or a Misha or an Andrei—a cherubic punk who Maria swore looked like the 1980s actor Richard Greico. In addition to the obligatory cutoff jean shorts and Vans, he wore a flannel button-down over a Flipper T-shirt and had a Hüsker Dü cassette playing in the car. Siberia, at least in the micro-culture of Andrei's car, was in the midst of a full-fledged 1990s revival. He would drive us the five hours to Tomsk. A train does go there, Andrei said, but "no one takes it."

It's proverbial that periods of reactionary politics can be the wellspring of creative protest, like the sharp political messages of Western punks in the Reagan and Thatcher eras. During that same period, Novosibirsk and Omsk were the centers of perhaps the only indigenous Siberian punk scene. Largely acoustic and based on *magnitizdat* (bootleg recordings), the small but influential circle centered on bands such as AIDS, Grazhdanskaya Oborona (Civil Defense) and its singer Yegor Letov, and the raw and charismatic songwriters Alexander Bashlachev (aka Sash-Bash, not Siberian but closely associated with the scene) and Yanka Dyagileva. The "suicide punks," as this generation of nihilistic Siberian musicians are sometimes called, shared a brutal, amateurish, and personal style. Letov described Bashlachev's gruff, toothless style as "dreadful, bright, and aggressive with no connection to aesthetics . . . a kind of voodoo that he found in his soul." Letov's own recordings were described by one listener, speaking to the musicologist Yngvar Steinholt, as having "that common Russian mud." Grazhdanskaya Oborona tapes, said another, were like "a raw, moldy cellar, like the ones they still have in the villages. You climb down into the cellar and there is this dank, black soil, this mould, this damp smell."

Bashlachev, who came to Leningrad from the northern Volga provincial town of Cherepovets, resurrected the *bardy* tradition of Vysotsky with a new intensity, and it was at one of his "house shows" in Novosibirsk that Yanka (as she became familiarly known) was inspired to pick up a guitar. Intense and reclusive, Yanka, sometimes called "the Patti Smith of Russian punk," was a tortured character who refused to give interviews. She was romantically linked with both Bashlachev and Letov (who remastered and rereleased all her recordings in 2008). One photo showed her with an anarchy symbol on her shirt and pointing a gun at the camera. Her songs, whose nearest Western analogue is perhaps early PJ Harvey or a low-fi Sinead O'Connor, were visceral ("From a beautiful soul/Only sores and lice/From universal love/Just mugs covered in blood), personal ("The television is hanging from the ceiling/And no one knows how fucking low I'm feeling"), and morbid ("The water will come, and I will sleep"). Neither she nor Bashlachev survived their twenties. Bashlachev fell from a ninth-floor window in 1988, and Yanka drowned in 1991. Both were officially suicides, though there are the usual suspicions. Some claimed that Yanka's body was recovered from the river with a crushed skull and no water in her lungs.

"It's really hard to find anyone who is still alive from those days," said Andrei, switching the Hüsker Dü tape out for Patti Smith. "Heroin was really cheap."

Andrei was from Novosibirsk and a northern Siberian family but had been born in Kazakhstan and raised there until the age of ten. He had spent some time in Boston on a work/travel visa working for the hardcore label Bridge 9, after quitting a construction job with some Poles in Dorchester. We pulled over at a rest stop where a dozen shirtless army guys milled around in the sun. I was about to make a snarky comment about the array of terrifying knives for sale until it occurred to me that any given truck stop in Oklahoma would have all that and more. (Though maybe it wouldn't have had the fifty vultures, circling something I couldn't quite see behind the building.) A sign read "2800 km to Chita."

"Chita," said Andrei. "I've got some stories from there."

"And?"

He didn't elaborate. "It's like a giant bad neighborhood. Everyone's trying to leave."

He turned over the Patti Smith tape as we passed an Armenian *shashlik* (kebab) house and stopped to use the bathroom. In the back, they were building a stage and dance floor that would hold hundreds. In the front stood a statue of an eagle crushing a snake. Next to that, two live bears—Misha and Masha—in an iron cage.

"Rock and Roll Nigger" came on the tape, and I started singing along under my breath. "You like this song?" Andrei asked.

"Yeah, it's a classic," I said.

"Is it . . . controversial in America?"

I explained that people understand the premise that it's about feeling like an outsider and a defiant outcast. He nodded and kept driving.

Tomsk, Krasnoyarsk, Irkutsk, and some of the other Siberian

cities have a distinctive local architecture of nineteenth-century rough wood houses, like aristocratic log cabins with ornate carved trim painted in fading ceruleans, purples, and reds. The buildings are deteriorating and sinking into the unsteady ground and facing an uncertain future. "The ones that aren't protected [by the government], they get burned down by developers," said Kostya. "If someone is living there, first they will burn the porch, as a"—he and Andrei briefly debated the translation—"as a hint."

A new big business in Tomsk was selling insurance against Lyme disease. The old big business was importing used cars from Japan. "A whole region lived on it," said Kostya. Many of the eastern Siberian cities teem with cars with steering wheels on the right, "Japanese style." Importers would ship the cars to Vladivostok, then move them westward across the country via train, selling them in the cities along the tracks, until Putin raised the tariff on auto imports to "encourage" the purchase of domestic vehicles.

"That must have been an unpopular reform," I observed.

"Yes," said Kostya. "There were riots. People burned Lada dealerships. I saw a picture with ten or twelve guys with machine guns protecting one of these stores."

Would you ever, I asked him, consider moving away from here?

"To Moscow or Saint Petersburg, no," he said. "I don't like cities, they are moving too fast. And people from Siberia, when they go to Saint Petersburg and take a shower, they're breaking out in pimples, because of the different water!" He paused. "It's hard here, though, if you want to make some change, that is—against the grain."

From the nineteenth century into the early twentieth, Tomsk was a way station for the tea trade from China to the Nizhny Novgorod market via Perm'. Custine detailed an annual delivery of "75 or 80,000 chests of tea, half of which remains in Siberia, to be transported to Moscow during the winter on sledges, and the other half arrives at the fair."[1] It was probably my favorite Siberian town: off the main train line, it was compact, charming, shaded, and full of those picturesque old wooden houses.

Chekhov disagreed, variously describing Tomsk in letters to friends as "not worth a brass farthing" and "a dull and drunken sort of place; no beautiful women at all, and Asiatic lawlessness. The most notable thing about Tomsk is that governors come here to die." He expanded on that opinion to his family: "Tomsk is a most boring town. To judge from the drunks I have met and the supposedly intelligent people who have come to my room to pay their respects, the local inhabitants are deadly boring. At all events I find their company so disagreeable that I have given instructions that I am not receiving anyone."

Kostya asked about the politics of other punks on the tour. The touring circuit we had been on since we arrived in Poland would be familiar to anyone from the German squat and youth center archipelago and the scene associated with American labels like No Idea and Plan-It-X Records: young, idealistic kids who love Fugazi and Hot Water Music, planning antifascist action days and running leftist infoshops and zine exchanges. Their politics were progressive; they were fighting what they considered the good fight. Notwithstanding the fact that they were entirely

---

1. A few decades later, Kennan complained of getting caught behind the caravans of "slow, plodding" sledges of tea from China—shades of today's Polish trucks.

tangential to the effective politics of the country, they had a valuable sense of camaraderie and moral grounding.

Kostya and Andrei, on the other hand, agreed with the old cliché that Russia needs the "knout or the pierogi"—or, as we might say, the carrot or the stick. It's the historical idea that, as Custine quotes a Russian aristocrat, Mongol despotism "established itself [in Russia] at the very period that servitude ceased in the rest of Europe. . . . Bondage was thenceforward established . . . as a constituent principle of society." This is the view that gives grudging respect to figures like Ivan, Peter, Stalin, and Putin—that only the iron hand of a stern but fair tyrant-*cum*-father figure, cruel in what used to be called the "Asiatic" model, can corral and control the sprawling and fractious Russian nation (including, of course, its colonized territory).

Kostya ran a small punk label and had been putting on shows in Tomsk for years. His great-grandfather was a Kazakh *kulak* ("wealthy peasant"), exiled four times. Another great-grandfather was an NKVD officer who worked with the Chinese army. "I've seen pictures of him. I think he was—not really a nice guy. He looked—typical." Kostya's father had been the head of the medical department of a local university but lost his job after he objected to a Putin policy that replaced a free prescription drug benefit for seniors with a cash stipend. Kostya left college and got a job working for an offset printing company to support the family. "It is hard to put on punk shows officially here—I mean [to publicize them] with posters and Facebook and so on. Some people will show up and wait for you after the show, you know what I mean? . . . I saw down by the beach a few years ago—the students like to have flash mobs there, and [at] this one they were wearing terrorist masks, and doing—" He mimed a Nazi salute.

Ultra-nationalist thugs, of course, are a danger anytime you have a stagnant backwater whose best days seem irretrievably past. As Christopher Hitchens put it, "nationalism and chauvinism are often strongest at their peripheries—Alexander the Macedonian, Bonaparte the Corsican, Stalin the Georgian"—and, he might have added, at the psychological peripheries, where dwell the economically tangential and the politically crippled. "Developing an overweening national pride is always a sign," Michel Houllebecq once wrote, "that you have nothing much else to be proud of." International punk has footholds in both the positive and creative and the negative and destructive axes of what Greil Marcus calls "the geopolitics of popular culture."

For all their devotion to and passionate advocacy for progressive Western punk tropes like veganism and antiglobalism, the punks I had talked to thus far had a disheartening aversion to, or apathy about, their corrupt and depressing local and national politics. Like Yegor from Saint Petersburg, there was a general disdain for the protests that sprang up in Moscow and Saint Petersburg in the wake of Putin's 2011 reelection. The common view was that they were of interest only to the urban, Westernized bourgeoisie, and doomed.

The feminist punk band–art collective Pussy Riot had already been arrested, but the international attention generated by their conviction and imprisonment wouldn't come to full force until the fall. When I asked the punks I met in Saint Petersburg, Moscow, and further afield about the controversy, their opinions were muted, verging on dismissive: the women were naïve; they weren't really a band, or at least not a band anyone knew;[2] what did they expect, and what are we supposed to do about it? In this apathetic light, their focus on Western-style punk ethics came to seem an escapist distraction with the veneer of protest, and a funneling-off of critical energy.[3]

Kostya lived on the edge of town in one of the gray concrete housing projects, built around an overgrown courtyard with a rusting playground. Driving to his place for dinner (borscht, potatoes with mushrooms, tomato and onion salad; a cold tea of mint, whole cranberries, lemon balm, lemon, and sugar), he asked if we'd met an American named Dave in Ufa. I said we had. Kostya said they had been friends until a "cultural misunderstanding." He and Andrei exchanged a meaningful look, and Kostya said he'd explain later.

As we brought our bags in, he pointed out graffiti: "Kill the Jews." "I saw the guy who wrote it. It was weird. Usually you expect that to be a young kid, but he was forty, fifty years old!"

After the show we stood outside a supermarket, waiting for their crew of friends to buy beer before they went and smoked weed on the beach of the reservoir under an orange half-moon. It was then they explained the "cultural misunderstanding" that severed their friendship with Dave. Andrei's band, who are on Kostya's label, is called Niggers. (This explained some stickers on

2. This was basically true. Pussy Riot the band was more a pseudonymous vehicle for performance art and protest by a larger collective than a band in the traditional sense.

3. The counterargument, as articulated by political scientist Kevin Dunn, is that the global idea of punk rock in the Internet age, with its egalitarian ethos and ability to repurpose international telecommunications to disseminate "counterhegemonic expression," offers a kind of alternative civil society in repressive

Kostya's mom's refrigerator.) Don't you agree, they asked, that punk rock is about provocation, and nothing provocative should be off the table?

You're going to have trouble convincing most Americans of that, I said—hypocrisy or no. Maria told them about her friends from New York who decided to call their band Ching Chong Song. After stubbornly sticking to the name through protests and boycotts, they eventually changed it after an incident in which the people with whom they were staying that night had been, unbeknownst to both parties, boycotting their show. They had clung to their contrarian anti-PC stance for too long, and it became a pointless expense of energy that led to conflict solely for conflict's sake.

Andrei said that didn't matter, that his band wasn't for the mass public anyway. He said it expressed how they felt, as Russians, as Russian punks, as outcasts, embattled at home and stereotyped overseas. Their record was called "Ugly Russians." Like the Patti Smith song—she used the word, why couldn't he? He pointed out that punk bands casually reference Hitler and the Nazis all the time. Richard Hell, I remembered, was quoted in the *NME* in 1977 saying, "Punks are niggers." Are both Hell and Smith examples of what scholar Julie Roberts called "the long European tradition of using art as a vehicle for the exploration of complex, uncomfortable and troubling issues . . . utilized by the dispossessed, the disenfranchised, the marginalized and the

---

states: "Punk rock is not just a medium of global communication; the medium itself becomes a subversive message in its own right. . . . While some observers occasionally bemoan the 'apolitical' nature of some punk rock scenes, often those critiques operate from a simplistic framework of understanding what can be regarded as political . . . the mere expression of punk rock can be regarded as a political act in itself."

reviled to speak out and assert their own position"—or just kids (so to speak) pushing a button that now sounds a sour note?

I said that using a discredited ideology as an object of or vector for satire was different from adapting it to an identity as oppressed outsiders—not least if you were coming from a historically imperialistic country. Kostya and Andrei seemed disappointed that I didn't agree that Dave was being unreasonable. Andrei remained in a sulk for the remainder of the evening.

I remembered "Kill the Niggers," the smash hit from "the most popular band in Rostov-on-Don." "Russian artists," wrote the American expat journalist Mark Ames, "going back to the Romantics like Lermontov and Pushkin, up through Dostoyevsky and experimentalists like Kharms, have always had a way of borrowing their aesthetics from the West, Russifying them, and taking them one step too far." And the vocabularies of provocation often resist translation. The fascination that some Western punks had with fascist symbols, in particular, became a problem for Soviet and post-Soviet punk.

Beginning in 1983, as Sergei Zhuk relates in his book *Rock and Roll in the Rocket City*, General Secretary Yuri Andropov, "concerned 'with the social control of young people' . . . declared war on Western pop music, [citing] 'repertoires of a dubious nature' . . . [and] the 'distortions, confusion, and antisocial patterns of behavior' associated with Western degenerate music." Rock clubs were closed, and bands were forced to perform at anti-American rallies to demonstrate "their loyalty and ideological reliability." The Soviet government policy against homegrown punk was similar to its war on rock in general but distinct in several important particulars. By purposefully or accidentally confusing and conflating punks in general with neofascist skinheads, the authorities amplified a dynamic of shifting boundaries between the two groups that continues to resonate.[4]

Punk imagery, which came through official channels mostly in its late 1970s British incarnation, arrived stripped of the (admittedly vague) signifying markers that distinguished genuine neofascists from leftists and from simple provocateurs like Johnny Rotten, Mark E. Smith, and Lou Reed, who used Nazi imagery for its shock value. The swastika, wrote Dick Hebdige in his book *Subculture*, "was made available to the punks (via Bowie and Lou Reed's 'Berlin' phase) [and] reflected the punks' interest in a decadent and evil Germany . . . which had 'no future.' It evoked a period redolent with a powerful mythology." He continued:

> Conventionally, as far as the British were concerned, the swastika signified "enemy." In punk usage, the symbol lost its "natural" meaning—fascism. The punks were not generally sympathetic to the parties of the extreme right. . . . On the contrary . . . the widespread support for the anti-fascist movement (e.g. the Rock Against Racism campaign) seem to indicate that the punk subculture grew up partly as an antithetical response to the reemergence of racism in the mid-70s. . . . The swastika was worn because it was guaranteed to shock. (A punk asked by *Time Out* why she wore a swastika replied: "Punks just like to be hated.") . . . . It was exploited as an empty effect. . . .

---

4. The following section draws upon the writings of Yngvar Steinholt and Sergei Zhuk.

Ultimately, the symbol was as "dumb" as the rage it provoked.

But the "symbolic" provocations were taken at face value by the Soviet press. The Russian music journalist Artemy Troitsky remembers that "the only thing anyone knew about punks was that they were 'fascists' because that's how our British-based correspondents had described them. . . . To illustrate this, a few photos of 'monster' [*sic*] with swastikas were printed. . . . The image of punks as Nazis was established very effectively."

Given the centrality of the apocalyptic anti-Nazi campaigns of World War II to the Soviet self-image, this was a powerfully negative association. Perversely, it only added to the subversive appeal of fascist imagery for some Russian punks: the enemy of my enemy is my friend, and to identify with the greatest historical foe of the Soviet state was to express the power of one's own opposition to Soviet Communism. "Fascism" as a synonym for pure evil became, by convenient or lazy association, "an epithet hurled at whomever the Soviet authorities happened to designate as the worst ideological foe of the USSR or its international interests," independent of actual political characteristics, wrote historian Mischa Gabowitsch. This decoupling of insult from meaning turned fascism into a useful shorthand for dissidence. Both Yegor Letov and a later 1990s group formed bands called Adolf Gitler,[5] the latter band adopting the stage names Goebbels, Gimmler, and Goring. Letov's second band, Posev (Seed), was named after a World War II–era anticommunist—and at

---

5. The Russian language, which has no *h* sound, substitutes a hard *g*.

the time anticommunist necessarily meant Nazi collaborator—
publishing house.

This led to some confusion about which bands were officially
condoned: the Clash, though iconic punks, were regarded approvingly by the Soviet state for the band's friendly relations
with the British left on issues such as labor and race relations.
Other scenesters, wrote Zhuk, protested the government bans
on grounds of aesthetic taxonomy: "When one of our disco-
theque enthusiasts interfered and told the KGB people that
AC/DC and Kiss were not punk rock bands, he was arrested by
the police and removed from the dance floor." But the net was
cast widely and none too perfectly. The band 10cc was banned as
fascist because the Cyrillic letter C is pronounced like the Latin
s, and thus the band was assumed to be referencing the SS in
their name (Kiss was blacklisted for similar reasons). A British
article contrasting punks and skinheads was vaguely translated
to conflate the two (identifying "shaven temples of the head" as
the distinctive marker of a punk). Ironic intent of any kind was
lost in translation.

Young people with a contrarian bent got the idea: punks
were fascists, fascists were anti-Soviet, thus if you were an anti-
Soviet punk the most effective vehicle for your disaffection was
fascist and right-wing imagery. "In 1983," Zhuk wrote, "the
Dnipropetrovs'k [Ukraine] police arrested ten students from the
local vocational school . . . [who] had made special white robes,
put the words 'Ku Klux Klan' on them, and tried to 'imitate acts
of this American fascist organization.'"

This conflation of punk and fascism in the official imagination
led to confusion and mistrust that exists to this day. Battles between so-called Fa (right-wing) and Anti-fa (progressive) groups

similar to those recalled with a kind of nostalgia in England to-day are present, visceral, and dangerous in the former Eastern Bloc, especially in its periphery.

Like the Soviet press, willfully or not, misinterpreting the British punks' swastikas, mistranslations become more aggressive in a world in which provocative concepts are available cross-culturally to people with vastly different frames of reference with which to interpret them. It's so easy to airlift an ideology, complete with a fraught vocabulary, wholesale off the Internet that it's equally easy to miss the context. The analogy is going to be inexact at best if one doesn't share the precise historical prejudices at play—and, I suppose, even if you do: I couldn't say precisely why something that feels OK for Patti Smith in 1978 would be off the table for a Russian in 2012, and the short answer may be that it should have been off the table for her as well. The result is a scattershot shooting gallery of offense: look at the tense, ongoing battle over the use of the word "gypsy," which many Roma consider an ethnic slur, others embrace, but which most Americans and British use freely. I heard an Asian American in Beijing brag about "jew[ing] down" a cell phone salesman. It's enough to make a guy say, "Fuck it" and buy everyone a Redskins jersey.

One man's life, in particular, makes a useful fable demonstrating the confusing way in which "punk" has been understood in the context of Russian political and cultural life. The writer, provocateur, founder of the quasi-fascist National Bolshevik Party, and self-identified "punk" Eduard Limonov has long blurred the line between radical politics and large-scale performance art. Because of the centrality of his experience with and interpretation of Western punk to the aesthetics of his politics, he provides a contrast with the later generation of young people, similarly inspired by Western punk but to radically different effect, who constitute the contemporary Russian punk scene. Limonov, exhilarated by characters like Johnny Rotten and of a Soviet generation mistrustful of any ideology, understood punk as an amoral license for confrontation and offense for its own sake. Today's punks (excepting, maybe, our friend Andrei), inspired by the anarchist, progressive politics of bands like Crass and Fugazi, imbibed not only aesthetics but a set of ideals and a progressive moral sensibility.

Limonov was born Eduard Savenko in 1943 in Kharkov and grew up in its gritty and violent Saltovka neighborhood, which he described in his third book, *Memoir of a Russian Punk*. In the 1960s "punk" meant petty theft and hooliganism, and Limonov describes an aimless world of gang scuffles, drinking, and runins with the "trash," or cops. His own father was a secret police officer who ran train convoys "transport[ing] punks to labor camps and prisons" in Siberia. So it was with a kind of oedipal commitment that he managed to get himself exiled from the Soviet Union by 1974. "Rat out your degenerate friends or go into exile," the KGB reportedly told him. He went to New York and managed to embed himself in the Lower East Side punk scene, befriending and idolizing scene luminaries including Richard Hell, Marky Ramone, and, yes, Patti Smith. It was a debauched period he used as material for his first books, *It's Me, Eddie* and *His Butler's Story*, which became sensations in France and Germany[6] and sold more than a million copies in Russia. The

---

6. The Dutch, French, and Italian editions of *It's Me, Eddie* were titled, in reference to Limonov's bisexual adventures, *The Russian Poet Likes Big Negroes*; the German, succinctly and inaccurately, *Fuck Off, America*.

exposure to the provocative downtown art world of 1970s New York shaped his self-conception permanently. To this day, he wears the "torn black sleeveless T-shirt or a button-down black T-shirt, black fake jeans unraveling at the seams, and Keds-like shoes" of an aging SoHo artist and "is clearly proud of being the sort of Iggy Pop of the right-wing literary world," according to journalist Mark Ames, a longtime Limonov apologist. He already had a *nom de punk*, thanks to a friend who had dubbed him "Limonov" or "lemon" because "he was very pale, almost yellow." He explained with no little pride that to a Russian ear the word sounds like "something punk, like Johnny Rotten."

In the 1980s, he spent a few years as a literary celebrity in Paris. "We were used to Soviet dissidents being bearded, grave, and poorly dressed," said French writer Emmanuel Carrère, who met him during these years and wrote a kind of "biographical novel" about him in 2011. "And here was this sexy, sly, funny guy, a cross between a sailor on leave and a rock star. . . . He sang Stalin's praises, which we chalked up to his taste for provocation." With the fall of the Soviet Union, he returned to Russia and immediately set about making himself infamous. He was invited by the clownish populist Vladimir Zhirinovsky, founder and leader of the Liberal Democratic Party of Russia, to join the LDPR shadow cabinet. After a brief stint as minister of the interior, though, he instead founded his own National Bolshevik Party (NBP), also known as the Nat-Bols. ("The name made no difference to Limonov," NBP co-founder and "ideologist" Alexander Dugin told the *New York Times*. "He wanted to call it 'National Socialism,' 'National Fascism,' 'National Communism'—whatever. Ideology was never his thing. . . . The scream in the wilderness—that was his goal.") The party unveiled a flag that was simply a Nazi flag with a hammer and sickle in place of the swastika. "Certainly it was irritation, provocative, outrageous punk, our flag," Limonov wrote. He named the party's newspaper *Limonka*, a pun on his name that was slang for a hand grenade. The Nat-Bols combined the far left, the far right, and the far out. "There's no longer any left or right," he told an interviewer. "There's the system and the enemies of the system"—and by "system," he explained, he meant Western liberal democracy.

The party slogan was "Russia is everything—the rest is nothing." Limonov's young skinhead bodyguards referred to him as "Leader," a term once used for Stalin. Party ideology was haphazard, opportunistic, but always oppositional. Party members were, said the *New York Times*, "part Merry Pranksters, part revolutionary vanguard," who

> have found in the NBP a satisfyingly fierce ideology, often mediated by black humor, that can be refashioned, as Limonov readily admits, "to fit anyone and anything." . . . His message has changed—from anti-Americanism and anti-capitalism to anti-Putinism and anti-fascism—though rabid nationalism has dominated. He has sought the mantle of everyone from Mikhail Bakunin, the 19th-century anarchist, to Jean-Marie Le Pen, the French ultranationalist. He has shifted course so often that by now only the goal—revolution—and the means—young people—remain constants. . . . Disaffected youth are Russia's "most exploited class" in Limonov's view and, as he readily admits, his core supporters. There are young men with shaved heads in the party, though

these days they are more likely to be left-wing punks
than right-wing skinheads.

The mixture of the absurd, the righteous, and the belligerent
was intoxicating to the disaffected youth of Russia's provincial cities, and in the pre-Internet era that ethos reached people via copies
of *Limonka*, which became a shared secret, a window into a garish
underground, like heavy metal or science fiction. "There was every reason to be blown away by its gaudy layout, vulgar drawings,
and provocative headlines," wrote Carrère, describing the impact
of the newspaper on the writer and NBP party member Zakhar
Prilepin. "*Limonka* dealt less with politics than with rock and roll,
literature, and above all, style. What style? Fuck you, bullshit, up
yours style. Majestic punk." Prilepin explained to Carrère,

> You have to imagine what a provincial Russian city
> is like. The sinister life young people lead there, their
> lack of a future, and—if they're at all sensitive or
> ambitious—their despair. All it took was for a single
> issue of *Limonka* to arrive in a city like that and fall
> into the hands of one of these idle, morose, tattooed
> youths who played the guitar and drank beer under
> his precious posters of The Cure or Che Guevara, and
> it was a done deal. Very quickly there were ten or
> twenty of them, a whole threatening gang of good-for-
> nothings with pale complexions and ripped black
> jeans who hung out in the squares. . . . [*Limonka*] was
> their thing, the thing that spoke to them. [Limonov]
> said to them, "You're young. You don't like living in

this shitty country. You don't want to be an ordinary
Popov, or a shithead who only thinks about money,
or a Chekist. You're a rebel. Your heroes are Jim Morrison, Lenin, Mishima, Baader. Well there you go:
you're a *nazbol* already." . . .

[They] were the Russian counterculture. The only
one: everything else was bogus, indoctrination and
so on. So of course the party had its share of brutes,
guys recovering from military service, skinheads with
German shepherds who got their kicks from pissing
off the *prilitchnyi*—the upstanding citizens—by giving the Nazi salute. But the party also included all the
frozen backwaters of Russia had to offer in terms of
self-taught cartoonists, bass players looking for people to start a rock band, amateur video freaks, and
timid guys who wrote poetry in private while pining
after girls who were too beautiful for them and nurs-
ing dark dreams of wasting everyone at school and
then blowing themselves up, like they do in America. Plus the Satanists from Irkutsk, the Hell's Angels
from Kirov, the Sandinistas from Magadan.

Limonov issued provocative policy proposals, including po-
lygamy and mandatory childbirth for women ("like military service for men")—and then retracted them: "Fuck, I even forgot
I wrote that." Indulging a Hemingway-esque infatuation with
the military, he appeared, wrote Marc Bennetts in *The Guardian*, in a documentary film "shooting a machine gun into a besieged Sarajevo in the company of Bosnian Serb leader Radovan

Karadžić.[7] The incident . . . shown at Karadžić's trial at the Hague, cost Limonov publishing contracts in both Europe and the US." The Nat-Bols embarked on a program of what Limonov referred to as "velvet terrorism." These were direct actions of the kind the anarchist writer Hakim Bey calls "poetic terrorism": situationist, absurdist public pranks, in which, as Bey says, "the audience reaction or aesthetic shock [is] at least as strong as the emotion of terror . . . art as crime; crime as art."

Nat-Bols doused a politician in mayonnaise, occupied the Ministry of Health, rushed the Ministry of Finance yelling, "Return the money to the people!" and scattered leaflets encouraging Putin to "Dive After the Kursk"—the Russian Navy submarine that sank with its crew in 2000. As far back as *Memoir of a Russian Punk*, Limonov had been taken with the romance of a small, disciplined group in a time of anarchy, writing about himself (as he usually does) in the third person: "Eddie-baby is convinced that if the leading people in the state are liquidated, there will be chaos in the country and a well-organized gang can seize power. . . . Eddie-baby doesn't see anything impossible about his idea. Lenin and the Bolsheviks also had a very small gang in 1917, but they still managed to seize power." The authorities took him seriously, and he wound up serving two years in prison for smuggling arms as part of a supposed plot to take over northern Kazakhstan ("We live in a terrible climate. . . . Russia should

---

7. "I've always loved bright and handsome gangsters," Limonov said of one of the Serbian paramilitaries, echoing Rebecca West's swoon over Yugoslav masculinity in general—"beautiful, with thick, straight, fair hair and bronze skins and high cheekbones pulling the flesh up from their large mouths, with broad chests and long legs springing from arched feet. These were men, they could beget children on women, they could shape certain kinds of materials for purposes that made them masters of their worlds"—and the Serbs in particular.

swallow Kazakhstan territory if we want our children to have sunshine," he later explained), and the Nat-Bols were outlawed in 2007 after seizing the reception office of the Kremlin.

Limonov's time in 1970s New York, and specifically its punk scene, remains his aesthetic and nostalgic touchstone. He "was never political," an old friend told the *Times*. "New York politicized him. This city was his awakening." Limonov himself told the *Times*, "The Ramones, I knew them. Not just Joey. All of them. It was a rich life then. . . . It was a great time, a legendary time. I have now a certain nostalgia. It's exciting, and dangerous of course, what we're doing now. But to have lived in the seventies in New York, it means a lot. Still." In one of several defenses of Limonov, Ames explains the through line between the provocations of the early punks and Limonov's reinterpretation in the political sphere of what he understood to be their modus operandi:

He told me that the first English poetry he translated into Russian after moving to New York was the lyrics of Lou Reed. Reed, both as singer of The Velvet Underground and as a major figure in Andy Warhol's Factory scene, was aggressively anti-bourgeois and anti-liberal, taking much of his aesthetic from the sado-masochist underground, from the violent fringes of society, from fascism and revolutionary aesthetics, in order to confront contemporary Western culture. Soon after Lou Reed and Iggy Pop, Limonov fell in with the punk movement in New York, which also agitated against liberal middle-class culture and values, relying heavily on violence and the threat of violence, though also more often than not on outrageous humor. Limonov never changed his heart or tastes; indeed, much of his sympathy with the skinheads goes directly back to The Sex Pistols, The Clash, and Lou Reed, a Jew from Long Island who carved a giant iron cross in his skull and strutted around stage in a black leather uniform singing "Kill Your Sons."

The use of Nazi imagery for shock was rampant in the UK punk scene. Steinholt gives such examples as "the Sex Pistols' 'Belsen Was a Gas,' Siouxsie Sioux's and Mark E. Smith's swastika armbands, [and] the origin of band names such as Joy Division." Johnny Rotten also toyed with swastikas as a fashion statement. "I believe [NBP membership] could be given to Sid Vicious and Johnny Rotten (the Johnny Rotten of 1977) and such membership would be accepted," Limonov said. While denying that he necessarily still considered himself a punk ("How can one be a punk after 60? That would be silly"), he explicitly confirmed, in his essay "Punk and National-Bolshevism," the influence of his youthful heroes on the NBP's aesthetic:

> Punks were skeleton of Party organizations in first years of our existence. Loud denial of so-called values of civilization, grotesque, trash, screamings, some borrowings of Rightist aesthetics, were common for New York City punk movement of 1970s as well as for first National-Bolsheviks in 1990s. . . . Newspaper of National-Bolsheviks Party "Limonka" was in 1990s the most radical and most punkish of whole world. With its slogans like "Eat the Rich!" or "Good bourgeois is a dead bourgeois!" or "Capitalism is shit!" We were in punk tradition, what else? . . .

NBP's actions, however non-violent, are bearing aesthetics of punk, for example occupation of Bolshoi Theater on May 7, 2004, the day when Putin was inaugurated. Putin was expected at Bolshoi that evening, so National-Bolsheviks erupted on stage, took over president's box. They were burning fires as football hooligans, wearing flags and screaming slogans. That was beautiful. That was punk. . . . Many heavy books will be written on subject "NBP and Punk." I just made a sketch.

Limonov may not be *a* punk anymore, he said, but "I believe that I am most punkish person on whole territory of Russian Republic and probably on all territory of ex-Soviet Union too. Maybe Shamil Basayev is comparable to me," referring to the deceased Chechen terrorist who claimed responsibility for the infamous Beslan school massacre.

Musicians were prominent in both the leadership and membership of the NBP—one account of an NBP rally noted that "Mr. Limonov's speech drew a number of leather-clad rockabilly fans and thrash metal musicians." Yegor Letov, whose *Independent* obituary called him "the father of Russian punk" and whose unimpeachable countercultural and dissident status included forced commitment to a mental hospital, was issued NBP membership card number four. He and Sergey Kuryokhin of the legendary band Akvarium[8] became two of the NBP's most prominent members, running its "cultural wing," and the party became a magnet for a certain strain of the aging avant-garde.

---

8. Kuryokhin was also a fluent practitioner of absurdist pranks like "proving" on a talk show that Lenin had transformed into a fungus after ingesting hallucinogenic mushrooms.

Letov's presence and credibility, said Limonov, gave the party "thousands of recruits over the years."

But their motivations and goals were not entirely in sync. The narcissistic Limonov saw himself, Steinholt argues, as the auteur of "a massive *Gesamtkunstwerk* that would cement his position" as a provocateur, "concentrating first and foremost on ideological taboos." Letov, on the other hand, was a psychedelic nihilist, combining "glowing, universal misanthropy [with] anti-social tendencies" and a weakness for "territorial nationalism"—the old self-destructive and self-hating Russian patriotism at work.[9] "Letov, as all punk artists, proved to be inconsistent, capricious, and unpredictable," said Limonov, not without sympathy. "He quarreled with us in 1996, came back to party later, then went to his own punk solitude. Sometimes he is declaring himself Red and National-Bolshevik, sometimes he makes believe he doesn't know us." In the last years of his life, Letov cycled through ideologies—he left the NBP for Zyuganov's revanchist Communists and then, as his political notoriety crippled his performing career, he renounced politics and, feeling misunderstood, retreated into a sullen silence.

Limonov, Letov, and Kuryokhin all belonged to what filmmaker Adam Curtis calls "a post-political generation," raised in the stagnant Soviet 1970s, "who retreated from all conventional ideologies, both communist and western capitalist, and instead turned to radical avant-garde culture . . . to try and protest against the absurdity of the system . . . something they be-

---

9. There is an implication in the commentary that Kuryokhin, for his part, was taking the piss: one of Kuryokhin's longtime associates told Steinholt "that his jokes had finally gone too far and made him friends among the wrong kinds of people."

lieved politics was incapable of doing. . . . Limonov has explicitly said that his aim is to take ideas and attitudes from avant-garde art and music and use them to try and create a new kind of confrontational politics."

A coping mechanism and way of public expression distinctive to this generation in the waning years of Soviet and Eastern European communism, conscious of the emptiness of Soviet symbology and language but pessimistic about its opportunity to foment change, was an attitude colloquially called *stiob*. Alexei Yurchak defined *stiob* as "an ironic aesthetic . . . [that] differed from sarcasm, cynicism, derision or any of the more familiar genres of absurd humor [in that it] required such a degree of *overidentification* with the object, person, or idea at which [it] was directed that it was often impossible to tell whether it was a form of sincere support, subtle ridicule, or a peculiar mixture of the two. The very practitioners of *stiob* refused to draw a line between these sentiments . . . refusing the very dichotomy." *Stiob* was parody so deadpan, so straight-faced, that it became indistinguishable from the real thing.[10] The authorities would be aware of and reactive to traditionally or literally dissident language. But since the "highly formalized language . . . [of] late socialism" meant that it was more important to reproduce approved phraseology "than to concern oneself with what [the words] might 'mean' in a literal sense," Yurchak explained,

---

10. In a journal article on *stiob*, Dominic Boyer and Yurchak wrote, "In the post-Soviet period the meaning of this term widened considerably, and today is often used in Russian media to refer generically to irony, sarcasm and absurd humor." The oft-noted tendency of postcommunist Eastern Europeans to hold those attributes may also go a long way toward explaining that generation's fondness for Frank Zappa.

official lingo proved a useful Trojan horse in which to insert subversive meaning.

An inexact parallel in contemporary American life was Stephen Colbert's past embodiment, on his Comedy Central show, of a Bill O'Reilly–esque right-wing blowhard. The comparison is inexact because *The Colbert Report* was clearly presented as a comedy program, with an audience explicitly let in on the joke. Imagine an unknown Colbert, in undercover character, hired as an actual Fox News commentator. Musicians showed a particular skill at this sort of thing—the Slovenian band Laibach, who in 2015 became the first Western band to play a concert in North Korea, remain well-known practitioners. In 1987, Kuryokhin managed to have published in *Leningradskaya Pravda* an ideologically impeccable attack on rock music, written in irreproachable Soviet jargon: rock musicians, he wrote, show a "complete lack of talent and very little skill in playing musical instruments. [The] deafening noise . . . reveals overall helplessness, the silliness of their texts reveals banality . . . their false pathos reveals social inadequacy. . . . It is time that the Komsomol takes a very serious look at this problem." The confused reaction of officials, wrote Boyer and Yurchak, proved that "a text written in that language . . . could be simultaneously an exemplary ideological statement and a public ridicule of that statement."[11]

The centrality of the official antifascist line made it an ideal target for *stiob* actions. To the *stiob* generation, "all political doctrines and sentiments (multiculturalism as well as conservatism,

---

11. Another Western analogue would be the articles in parody newspapers such as *The Onion* that, because of their pitch-perfect parroting of journalistic jargon, are mistakenly shared as real news.

liberalism as well as socialism, fundamentalism as well as athe-ism) [were] equally corrupt, deformed, and hypocritical," wrote Yurchak. And if fascism were divorced from its sacrosanct place in the Soviet hierarchy of evil, it too could be repurposed as just another empty ideological aesthetic.

Is Limonov, then, a subtle and committed practitioner of *stiob* (though to ask the question is to misunderstand the game)? Jour-nalist Matt Taibbi, the co-editor (with Mark Ames) of the amoral expat journal *The Exile* in Moscow in the 1990s, described Li-monov's imprisonment as having been "for faux-fomenting real revolution, or really fomenting faux revolution." Is he, as Ames has described him, an opportunist and self-promoter, "a cynical marketing whiz looking to . . . maintain his fame?" Were he and Letov examples of a tendency of a kind of aging contrarian to find in political strength-worship a culmination of the libertar-ian self-sufficiency that defined their dissident youth? Perhaps he should simply be taken at face value—actions and words do exist independent of intent—as the French writer-provocateur Michel Houllebecq once wrote of himself, as a "nihilist, reac-tionary, cynic, racist, shameless misogynist: to lump [him] in with the rather unsavory family of 'right-wing anarchists' would be to give [him] too much credit."

Or, as Ames wrote in an impassioned defense, was Limonov a principled, almost pathological contrarian, and the criticism of his political theater the cowardice of aesthetic dilettantes? Ames described a call he received from Limonov on the occasion of *Limonka*'s fourth anniversary: the paper was throwing a party at the Mayakovsky Museum, and Limonov wanted to invite his old hero Johnny Rotten. Rotten, through his agents, begged off, cit-ing jet lag and Thanksgiving plans. Limonov, said Ames, was a

living contrast to formerly extremist artists like Rotten who had
been co-opted into the bourgeoisie.

After the departure of Dugin from the National Bolshevik
party—he went on to become a Kremlin-funded primary ideo-
logue of the Russian incursions into Ukraine—and Limonov's
prison term ("For a man who sees himself as the hero of a
novel," his biographer wrote, "prison is one chapter that can't
be missed"), the latter disavowed the more xenophobic and far-
right rhetoric of the NBP, which was banned by the government
in 2007. As promiscuous in his political alliances as in his personal life (he's been married six times), in 2010 he joined forces
with the chess champion and Western-style liberal Garry Kasparov in an umbrella group they called the Other Russia. "Russia is rich in generals without armies," Kasparov told the *Times*.
"But Limonov has foot soldiers. He commands street power." But
the Other Russia coalition crumpled in the wake of its ineffec-
tual resistance to the election of Dmitry Medvedev in 2008, and
the *Times* found Limonov seeming lost, adrift, "a performance
artist who could not perform." The massive anti-Putin rallies of
2011 were largely attended by a serious, Western-looking urban
middle class, not a ragtag collection of contrarians and ironists.
"Limonov held his own rally alongside," said Curtis, "obviously
hoping that he would be the vanguard for this new insurgency."
But Limonov was a man of the anarchic 1990s. The role of "virtuous opposition figure," wrote Carrère, turned out to be a kind
of booby prize, the only option left for a would-be political leader
trumped by more cynical Putinists on the right and by genuine
idealists on the left: "the defender of values he doesn't believe
in (democracy, human rights, all that crap), alongside honest
people who embody everything he's always despised." But the

nouveau bourgeois protesters had their own chosen mouthpiece, the blogger Alexei Navalny, and wanted consistency, not chaos. "[Limonov] and his supporters were completely ignored. The protests swept on past them."[12]

Ames asked Limonov "what happened to that punk-fascist element in the National-Bolsheviks after he got out of jail [in 2003] and he told me: 'Why would we bother playing with fascism anymore when the Kremlin is already fascist? We are an opposition party. And today the most radical position of all is to fight for democracy and elections—against Putin's fascism. It's far-right fascism that is banal and oppressive now.' To quote Yegor Letov's great anthem: 'Я всегда буду против!' ('I will always be anti-!')"

Maybe. But for all his contrarian rhetoric, Limonov's greatest fetish was always for power. A friend once told him that his "habit of dividing the world into failures and successes was immature and . . . [would] only result in perpetual unhappiness." To have aligned with the emasculated Russian liberal left must have seemed like a final miscalculation, leaving him politically sidelined, an inconsequential relic. "A shitty life" was his assessment to Carrère in 2009.

---

12. In 2012, Curtis proposed that Limonov's true political legacy could be found in the half-Chechen fixer Vladislav Surkov, a member of the *stiob* generation who wielded more actual power than any of his counterparts in the opposition. Surkov became the mastermind of "managed democracy," helping to create both Putin's party and its Potemkin opposition. He co-opted Limonov's paramilitary nationalist youth movement, forming the similar Kremlin tool Nashi, which used slogans borrowed from the NBP. Meanwhile, he wrote essays on conceptual art, ghostwrote lyrics critical of the government for a rock band, and dispensed patronage in the art world. His aesthetized, amoral power games took the *stiob* attitude of the interchangeability and hollowness of ideology to another, more insidious level, replacing apathetic *stiob* detachment with a puppetmaster's will and a nihilist's ruthlessness.

And so, with power in mind, he pivoted toward Putinism. For decades Limonov had advocated for the annexation of Crimea and the return to Russia of all the territories—especially those with residual ethnic Russian populations, such as the Baltics, eastern Ukraine, and northern Kazakhstan—lost in the disintegration of the USSR. As the Ukrainian antigovernment "Euromaidan" protests of 2013–14 climaxed, he called on Ukrainian president Viktor Yanukovych to crack down. When Putin moved into Crimea, Limonov publicly and vociferously cheered, urging him to openly employ the Russian army to seize eastern Ukraine (including his hometown of Kharkov). Alexey Pesotsky, a member of his Other Russia party's executive committee, wrote that the "Russia Without Putin" opposition slogan had become an "empty mantra" and that Putin "has started to make steps in the last years that deserve respect. It is difficult to deny Putin's accomplishments, such as preventing a war in Syria, victorious Olympic Games in Sochi and the reunification of Crimea with Russia." The Other Russia, which had for years been denied official registration and whose freedom-of-assembly rallies had regularly ended in arrests, was suddenly granted permission to organize public gatherings.

The party splintered, with some volunteering to fight in eastern Ukraine and others leaving, denouncing what they saw as Limonov's accommodation. Limonov traded insults with the classic-rock musician Andrey Makarevich, a onetime Kremlin supporter who wrote songs in support of Ukraine and performed in the war-torn region. (Limonov called Makarevich old and impotent, and Makarevich offered to "prove his sexual prowess" to Limonov in person.) Limonov turned up in "Novorossiya" (the separatists' aspirational name for southeastern Ukraine), still unable to resist the allure of the military encampment. Instead of writer-as-leader, he became writer-as-cheerleader—not Havel, or even D'Annunzio, but Pound. Whether out of a fear of irrelevance or a simple alignment of goals, the arch-oppositionist and revolutionary fantasist had been co-opted into the regime, finally aligned with the side of arms and cynical power.

A hot and dusty haze hung over the road to the old silver-mining town of Barnaul, by the Mongolian border. We were well off the main Trans-Siberian line, so Andrei had put us on a bus. There was a north–south train line from Novosibirsk, but, Kostya explained, the line ran in sections, and you had to change trains at each station.

After Dostoyevsky's release from prison in 1854, he was still forbidden from returning to Russia proper and took a tutoring job in Semipalatinsk (now Semey in Kazakhstan, home of the Soviet atomic bomb test site). He married his first wife, the widow Maria Isaeva, and moved with her to Barnaul.[13] He reminisced with fondness about that time and the region in the opening of *House of the Dead*:

> One may find a blissful existence in Siberia. The climate is excellent; there are many extremely wealthy and hospitable merchants; many exceedingly well-to-do natives. Young ladies bloom like roses, and are moral to the last extreme. The wild game-birds

---

13. Barnaul was also the urban jumping-off point for Limonov's abortive Nat-Bol training camp, established with the vague goal of fomenting Russian separatist rebellion in Kazakhstan.

fly about the streets and positively thrust themselves upon the sportsman. The amount of champagne consumed is supernatural. The caviar is marvelous. In some parts the crops often yield fifteen-fold. In fact it is a blessed land. One need only to know how to reap the benefits of it. In Siberia people do know.

The farther we got from Saint Petersburg, the more catch-as-catch-can the venues became. In Barnaul it was a classic rock bar. The owner, who introduced himself as Michael Rappaport, had a collection of reel-to-reel bootlegs of Quiet Riot, White Lion, and Queen labeled and stacked on metal shelves in the dressing room. His "vice president" was a young guy whose band did ska and reggae covers of classic Soviet rock and schmaltz—Kino, Akvarium, Alla Pugacheva. Michael bought two of each of our records and sent us over to the local Intourist hotel, where the desk clerk had us listed as "two foreigners, from Michael Rappaport."

In the morning we were incapacitated by stomach cramps, which brought with them all the additional symptoms you might expect, and I considered calling ahead to cancel that night's show. Was it the water? The multi-fruit juice on an empty stomach? The zinc tablets? Who knows, but the effects were gone two hours later, and we made it back to Novosibirsk for the third time in three days. That night's show was at a chrome-and-mirrors dance club called Lebowski Bar, with a mosaic of the titular character on the dance floor and murals from the movie on the walls. A group of teenage girls celebrating a birthday ran to the front of the room to clap for our faster songs, melted back into the shadows for the ballads, and called me to their table afterward for shots of a hideous red, flavored vodka. The club stiffed us on the guarantee, and I slept poorly on the airless train.

Krasnoyarsk has a reputation as one of the more beautiful Siberian cities, and our approach confirmed that. There was more mountainous terrain than I'd seen in weeks, and my ears popped. When Chekhov reached this point in his journey, he wrote to his family:

> In [my] last letter . . . I said that the mountains around Krasnoyarsk resembled the Don ridge, but this is not really the case: looking at them from the street, I could see that they surrounded the town like high walls, and they reminded me strongly of the Caucasus. And when I left town in the early evening and crossed over the Enisei, I saw that the mountains on the far bank were really like the mountains of the Caucasus, with the same kind of smoky, dreamy quality. . . . The Enisei is a wide, fast-flowing, lithe river, more beautiful than the Volga. . . . So the mountains and the Enisei have been the first genuinely new and original things I have encountered in Siberia.

It was another famous gulag town: Lenin spent a "couple of months" here during a period of exile, according to Ian Frazier, and "the research he did [in Krasnoyarsk] helped in the writing of his *Development of Capitalism in Russia*."

Our handler Yegor, wearing an obscene shirt advertising the American punk band NOFX, had a deadpan idea of what constituted local landmarks: our first agenda item was a hike out to the local hydroelectric dam, next to which was a truck parked atop a thirty-foot pedestal with the words "Glory to Work" painted on its side. Next he pointed out a twenty-four-story office building left incomplete in the late 1980s on which work had just begun again. The local council had been planning a metro as well, but then the government changed hands, and the new mayor "spent all the money on fountains instead." Yegor pointed out a bronze sculpture of three elk, coated in leafy ivy like giant Chia Pets, and life-size "electronic trees" whose LEDs flashed in the night. "The mayor likes stuff like that," he said. "Especially fountains." But the mayor had just been elected to the Duma, the parliament in Moscow, "so probably he won't go to jail."

Intrigued by Yegor's bluntness, I asked him what he thought of the recent anti-Putin protests, and he repeated the same glum assessment I'd heard elsewhere: the protests are just against Putin and only for the urban elite, there are no alternatives, all the other presidential candidates were "just part of the same gang," allowed to exist by the Kremlin as a (so to speak) Potemkin opposition. Navalny, the opposition blogger who got a lot of attention in the Western press, was a "bastard" only in it for money and attention.

Were there, I asked, any politicians he liked? "Zhirinovsky"— the radical populist and xenophobic nationalist—"is the only one who says anything interesting, but he will never get elected," he answered.[14]

We drove to one of the genuine landmarks of Krasnoyarsk, a chapel on a hill that appears on the ten-ruble note (alongside

---

14. "Sick and twisted as he was, I liked Zhirinovsky," said Taibbi. "I knew that, for the greater good, he should probably be shot, but he's at least funny—really funny, funnier than anyone in American public life. . . . His party was the Oak-

the hydroelectric dam). "Here," said Yegor, gesturing to his left, "are drugs."

In those beautiful wooden houses?

"Well, rich people too, but also gypsies on drugs."

The main road is Ul. Sovietskaya. It would be nearly impossible to get lost in any major Russian city, I thought: just ask for the intersection of Sovietskaya, Lenina, and Karl Marxa and you are guaranteed to find a train station and a giant square. Was there—to cross off the last box in Russian street-name bingo—also an Ul. Pushkina? Not in Krasnoyarsk, but, as if to make up for it, there was a Pushkin statue.

We passed the "Island of Sport and Recreation" and picked up Yegor's three cheerful and enthusiastic friends, who placed my guitar across their laps as they sat in the backseat.

"He"—Yegor indicated the guy sitting behind him—"loves to change guitars for drugs."

Sorry?

"He sells guitars and buys drugs."

The guy with my guitar in his lap?

"He used to make a living playing Internet poker, but they blocked Americans last year, and now it's harder for him to make money."

The chapel hilltop looked out over a vista reminiscent of Los Angeles: hot, hazy, ringed with hills and apartment towers. Dozens of brides and grooms in shiny suits were posing for photographs. A pair of caged white doves, off duty as props, fluttered on the hood of a jeep. A peddler sold magnets, custom-stamped

land Raiders of politics—the place you go when you've fucked up one too many times. Its Duma headquarters had a great reputation for parties."

coins, and heart-shaped locks that lovers could attach to the iron fence.

The haze was at least partly due to forest fires in the national forest—though, as Ian Frazier pointed out, "Krasnoyarsk puts out an impressive smoke haze of its own." The forest was infested with encephalitic ticks, which were beginning to migrate into town. Rumor attributed the ticks to the remnants of a Japanese biological warfare campaign.

Yegor, we discovered, worked as a flight attendant on one of the legendarily dangerous Russian domestic airlines, after having gotten himself excused from army service for being underweight—he had starved himself for two weeks before his draft physical—and excused again later because he was the sole support for his pensioner mother.

"You look like Michael J. Fox," Maria told him, which was true.

"Who?"

"The actor, from the movie *Back to the Future*?"

"Ah. He had a shitty car too."[15]

We were playing in the basement of a café that night, and the opening act was a bayan-fronted trio who did a credible Bowie cover. It was a fractious show with a raucous crowd. A tuning peg on my banjo exploded into shards of plastic, rendering the instrument unusable. My jacket and some cables disappeared from the back room. I lost my temper at the unresponsive local sound guy, and yelled my way through the set with all my excess

---

15. "Melancholy, disguised as irony," Custine observed, "is in this land the most ordinary humour."

frustration and aggression. "Fatigue," said Custine, "renders a man almost as ungrateful as ennui." We slept late.

In the morning, Yegor found what they called a "guitar master"—a repairman—at a guitar/accordion store with some Soviet-era Jaguar and Jazzmaster knockoffs. He set to work carving a new tuning peg out of wood. Meanwhile, we went to the "city day" festival, a cluster of Uzbek food stalls and Buryat dancers. We picked up my banjo (one of Yegor's friends paid for the repair, feeling badly about the missing cable) and boarded the seventeen-hour train to Irkutsk.

> *There seems no end to the journey. There is little of novelty or interest to be seen, but I am experiencing and feeling a lot. . . . Between Krasnoyarsk and Irkutsk there is nothing but taiga. The forest is no denser than at Sokolniki, but no coachman can tell you where it ends. It seems endless. . . . When you are going up a mountain and you look up and down, all you see are mountains in front of you, more mountains beyond them, and yet more mountains beyond them, and mountains on either side, all thickly covered in forest. It's actually quite frightening.*

> *—Anton Chekhov*

If pressed, I could describe Siberia with just a list of four natural items: birch, pine, purple wildflowers, and that mutant Queen Anne's lace. The heat had broken, and the meadows and Easter-egg villages looked idyllic. Two teenage boys stopped by our compartment to hawk a dubious lottery-ticket scheme: "Ten rubles can feed ten babies." The local train stations were encased in massive yards of tree trunks and rough-cut lumber.[16] In fact, the only other train traffic at this point was the lumber cars and the oil trains, with slick spill stains down the sides of stenciled tanker cars.

The *provodnitsy* on this train were unusually young, and a few seemed to have their significant others along for a romantic ride. Or at least they had managed to cultivate a significant other in every port to come meet them for a few minutes at the platform. While one of the young men in uniform stood by the doors with his leather-and-wood signal flags, a bored girl in shower shoes uncoupled herself from him and stood aside as ticket-bearing passengers reboarded.

One of the less plausible but most tenacious tropes of writing about trans-Siberian travel are sexual fantasies about the *provodnitsy*. In Carrère's Limonov biography, the protagonist "hears the female conductor moaning as two little punks take turns doing her in her cubbyhole." On the recommendation of one of the Siberian punks, I read the British writer John King's *Human Punk*, a roman à clef (and endless tapestry of run-on sentences) of peripatetic summer-of-'77 punk youth, including a job in Hong Kong and a trans-Siberian ride from Beijing to Berlin. The youthful working-class violence of the early sections may ring true—I wouldn't know—but the train romance with the blonde Slavic stereotype Rika is pure fantasy: "I see . . . Matron standing by the door of her cabin, trying to open a bottle. She asks me to

---

16. "American companies have tried to put together deals to harvest Siberian timber, but as a rule the deals go wrong," wrote Ian Frazier. "Executives of these companies eventually give up in disgust at Russian business practices, particularly the corruption and bribery. . . . Some environmentalists say that Russian corruption is the Siberian forests' true preserver and best friend."

help and I unscrew the top without any problem. She asks if I'd like a drink, and I don't see why not. . . . For the first time I see her as a woman. . . . Before, she was the commandant, someone in a uniform off the films, a lifetime of cold Eastern Bloc women with thick calves and weightlifter faces, but now she's Rika, with short blonde hair and nice legs."

Of course, it's not ridiculous that men traveling alone (and it's all men who write these stories) would let their minds wander; fantasies about airline stewardesses or even motel clerks and cleaning ladies are even more common and fully international. King limits himself to the imagining. If Paul Theroux's *The Great Railway Bazaar* is to be believed, the author cornered a kitchen girl in an empty compartment somewhere east of Yekaterinburg: "I put my arm around Nina and with my free hand took off her white scullion's cap. Her black hair fell to her shoulders. I held her tightly and kissed her, tasting the kitchen. . . . But the compartment door was open, and Nina pulled away and said softly, 'Nyet, nyet, nyet.'"

For our part, we experienced none of the clichés of trans-Siberian romance: no vodka shared with strangers, only a few hallway hawkers; no crowded, boisterous restaurant cars, just people going where they were going and trying to do it as simply as possible. At Ilyinskaya, we bought a bag of tart blue berries (later identified as "bog whortleberries") from a baba on the platform and reboarded without incident.

The flag of Irkutsk features an all-black cartoon of a Siberian tiger with the all-red corpse of a sable in its jaws. The aristocratic, anti-tsarist Decembrists, exiled to Irkutsk after their failed plot in 1825, made the city the cultural center of Siberia—admittedly a low bar in a region which was at the time home almost exclusively to prison colonies and nomadic herders. An entire generation of would-be liberal revolutionaries from Western-looking Saint Petersburg, fresh from the Russian defeat of Napoleon, thought they would cap the fall of a foreign emperor with the overthrow of their own, only to end up in Siberia. But more than the rebels Volkonsky, Trubetskoy, and their compatriots, it was their wives—who had voluntarily joined them in exile—who became icons and romantic avatars of loyalty. The men were acclaimed by the Bolsheviks as proto-revolutionaries, and the Volkonskys in particular were embraced by the literary world: Tolstoy reportedly based the character of Bolkonsky in *War and Peace* on Andrei, and of his wife, Maria, Custine commented, "Pushkin rhapsodized that her hair was more lustrous than daylight and darker than night." Maria Volkonskaya hosted a famous salon in her log house, maintaining as best she could the cosmopolitan culture of her and her husband's hometown in what must have seemed like the other side of the world.

Ivan the bloody unifier, Peter the bloody modernizer, Catherine the bloody conqueror, Stalin the bloody globalizer—all iconic Russian leaders can share that adjective. It was around Irkutsk that the moral objection of the international liberal class to the Russian monarchy began to coalesce. They found in the Decembrists their aristocratic and intellectual peers, an empathetic face for the thousands who were poured into the near-infinite oubliette to the east as a pressure valve protecting a rotten regime. Custine was no democrat ("I went to Russia to seek for arguments against representative government, I return a partisan of constitutions"), but he saw in the Decembrists an elite of aesthetes with whom he could identify. Their fate appalled him and hardened his ultimate judgment against a tsar he otherwise respected. Likewise, for George Kennan (whose 1891 book *Siberia and the Exile System* was called the "*Uncle Tom's Cabin* of Siberian exile," though that was a promiscuously applied honorific in the nineteenth century), exposure to the political prisoners in Siberia turned his erstwhile support of the government to disgust and condemnation.

"The best of the Siberian towns is Irkutsk," declared Chekhov—not much of a compliment since he complained about virtually every other stop on his journey.

> Irkutsk is a splendid town, and very civilized. It has a theatre, a museum, municipal gardens with music playing in them, good hotels. . . . I see a lot of Chinese [there remains a substantial, crowded Chinatown today]. . . . Last night the officers and I went and had a look round the town. We heard someone shouting for help about six times; it was probably somebody being strangled. We went to look, but didn't find anyone.

It was a compact old city and felt relaxed—it was a Sunday, and anyone not at their out-of-town dachas was at the market or on the waterfront. Promoter Valeriy and his ponytailed friend Dima took us down to the Angara River embankment. It was new, part of a development boom tied to the 350th anniversary of Irkutsk. "Well," explained Dima, "the government did nothing for twenty years, and people were really complaining. So they had to build some things. Like a bribe, for people to calm down." (Perhaps one of these buildings was the isolated, glass-fronted skyscraper on a bluff overlooking the city, where we went for oligarch-priced coffee in a spectacular, and completely empty, penthouse restaurant.)

Yet it was a lovely riverfront, and a dance band played on the plaza under a statue (also new) of Alexander III. Old ladies danced in pairs with other old ladies. The sad demographic fact of Russia is that for a long time most men haven't made it out of their fifties, largely due to alcoholism and World War II, which decimated the males of that generation, and the elderly population skews female by a large margin. On a small spit of land sat an angular white bandshell—"our version of Sydney Opera House," said Valeriy dryly. "A miracle of Soviet architecture." The bandshell was covered in graffiti and faced a rotting wooden dance pavilion beginning to grow over with grass. It stood on what they called "Youth Island," across a small bridge, where artificial beaches for tanning and drinking encircled a bedraggled arcade. Youth Island could stand alongside Asbury Park and Coney Island in the esteem of any connoisseur of down-at-the-heels amusement parks.

"Here is the new bridge." Valeriy gestured toward it. "We are very disappointed because it is such a boring bridge. Come on, it's the twenty-first century, you can make a cool bridge!" Across the river, the bridge terminated at a black glass pyramid. "It was supposed to be an ice skating rink, but they ran out of money ten years ago and didn't finish. It's a typical situation in Russia— they can make more money starting to build and quitting"— and pocketing the balance, it was implied—"than finishing and selling."

We had an extended debate about relative tax rates while we rented a small motorboat and went on a ride around the river. Russia trumpets a 13 percent flat rate on income, but Dima and

Valeriy said that so much is withheld for pensions and health care that it ends up adding up to a 50 or 55 percent effective tax rate. "Except in the U.S., you see something for your taxes. Here the roads never get better."

The boat ride over, we disembarked and walked past (another!) bar called Bar Akobama. I asked our guides if either of them had spent time in the United States. "We did work-study in Los Angeles," Dima replied—the same work/travel program we'd heard about from others. "At first we had a job at Six Flags, but it was like slavery. Then we got a job in the warehouse at a 99-cent store, and that was much better. Hard work, but it was fine for us. Then we went to New York and we were buying weed from a guy, and he said we could stay with him in Brighton Beach, so that was good."

"Did you like New York?"

"Honestly, I didn't like New York as much as LA. It was more like Russia—like Moscow—everyone is closed off and depressed. Everyone said, 'Oh no, LA, it's so dangerous,' but I think a bad neighborhood in the U.S. is like a good neighborhood in Russia. We lived in East LA, by Compton, it was no problem. I was ashamed of the Russians in Brighton Beach. It is a different kind of Russian. All the women only care about money, and I think the guys are bad guys." (Brighton Beach, while a center of Russian expat life in New York, also has a reputation as a hub for Russian organized crime.)

Just past the dam was the inevitable Lenin, in a pose I hadn't seen before, palms up and beckoning. "There are infinite poses of Lenin," Valeriy told us. "My teacher said in one city they made a Lenin with two caps, one on the head and one in the hand. In Ulan-Ude"—opposite Irkutsk, on the eastern side of Lake

Baikal—"is a giant head [of Lenin]. In Soviet times they said it was hollow, so KGB guys could get inside and spy on people through his eyes."

Valeriy played in a band (that included a bayan) called Radio Mayak after the Soviet-era monopolist radio station. For a while, their practice-space neighbors were the local Mormon missionaries who are a noticeable presence in this part of the world and often the only Americans locals have ever met. "I used to drink a lot, and then I would tell them all my opinions." He snickered. "It would take a while."

Anyway, Dima and Valeriy had met more eminent Americans while in the States. "We took off work [at the 99-cent store] one time to meet Tommy Chong at a bookstore. Our supervisor wouldn't let us off, so we just didn't go [to work]. It was important enough. He's a good guy!"

We were up by seven thirty to catch a seven-hour bus to the ferry to Olkhon Island, a backpacker destination in the middle of Lake Baikal, but Valeriy had forgotten to call a taxi to get us to the nine a.m. bus. We sat outside the apartment building for over an hour while he ran to various corners and called various numbers. When a car finally appeared, he got the bus company on his cell phone, saying, "Don't go anywhere: I have two foreigners who are running late." We arrived at the market, which was chaotic with unmarked buses—more accurately, small vans, crowded at a dozen occupants, with luggage racks on the roof. While Valeriy disputed with one van driver, another beckoned us across the street. We followed and flung our bags on the roof. He secured them with a rope net, the door closed, and we were off. So long, Valeriy. At least we had the backseat to ourselves.

That relative bliss lasted all of five minutes, until the driver pulled over, got out, crossed the street, and lit a cigarette with other drivers. Amid general grousing, most of the passengers got out and started smoking as well.

After another couple of minutes, the driver returned and told us all to get out, that we were being consolidated onto another bus. He ignored the bags on the roof and wandered off, so I clambered up myself and threw them down. A ruddy and malevolent drunk in a tracksuit wandered up to our new bus and negotiated himself a discount ride.

"We'll drop you at the highway," the driver told him.

When we got to the highway, the drunk reconsidered. "Ah, I'll go all the way."

"You're going to ride all the way there?"

"I know a guy."

He began harassing a slight Swiss woman, part of a mother-and-son traveling pair who didn't speak Russian. Some helpful fellow riders chipped in that he was drunk and an idiot besides. He offered the woman a plastic water bottle full of schnapps and wouldn't let up until she gave him the window seat. There was general tittering.

"This is the problem with this part of the world, with Russia, and Ukraine," Maria fumed. "They just laugh at these drunks and let them get away with everything." Dostoyevsky wrote in *The House of the Dead*, "Everywhere among the Russian people a certain sympathy is felt for a drunken man; in prison he was positively treated with respect."

Seven hours were left to drive. The drunk passed out with his arm slung over the (occupied) seat in front of him, and we finally rolled out of town. The first two hours were dull, grassy land reminiscent of Nebraska. Once I saw a mounted cattleman with a herd. Otherwise there was no sign of life besides a cluster of white butterflies at the beginning of a long stretch of coniferous hills. The van struggled up them and coasted down. Forty kilometers north of Irkutsk, we passed a field full of (retired?) biplanes. AC units hung from the sides of yurts.

The driver, it became obvious, was running a "drunk transport" for his friends. The first drunk got off and greeted a toothless and bearded friend across the dirt street. Another opened negotiations to board, but a local lady slipped quietly into the empty seat.

"Local," by now, was solidly Buryat, the Mongolian Buddhist people historically centered on the eastern bank of Lake Baikal. The outskirts of the villages were studded with ribbon-wrapped posts supporting frayed prayer flags. The altitude was apparent in the landscape: barren, rocky hills overlooking grassy valleys and scrub trees, wandering cows, split-rail fences, and exposed shacks. The treelessness exposed things that most communities hide, like the open valley that served as the town rubbish dump: you drove through a nominal gate but then dumped your trash anywhere, and the wind spread it over a couple of surrounding acres. Across the road was a neat and colorful cemetery, organized in discrete and fenced-in squares.

Soon rock formations started to poke through the grasslands, and we reached the top of the highlands on a long plain. We passed some salty-looking ponds, and the asphalt disappeared. Picture driving the length of Montana on a one- (or one-and-change-) lane road.

And then before I realized it was upon us, I saw past a hill the cold blue of the lake, gradient from ice-white by the shore through pine green to dark cobalt as it deepened. Baikal, wrote Edward Gibbon, "disdains the modest appellation of a lake," claiming that native fisherman adhered to the fable that "the *holy sea* grows angry and tempestuous, if anyone presumes to call it a *lake*." We boarded the ferry, the air impossibly clean after weeks of smoggy Siberian cities. Maria struck up a conversation with a woman with a mouthful of gold teeth who was from south of Vladivostok. It had taken three days on the westbound train for her to get here. Her husband was a fisherman on the Sea of Japan, which she said was beautiful but smelled of iodine.

Chekhov tells a sob story ("I'm having the most frustrating time") about leaving Irkutsk for the Baikal shore to catch a steamer across the lake but finding no horses, missing the boat, and learning there wouldn't be another for four days. "All we could do was sit on the shore until Friday, look at the water, and wait." While grouchily wandering the bank, though, he saw a boat loading up, made a quick arrangement, ran back for his traveling party, and boarded: "People say that in the deepest places you can see down almost as far as a mile, and indeed I myself saw rocks and mountains drowning in the turquoise water that sent shivers down my spine. The trip across Baikal was wondrous, utterly unforgettable. . . . What ravines, what crags!"

Olkhon Island is a barely disconnected bit of land off the west shore and about halfway up Lake Baikal. It graduated from peninsula to island at some point after the Ice Age, in a freshwater lake that at some point will itself join the sea when the continent splits. The island has been a shamanistic center since prehistory, and the Buryats worship it as the final resting place of Genghis Khan. The waters of the whole region are generally assumed to have medicinal properties. There was one ragged village,

Khuzhir, dominated by a backpacker complex called Nikita's Guesthouse. The eponymous owner was a former table-tennis champion. Maria had negotiated for a discount on the room and food in exchange for a concert at a local music school for children. The staff was a sheaf of willowy young girls in sandals and flowing skirts, shuffled and directed by an alpha yogi with a shaved head and a shawl over her shoulders. Giovanni, a shaggy and excitable college-aged Frenchman volunteering here in exchange for free board, showed us to our room. We speculated about intra-staff intrigue, and sure enough it wasn't minutes before I spotted Giovanni in a spirited exchange with an aggrieved local blonde.

The rest of the town was a ramshackle collection of wood houses and alternately dusty and muddy dirt roads riddled with potholes. Its centerpiece was a standing pool of stinking water. Townspeople had taken note of the success of Nikita's and were engaged in a rush of construction. There was something of the coastal Alaskan fishing village about it, and also something African. The proprietress of the local general store, a Buryat woman, broke off her conversation as we entered, muttering, "Foreigners . . ." to her other customers.

We rented mountain bikes and went on a torturous, though stunning, lakeside ride. The lake was ringed with hills, the water deep and eerily still. Just offshore, the water was pierced by crags that looked like stone icebergs, topped by short conifers decorated with the primary-color ribbons of Buddhist observance. Within a single kilometer the landscape morphed from sandy beach to grassland, with the occasional gnarled tree, to pine grove. I went to explore the highlands and found the forest floor covered in trash: punctured sacks of refuse, the fluttering snow of shredded plastic bags, a dead dog in a trash can, the corpse of a cow half-covered with a tarpaulin. The circular concrete foundation of a never-finished home had been repurposed for landfill. A kid leaned over its edge and yelled to his mother, "Hey look, our old couch!" This is what anarchy actually looks like: the absence of a local governing authority, the tragedy of the commons in stark material form. With no town dump, people just drive up into the woods and throw trash off the back of the truck for the wind and the elements to do with what they will. Acres of woodland in the middle of "Siberia's jewel"—a national forest, in fact—covered in detritus, the rest thinned to a sandy meadow from logging for firewood and for raw materials for development. ("When I think of the consumption of wood in this country, both for the construction and warming of houses, I am astonished that any forests remain in the land," wrote Custine in 1839.) This was the not-so-hidden back door of Russian capitalism. The power of the government limited itself to action on its own behalf and in its own defense. The rest of society, and the land itself, was left unregulated and, by all evidence, unmourned. The towns, large and small, were graveyards of abandoned and wrecked concrete, undemolished except by lassitude and time, slumped buttresses of a sense of collective failure despite individual innocence. When a state takes full control, it assumes full responsibility; the corollary is that individuals completely relinquish the same. When the state melts away or abdicates, there is no entity to handle the leavings. A communal original sin hangs over everything, beyond the lifetimes of the young people who nonetheless grow up in its shadow.

Is there a weaker sense of mutual civic responsibility in Russia? Are there, say, church groups for the common good, like you see in Protestant America, or is that an impulse specific to Puritan ideas of work and charity? Is it a result of a protective or apathetic passivity learned in the Soviet era, or is it older, descended from centuries of class immobility, in which no matter your achievements or your talent, you would never leave the world with more than you entered? Forgive my descent into florid language, when the question is so prosaic: who's going to pick up the trash if it's not specifically their problem?

Twelve kilometers down the shoreline was a beach enthusiastically recommended as "slightly warmer than the rest of the lake." At the first cove, the water was covered with a beige growth I hoped, but couldn't quite believe, was an algae bloom rather than raw sewage. We pushed on, soggy with sweat, as it began to rain. I'd promised myself, as a reward at the end of this trailless, thigh-scorching ride, a dive into the deep freeze of the lake. As the rain picked up and I envisioned the two-hour ride home, I figured it was now or never, stripped down, dodged the dodgy algae, and plunged in. The skin on my shaved head went instantly numb, giving me the sensation of wearing a tight high-diver's skullcap. After my heart restarted and I left the lake, we wheeled the bikes up a hill to a yurt-shaped shack labeled "Kafe" in the hopes of a snack, a drink, and a roof from the rain.

It was a "kafe" in the sense that there were tables, but not in the sense that they had food. What they had were two garrulous drunks, shirtless Sergey and one-eyed Peter, sitting on a plank outside the kitchen, with a two-thirds-empty bottle of vodka between them. They were workers, they said, preparing the premises for the tourist season. Peter claimed, not entirely convincingly, to be the owner of the place, and he offered to fix us some bread and hot tea.

We devoured some chocolates, shortbread wafers, and instant coffee in the café, which was otherwise stocked with fifteen bottles of vodka, five packs of cigarettes, and no food. ("The local population eats nothing but wild garlic," grouses Chekhov. "There's plenty of vodka though! Russians are such pigs. If you ask them why they don't eat meat and fish, they will tell you that there are problems with supplies and transport and so on, but you'll find as much vodka as you want even in the remotest villages.") Sergey stuffed two dried whole fish (omul, the native whitefish salmon) in Maria's bag and offered us some "Russian energy drink"—vodka, inevitably. He'd "frozen his balls" jumping in the lake that morning, he said, and then floated for a while on an inflatable mattress. The Russian energy drink did give me the heart to cycle home, dodging vans packed with new guests on their way to the hostel. We passed a kid in a convertible, blasting hip-hop. He wore a T-shirt printed to look like a Young Pioneers uniform, complete with faux red scarf and Lenin shoulder badge. Maria fed the dried fish to a stray dog, and we drank beers under an aluminum roof to the accompaniment of the dance-pop hits of the day. I was up all night, the tinnitus of anxiety ringing shrilly.

A good percentage of the town came to the show the next night. We performed in a one-room schoolhouse, the crowd seated in rows of benches with the rest stuffed into standing room in the back. Teenage girls peeked in the windows and giggled. The scruffy guy in the David Foster Wallace bandanna who had booked the banya left after a few songs. An elderly gay French couple filmed the whole set on their iPad. Nikita, the courtly, white-haired and bent proprietor, comped our stay and invited us to the "VIP breakfast" buffet for staff and special guests. The next morning we headed back to Irkutsk.

VI.

❧❦❧

The Hall of Sufficient Looking
(Trans-Mongolian)

B oat to bus, bus to train, station to station. The return bus from Olkhon delivered us to the train station, where we boarded for a two-day journey to Mongolia via the Buryat capital of Ulan-Ude, home of the hollow Lenin. Dima and Valeriy showed up in the rain to see us off, bearing a cedar air freshener and an Irkutsk refrigerator magnet by which to remember them. A low, thick fog hung like cotton batting over the Angara River.

Thus far we had been lucky to be off the regular tourist track—no longer. "A traveler's worst nightmare," wrote Theroux, is "meeting another traveler." Proust agreed: "Most of the companions you chance to meet on the road are more an encumbrance than a pleasure." For the first time, the train car was full of Americans—from here to Beijing, it became pretty clear that the Westerners were segregated into tourist cars. (The other cars, and the station benches and floors, were dominated by young Russian soldiers bent over their ration boxes, headed for a stint at the border. Civilian Russians, I suppose, had little business in Mongolia.) Between Irkutsk and the far eastern end of the line in Vladivostok lay three days of Siberian monotony—what Custine called "a forest without trees, interrupted by towns without life"—so most travelers choose the more romantic Trans-Mongolian branch, which swings south and east through Ulaanbaatar to Beijing. Tall, energetic, bearded men in sandals made each other's acquaintance; serious women in glasses, traveling alone, fiddled with complicated cameras.

I had another difficult night's sleep. Touring is both a crucial component of most musicians' annual income and the gathering sieve when prospecting for material for songs. It is also a waste of time, especially creative time, and of energy that could be spent on producing new work. I had a fresh album coming out in England in a matter of weeks, and organizing artwork, publicity, and logistics from Siberia was a challenge. Concerned about weight and security, we hadn't brought laptops and were constantly borrowing other people's to conduct pressing business.[1] Yet a smartphone, given the etiquette of the day, makes a fantastic clandestine note-taking tool. If I was forever pulling out a pencil and notebook, it would be at a minimum distracting, whereas pulling out a phone in the middle of a conversation

---

1. Much of this book was written in the Notes app on our iPad or on my iPhone, leading to an entrenched battle with autocorrect, frustration that the apostrophe is on a different keyboard screen than the letters, and a manuscript that began life in a ludicrous font. I would almost rather have carted around a manual typewriter.

to tap out a few lines is scarcely even considered rude and draws
no comment.

   I was up reading until about four, awake again by six.
"Sunrise," said Proust, "is a necessary concomitant of long railway journeys, just as are hard-boiled eggs, illustrated papers,
packs of cards, rivers upon which boats strain but make no progress." We got out at the Ulan-Ude station just long enough to use
the bathroom. Since most public toilets are pay toilets, this left
us with a stack of ruble coins we wouldn't need much longer. In
the weak light of sunrise, the frictionless alchemy of the market
turned the coins into a couple of potato-filled puffs of oily fried
dough and a piece of almond cake, and we went back to the train,
to the bunks, and to sleep.

   The train turned south toward the Mongolian border, and the
landscape contained barely enough detail to be describable: dry
grassland, low mountains, the same brown wooden-shack village with pastel highlights and backyard garden plots endlessly
repeating ("It may be said," noted Custine, "that there is but one
village in all of Russia"). We passed Lake Gusinoye, unexpectedly large, a power station looming foggily on the far shore. The
birch and pines were now gone, and the land oscillated between
the poles of positive marsh and negative desert.

   Besides the tourists, there were some practical and aesthetic
differences between this train and the stolid Trans-Siberian
workhorses of the past few weeks. The teacups on the Russian
trains were glass, nested in pressed-tin holders; those on the
Trans-Mongolian were paper and disposable. The mattresses
and pillows were a vivid maroon and gold but so thin as to
be merely decorative, and my primary sensory impression after a night of half-sleep was the itch of a wool blanket pricking

through the sheet. Say what you will about the stained and in-decorous bedding on the quotidian Russian lines, but it was thick and functional. This was the future of rail, though: in 2015, China announced that it would build a $242 billion high-speed line from Beijing to Moscow. It would cut the travel time be-tween the two cities to forty-eight hours and render most of the legendary old line, and its languorous rides, obsolete.

A German guy in his twenties set up court outside our door and bragged lordishly about his travels through Belarus, where "you can go to a club and get a table and a bottle of vodka for $20, and all the Belarusian girls come over and hang around you, huh-huh-huh-huh." He had an ingratiating chuckle that took me about two iterations to detest, a guttural quatrain of hail-fellow condescension. "I think many people are coming to Russia for reasons like that, huh-huh-huh-huh . . ."

In theory, it's a four-hour ride to the border from Ulan-Ude, but ours was running six and counting. It was a fickle train, tak-ing short stops at large towns and a long stop for no obvious rea-son where a lone mahogany stallion drank by a bend in the river, then again at the next bend where a dozen more simply stood, facing south, up to their fetlocks in the current.

We approached the border, passing a home garden fenced on one side by the vertical, end-to-end carcasses of four dead La-das. Actual fences made a slow stylistic shift from long logs laid lengthwise to a threnody of vertical twigs lashed together in the African style. The valley was verdant floodplain, though the cen-tral river seemed too meager to merit such a retinue. A German did a lengthy series of deep knee bends, blocking the hallway.

We were released for two hours in the border town of Naushka, where we found a couple of decent vegetable stands and a sullen café. I ordered microwaved mashed potatoes and eggs. Someone stole my sunglasses. The one overgrown and under-watered park was home to two weathered statues cast in concrete and spray-painted silver: one looked like a moose but may have been two camels; the other was a classical female nude with both hands broken off to reveal rebar claws. In theory, border towns could embody the face a country would like to present to its neighbors. In practice, they are, like airports, often a drained, liminal breach—the space between two calloused palms, not the point of contact. We returned to the platform, through the station's Zal Dosmotra, which Maria said probably meant "Inspection Hall" but read to Ukrainian eyes as "Hall of Looking Until We've Looked Enough" or "Hall of Sufficient Looking." Having had more than enough of looking at Naushka, we reboarded the train.

This was premature. Three hours into our wait at the Naushka station, the rest of the train had decoupled and we were the only car left on the track. The Russians had collected our passports an hour and a half earlier. The German was doing calisthenics again. One of the American girls strummed a ukulele. A genial Mongolian border guard strolled down the hallway with an adorable drug dog, a little black terrier. Only five hours later, we were on the move. For fifteen minutes.

Sükhbaatar, the first Mongolian border town opposite Naushka, felt by comparison rather a happening place. ("One is apt," said George Kennan, "upon arriving after a long voyage in a strange country, to form a more favourable opinion of its people and scenery than his subsequent experience will sustain.") We passed through a few kilometers of marshy river valley, then past scattered white yurts like low, wide mushrooms ringed by sprays of bovine spores. On the east bank, a circle of spotlights illuminated a gold statue of something or other. Farther down the hill a silver globe sat atop an obelisk. As we pulled into the station, out walked a young dude—and "dude" is the appropriate term—in a tight black-and-gold outfit and equally tight hair. Behind him was another dude with big white headphones, a backwards Kangol hat, a Jordan shirt, one black Jordan sneaker with red highlights, and one white Jordan sneaker with red highlights.

The Mongolians were stylish. The older gentlemen wore suits with pants tucked into knee-high rubber boots and cocked pinstripe fedoras or cowboy hats, and had the bowed legs that come from a lifetime on horseback. It was a town full of Asian Tom Waitses. I saw an old woman with a crew cut and a Clint Eastwood face wearing capri pants over red wool socks tucked into heels.

A Mongolian soldier saluted as the train pulled into the station, and my mood lifted just being there and out of Russia. A woman swept the taxi stand with a twig broom—they take care of their public spaces! The crummy public housing blocks were painted fresh pastel and seemed kept up! There were kids in the street! People seemed to be in (even at the time I realized how subjective this was, and how I was projecting) a fundamentally better mood. I hadn't realized how weighed down I'd become by the underlying cruddiness of Russian provincial urban living.

Twelve of the cities we had visited in Russia and Ukraine were included in a 2012 UN report on a list of the twenty-eight most endangered large cities in the world (based on productivity, quality of life, infrastructure, environmental degradation, social justice, and negative population growth through declining birthrates, increased mortality, and emigration). Dnipropetrovs'k, Donetsk, and Kharkov in Ukraine, and Russia's Novosibirsk,

Omsk, Perm', Rostov-on-Don, Samara, Ufa, Voronezh, and even Saint Petersburg were considered in danger of shrinking to the point of disappearing.[2] And the overall list is dominated by Russia and Ukraine: of the twenty-eight endangered cities, eleven are Russian, five Ukrainian, three Italian, two South Korean, and one each in Armenia, Georgia, Hungary, Cuba, Liberia, Romania, and the Czech Republic. The population of Russia as a whole is also under threat: deaths exceeded births by 12.4 million between 1991 and 2007, and if projections hold true, by 2025 it will have lost 20 million people.

Like Detroit, single-industry cities (in Russian, *monogorod*, defined by Svetlana Gomzikova as a city in which "more than a quarter of the population is employed in the same industry, and more than a quarter of all economic output within the city created [is] in the same industry"), are particularly vulnerable. And single-industry cities are particularly endemic in Russia and Ukraine as a result of Soviet industrial policy, which compartmentalized production to such an extent that entire cities were created to serve a single purpose—mining, lumber, coal— often reflected in their names. With the fall of the Soviet Union and the end of the planned economy, those cities were left at the mercy of the market and the varying competence of their newly privatized bosses, uniquely vulnerable to devastating urban contraction.

Russia is easy to slander in an epigram. It is a sad country, a morbid country, as Theroux once said, "exactly . . . as it had ever

---

2. The one major Russian city besides Moscow to see uninterrupted positive population growth since the 1990s was Krasnoyarsk. Maybe the mayor who loved fountains was onto something.

been: a pretentious empire with a cruel government." Beyond the stereotypical fatalism and romantic, alcoholic self-destruction, there is something in the typically Russian rude bluntness that appeals, alongside what Mark Ames called "the sheer energy and *pride* in Russian self-hatred." It's the kind of affection one might feel for a broken, alcoholic neighbor who has nonetheless decorated his walk with a mosaic of shattered glass embedded in concrete, or an obnoxious bachelor uncle who airs family secrets at dinner. Russia, Ian Frazier said, is "the greatest horrible country in the world. . . . We all know of famous authors who gave the world great works of literature yet were not such good people themselves. I supposed maybe Russia was an entire country like that."

Russia and America, the two great imperial land powers of the last century, both project to the world equal parts injured dignity and inadvertent buffoonery, and both are easy targets for the jibes of a sarcastic traveler. Boilerplate romantic generalizations about the poetic and passionate Russian soul or freedom-loving Americans spring easily to the page, but either country is just as easily defined by flag-waving and fried food. I don't mean to imply a false equivalence, though. If the temper of Russian society is cynical, and the European pragmatic, the American remains, somehow, optimistic. You still find in America, despite much evidence to the contrary, the idealistic, naïve sense that if you just get the right person in charge or out of office that everything will be set right. And so we ride eternal cycles of hope and disillusionment.

I had a train dinner: paprika chips, a pear, a cucumber, and a beer. The sunset was magnificent as we withdrew from Sükhbaatar through another massive green river valley. Mongolians on horseback and motorbike gathered herds toward yurts that parked like UFOs on the hillsides. Where Russians had over-stuffed backyard gardens, Mongolian village houses had paddocks of half an acre or more, marked out with split-rail fences. Where old Russian train stations pumped crackling, martial music through the arrival-platform PAs, as we stepped off the train in Ulaanbaatar, disoriented in the early morning after days on the train, the speaker blasted Namjilyn Norovbanzad, the diva of Mongolian long song (*urtiin duu*).[3] The otherwordly vibrato cemented the hallucinatory feeling that we'd stepped out of this metal tube into somewhere quite foreign indeed.

"When one drives into a large city, even a capital city," Gogol wrote, "one's first impression is always of drabness, of grayness, and monotony: at first there are endless factories and mills all grimy and soot-covered. Only later will there appear the corners of six-story houses, stores, signboards, the broad vistas of avenues and squares with steeples, columns, towers, and statues, the glitter, the noise and roar of the big city, and all the other marvels that the mind and hand of man have created." As the buzz-cut grasslands cross-faded into the outskirts of Ulaanbaatar, we passed the twin towers of a nuclear power plant, and a lot full of chipped concrete walls salvaged from demolished buildings, stacked against each other for reuse. I would prefer to say that the drabness and grayness faded too. But Ulaanbaatar is one of a type of Central Asian capital, like Bishkek and Dushanbe, with a short and uninspiring history, where nomads of centuries'

---

3. The genre is called "long song" because of the melismatic extension of the syllables, not because of its duration.

provenance were encouraged—forced—to settle in Soviet-built concrete housing projects. (Ulaanbaatar was a "moving capital" for its first 150 years, before permanently settling in its current location.) A people not culturally urban, settled in a city built by foreigners, pre-stocked with monumental (if not beautiful) statuary in an imported style, will not feel the same sense of ownership and pride of place as the residents of, say, Paris.

"People here still think like nomads," said Jay, an expat of colorful background and opinion we met a few days later at our show. "When you're moving four times a year," he pointed out, you might well say, "'OK, the grass is worn down [from grazing], we'll move 120 kilometers.' They leave their trash [on the steppe], no problem, some vegetables, some sheepskin. But if they move to the city [and act] the same—they put their trash out the front of the door and leave it. 'It's a public space, someone will take care of it!'"

To be fair, a lot of the city's ugliness can be laid at the feet of the Communists, who conducted brutal persecutions of the Buddhist clergy (who also constituted the political authority) in the late 1930s. As a result, the beautiful old things in Ulaanbaatar are few, residing in the midst of dusty concrete housing blocks and construction sites. The Bogd Khan palace, the multipagoda home of the last religious (third in line in the hierarchy of Tibetan Buddhism behind the Dalai and Panchen Lamas) and political monarch of Mongolia, is overgrown with weeds. The few still active monasteries sit at the ends of rutted alleys.

The architecture that you notice is the Stalinist development around the central square, which features a slim equestrian statue of the nationalist liberation hero Sükhbaatar, dwarfed by government buildings on three sides and the state drama theater across the intersection on the fourth. But what you really can't miss is the colossal seated statue of a corpulent and lizard-eyed Genghis Khan atop the steps of the Government Palace, flanked by smaller statues of two of his sons.

In 2008 there were antigovernment riots in this square to protest questionable elections, and five people died. I asked Jay if he'd been there.

"You can call them 'riots' if you like," he said. "Three thousand students in the square for a day. I stopped and joined in, then I went to visit my friend in a restaurant on the sixth floor of the hotel on the corner. All the people that 'died' in the riots—they died later that night, after everyone went home. So!" He gave me a meaningful look that meant "killed in government custody."

We found a hostel—it was yurts on the roof with en suite toilets—and went out for Indian food. After a month of cabbage salad, black bread, and beer, UB seemed dizzyingly cosmopolitan, with Thai and Indian restaurants, Irish pubs, red wine even. There was a particularly strong association with Korea: Korean beauty salons, 99-cent stores stocked with Korean goods, Korean restaurants, even a Seoul Street. Ethnically and linguistically related, Korea and Mongolia are increasingly exchanging trade and labor (including North Koreans, both official guest workers and refugees). Korea is where Mongolians go to work: thirty thousand Mongolians live in Korea, the biggest Mongolian expat community in the world. They don't go to Russia, said Erden, the desk clerk at the hostel. "I have heard Russians are very rude. For example, you can be robbed, and no one will help you. I have heard this many times." Tourists in Mongolia are Germans, French, and increasingly Israelis. The Chinese come "as workers—they are very hardworking in construction," Erden added.

The big business is in mining, which makes up 20 percent of GDP and 80 percent of exports, driving growth that had been pushing 10 percent before the worldwide economic collapse in 2008. Ulaanbaatar still has the feel of a boomtown about it, which isn't dispelled by the rumors of money laundered through the hundreds of backpacker-bait pubs. The current president is the fourth of the postcommunist era. His predecessor was jailed for corruption. ("Well," said Erden, "we are a young democracy.") The streets of the capital are full of 4x4s and SUVs, another contrast from a Russia that ran on rag-and-bone Ladas from the 1980s and used-car imports from Japan. One cabbie drove a Prius. These people are doing pretty well, I thought.

On our second day, it rained, and I realized what the 4x4s were for. The dirt roads became muddy waterfalls and the paved roads became pools. A bank stacked sandbags around their front door, and pedestrians used them as a bridge. The SUVs were up to their wheel wells in water on the main streets, and I was up to my knees. Boomtowns can still be the Wild West when it comes to drainage infrastructure.

It was pretty clear we were going to have to get out of town if we wanted to see any objective beauty. We asked Erden for suggestions, and he offered himself as a guide for an overnight trip to the village of Terelj and the adjoining national park. He was marshmallow soft, with a limp and a lame hand, his pinkie and ring fingers indented and curled. He taught English during the school year and worked at the guesthouse over the summers. He was educated by Mormons, who made a deal with the government to come into primary schools and teach English. They were forbidden to proselytize in school, but after hours was fair game, and they duly set up after-school clubs for the particularly enthusiastic English learners.

"I did go to the Sunday sacraments when I was in fourth grade," Erden told us. "I think most Mongolians think Buddhism is the best in their hearts. There are more shamans again these days, but I think they are doing it just for the money. Like, so someone can come to them with their problems and they can say, 'I will fix it, if you give me one million *togrog*.' I think that is not really good. . . . When I have problems, I go and talk to the monk, and I give a donation to the monastery. But I'm not going to the temple regularly. I guess that isn't being a good Buddhist."

The Mongolian language is a gentle, sloshing, and guttural gurgle, like the cooing of mourning doves, and when Mongolians speak English it sounds soft and almost tender. They seemed generally aware of the difficulty of their language for foreigners. I thought I'd identified an essential goodwill among the Mongolians (at least compared to the brusque Russians) when I realized I'd never had so many people in a foreign country help me with my pronunciation.

Erden was keen to show us the Hotel Mongolia, a five-year-old luxury resort on the outskirts of Ulaanbaatar, and we stopped and admired the swollen Tuul River on the way. After the rains, it was up and over the banks, muddy and forceful. The roads to the monastery we had planned to visit on the third day of our trip were washed out.

"It is unusual," said Erden. "It is more, bigger rains this year."

The roads outside the city were barely that, more rough trails that branch and contract as drivers blaze new trails around potholes and washouts, then return to the main track. Erden,

Maria, and I were in a van with an elderly driver with a grin but
no English, bouncing and shaking up a path that you'd consider
a rough go even for hiking. The van strained up a low mountain and through a forest of pines feathered with blue Buddhist
prayer ribbons. We stopped at the crest of the ridge and got out,
into a cloud of small flies. Here was a four-foot conical pile of
rocks, topped with sticks bound like a tepee and garlanded with
threadbare blue silk that is meant to symbolize the sky: an *ovoo.*
We were to add a rock each and walk around it, counterclockwise, for good luck.

I took this for a fake tourist ritual, but a truck of locals drove
up and did the same. The back of their pickup was full of sheep,
and as they drove away, the truck hit a bump and one of the
sheep flew over the side. The animal ran frantically in the mud,
dragged by a rope around its neck that was still tied to the back
of the truck. Our driver scrambled into the van and honked at
the departing truck. They stopped, tossed the sheep in the back,
and took off again.

We arrived at a small compound in Terelj, a village of fenced-
in yurts at the soggy bottomland of the river, on the border of
the national park. The host installed us in a comfortable yurt
with a woodstove and served dumplings and coffee. Erden said,
"We will have horse riding at three thirty"—in about an hour—
and promptly fell asleep for two hours.

At a loss, we sat around and read for a while. Finally we roused
Erden. He seemed so disoriented that we left on a walk by ourselves, got caught in a downpour, turned back, and spent most of
the next twenty-four hours in the yurt.

Nomads still make up some 40 percent of the population.
They travel one or two hundred kilometers four times a year,

following grazing land for the herds—mostly sheep and short, Mohawk-maned horses. The yurts (or *gers*; "yurt" is the Russian term) sit inside fenced compounds with the animals and contain appliances powered by solar batteries. Herders feed the animals by hand in the winters, when the grass is snowed under. Children are sent to town centers for school, to live in dormitories or with relatives, and rejoin their families to tend the lambs in the summer.

Erden seemed content to sit in the house drinking tea for two days. We asked if he could recommend a hike, and he gestured at the hills in every direction as if to say, "Just start walking."[4] It was clear both that he was no outdoorsman and that he considered his job done once he'd gotten us to the village. (He had organized a horseback junket, but instead of a long ride over the plains, it turned out to be a sullen young boy walking us, atop two sad horses, down the lane.)

Frustrated, we took off on our own again. The land in the river valley was flood-soaked and bounced like a soggy trampoline as we jumped from hillock to hillock, doing our best impression of the local goats. If we misjudged a landing, we might be sucked into a squelchy end. Kennan described this moss steppe as "a great, soft, quaking cushion of wet moss . . . as soon as the pressure [of the foot] is removed it rises again . . . and no trace is left of the step. Walking over it is precisely like walking over an enormous wet sponge."

---

4. The idea of "hiking" as a purposeful leisure activity along pre-blazed routes is, admittedly, a concept specific to cultures both rich in leisure time and divorced from regular contact with nature. The Slovak word for "hiker" is the same as the one for "tourist," the poetic conclusion being that only a tourist would walk so far without a specific material purpose.

We climbed one of the bare hills and looked down at the town. A kid in a Celtics jersey picked up a sheep by the scruff of its neck and the wool of its rump, swung it around like an Olympic hammer thrower, and tossed it about five feet. He ran over to where the sheep had landed, kicked it in its side, slapped it upside the head, then wandered off, bored of casual violence for now. Two other children played basketball with a dirty soccer ball on a patch of bare ground. Two two-by-fours bore a piece of plywood as a backboard—no hoop.

Erden finally roused himself for a bracing bout of tea-drinking with the proprietress of the yurt. After a few hours of this, Maria and I had enough and set off again, down the muddy path toward what passed for a town center. We hadn't gotten a quarter mile before we heard someone calling and looked back at Erden limping toward us and waving his good arm.

"I will come with you," he panted.

"Really," Maria said, "You don't have to."

"No, I must."

Our hike into the national forest became a stroll to the store. I bought a liter of beer to make our yurt night shorter. It began to rain.

Erden took a deep breath as if to say something, then stopped. I looked over at him.

"Tell me," he said bashfully, "how do you make a relationship work, for a long time?"

He was recently separated from his wife and their young son. He had moved out of their apartment and was sleeping on a couch.

"I think it's about communication," said Maria.

He sighed. "It is very difficult."

We took the long way back to the city. We stopped at a slender cave set in a freestanding rock formation, where a hundred monks hid from the 1930s purge, then at a massive stainless steel equestrian statue of Genghis Khan, over 150 feet tall if you include the museum that serves as its pedestal. The whole complex was isolated atop a low man-made hill, in the center of a large circular valley in the middle of nowhere, fifty-five kilometers from the city. It was erected in 2008, funded privately by a middle-aged oligarch who dabbles in politics. Unlike the squat, explicitly Asian Genghis statue at the government palace in Sükhbaatar Square, this is a generic image of a mounted hero, muscular, armored, and bearded.

I asked Erden about the Mongolian perceptions of the great Khan. His name, like Attila the Hun's, carries the whiff of fear and rape, pillage and destruction in the West, and indeed only his death spared Western Europe from the raids that blew through what is now Ukraine and Hungary. In the ranks of freestanding, man-made holocausts, the estimate of a 40-million-strong body count resulting from the life of this one man is unmatched but for the wars and famines of the twentieth century. But then, what would the Persians say of Alexander the Great, or the Gauls of Julius Caesar? What of Native Americans and Columbus and the conquistadors, or Central Asians and Catherine the Great? Throughout human history, the men and women who unite and expand nations do so at no small cost.

"People are proud of him," said Erden. "He is like George Washington for us."

The roadside attractions on the way back to the city were few: a couple of molting Bactrian camels harnessed for riding and sulfurous, shaggy vultures waiting for roadkill. The cities were overgrown villages, sprawling at random over the rolling steppe—primary-colored roofs set apart by cement or twig fences, the inevitable acre of windblown trash tossed over a ledge or riverbank (as long as it faces away from the house, even if it's toward the road). No buildings rose much above a story and a half: just a low factory, and some isolated housing projects that stood like lost Legos across a few miles of field, without access roads.

To our right was Ulaanbaatar. The name means "Red Hero"— locals nicknamed it "Utaan Bataar," or "Smog Hero." Most of the city is still heated by coal or wood, so anyone who can flees to the countryside in the winter to avoid the choking, carcinogenic smoke and soot. To the left was the road to the Gobi Desert: by the nomadic reckoning, a "*gobi*" is defined as steppe with sufficient foliage to support marmots. The desert proper begins when even a camel can't survive.

We turned back toward the city. The traffic was even more impenetrable than the usual four-dimensional game of chicken played by cars, motorbikes, horses, and pedestrians. There were police posted every half mile. Hillary Clinton was visiting, and one main artery was closed and secured for her motorcade. Horns were not so much an alert as a shorthand language unto themselves: "I exist and am present." "On your left." "Sweet ride, buddy."

"Two hundred thousand cars registered in the whole country, and no roads outside this city," said Jay. "It's all the same people, driving from the square to school to the shop and back, all on the same roads."

Old women on street corners tended barrels of roasted pine

nuts for sale, sifting them with plastic gallon scoops. The badass dudes here looked like *cholos*, their hair shaved on the sides and long on top under a folded bandanna. All the young children, male or female, got shaved heads when hot weather came. A middle-aged Mongolian rock enthusiast had funded an incongruous and inartistic monument to the Beatles in the middle of a pedestrian mall. George and Ringo were indistinguishable.

We spent the evening at the state opera house, a pink neoclassical wedding cake that was hosting a performance by the state dance troupe. It was a classic Soviet throwback—a series of five-minute demonstrations of overtone singing, dances from various regions, throaty narration. It culminated in a "Friendship of the Peoples" group dance in which pairs of performers, dressed in "authentic folk garb," held a kind of dance-off between the styles of the tribes and ethnicities encompassed by the Mongolian state. "Fakelore," Maria calls it.

Maria and I can both be grumpy, independent travelers, impatient with tour guides. We decided to take another shot at an Erden-free rural excursion, to the ruined monastery of Manshir Khiid, above the town of Zuunmod. Getting out of town was a wild yak chase. We were directed to a bus station on the west side, from whence buses did not go to Zuunmod. We negotiated a taxi to the bus station on the east side, though as it turned out the driver didn't know the location of the other station. (Cab drivers have a way, sometimes, of giving you the feeling that instead of paying them for a service, you've insulted their mother and then asked them to help you move into a fifth-floor walkup.) He pulled over in an alley and handed us over to two elderly strangers, a retired pharmacist and his wife. They spoke decent Russian—the husband had been in the military in Russia in his youth—and we ended up sharing an hour-long cab to Zuunmod. (An object lesson in contextual pricing: the hotel had quoted this cab ride at T40,000 [US $20], the first cab driver had asked for T80,000, when we shared with locals it was T4,000.)

The annual Naadam Festival (the "nomad Olympics"), Mongolia's biggest sporting event, was taking place that week throughout the country. The festival in Ulaanbaatar was the nation's biggest, but other cities held their own as well, and the pharmacist insisted we accompany them to the horse races in Zuunmod. He gave the cabdriver some directions, and we veered off the road and up some hills to a temporary village of teepee-like tents. Around them stood dozens of horses, tied to stakes like wet laundry set out to dry. He led us inside one tent and introduced us to the multigenerational party inside. The children squirmed, while the adults sat on rugs around a central table. It was piled with sweet breads stacked crosswise in metaphorical layers: the top and bottom layers for happiness, the second for sadness, and so on. On top of the bread tower were stacked homemade cheeses and shortbread cookies. I passed off the ceramic bowls of rice-and-mutton soup to Maria; she, in turn, slipped me the brass bowls of *airag* (the fermented horse milk that is the national drink) and vodka. They urged me to drink a bowl of vodka before we could do anything else—about four shots' worth. After I managed it, an old uncle with one tooth laughed and refilled my bowl. Everything was served and accepted with the right hand only, a hygienic tribal custom the world over in places where you eat with the right hand and wash your backside with the left.

The children played cards from a deck decorated like $100 bills. One young boy had a number strapped across his back that

designated him as a contestant in the horse races going on outside. I stumbled out into the still sunny afternoon, woozy with
vodka, and headed for the finish line. The whole affair was like
a Dakota-territory county fair or rodeo, complete with what you
might call midway attractions: burst a balloon with a dart and
win a stuffed animal, or dress up in traditional garb and get your
picture taken in front of a backdrop with a rainbow and Disney's
Tinker Bell. Young boys aired out their horses in informal races,
standing upright in their stirrups in a cloud of dust. Drunks
curled up in the middle of a field to sleep it off. People giggled
and relieved themselves in a ditch.

The elderly, as usual in this country, were paragons of style.
There was something Bolivian about the dark, weathered faces
in bright, primary-colored ranchwear. The men were in cowboy hats, the women in cloches. Both wore long black over-
coats with wide sashes in red, yellow, and blue. There was one
race left: an eight-kilometer for two-year-old horses ridden by
boys (and at least one girl) aged five to eight. We lined up along
the race's last kilometer, behind waist-high string barriers, and
a cinematic cloud of dust sprouted over the horizon line. Tiny
children on tiny horses began to crest the hill and fly by, hooves
hammering, leather whips flogging first one side, then the other,
of the animals. The spectators urged them on with a burbling
"coo-coo-coo" cheer. Two empty horses had thrown their riders somewhere along the way. One child lost his purchase on his
own horse on the far side of the track. A handful of judges scurried out and carried him to an ambulance.

We caught a taxi from the race site to the ruins of the monastery at Mandshir Khiid, on the upward curve of a great valley
chiseled with terraces. The cab dropped us at a parking lot, and

we hiked the last two miles. A spray of grasshoppers scattered in front of our every step, as if we were shuffling through grain. A single cuckoo sang in the pine forest to the west, and a pair of hawks patrolled the valley.

The main temple had been rebuilt in the 1990s but was still surrounded by the overgrown foundations of the old temple complex. Stinging nettles grew where three hundred monks had once lived. An iron cauldron, cast large enough to boil ten sheep at a time, sat protected from communist depredations by its sheer immobility. We hiked farther up the ever-steeper cliff, past a centuries-old rock painting of a Buddha, then past another of a bearded sage. Both paintings wore a kind of skirt of paper-money offerings, bills shoved under rocks to keep them from blowing away.

The staff was young and seemed put off by the idea of renting a *ger* to some visitors. It would distract them from hanging out with one another. Some played volleyball; one tended a "museum" of rotting taxidermy. It was a party scene, like a summer Saturday at a state park beach. Kids sang drunkenly a hundred feet up the hill. Cars ascended, honking, from the gate. The other guests at the camp were an extended Korean family settling in for a week or at least a long weekend. They organized a pickup soccer game—no small feat on a twenty-degree mountain slope.

To the east side of the camp was a circular, two-story wooden structure decorated in faded cerulean and gold. I went looking for beer and knocked, then entered. The first floor was an approximation of an American rec room, plus a half of a PA system. Upstairs was empty but for some posters of topless Japanese girls. I tried the other building in the camp, which looked like, and turned out to be, a deserted restaurant. The same kid with the put-upon attitude and the giant cold sore who had grudgingly checked us in was behind the small bar, futzing with a Winamp playlist of Mongolian hip-hop. He didn't look up as I walked over, but he closed a window of erotic—though not strictly pornographic—photos on his computer.

"Beer, two?" he asked, with two upraised fingers. I nodded.

He clicked on a walkie-talkie. "The foreigners want beer."

Another grinning creep, in a T-shirt reading "Maniac" in the style of the Metallica logo, came in a few minutes later.

"Beer?" he said, leering and miming drinking with his hand.

"Yes, beer, two."

He signaled that it was OK to serve us, and the first kid produced two bottles from under the counter.

Maria and I drank them on the stoop of our *ger*, shelling pine nuts and watching the hawks. When I went to get the second round, Cold Sore and I repeated the whole charade: Winamp, walkie-talkie, leer, service.

I asked Maria if he had some firewood and matches for our woodstove. He left, and returned with some sticks and a blowtorch. Despite blasting the birch with the torch, the fire didn't take, and I sacrificed the first chapter of my Victor Pelevin paperback as kindling. That did the trick, and I thought Pelevin would appreciate the irony. The beds were stiff and flat as sleeping on a floor, the pillows unaccountably hard, and the kids running the place stayed up all night drinking and singing. I was awake at six, listening to the rain and the angry and confused bees who had let themselves get trapped in the *ger* overnight. We hiked out and caught the local bus back to Ulaanbaatar.

There are many songs one doesn't expect to hear crackling through an overextended PA at the nomad Olympics. In our case, it was Aerosmith's "Mama Kin." It was no stranger than anything else happening on the stadium's field. The annual Naadam Festival celebrates the "three manly arts" of horse-racing, wrestling, and archery (which included some truly badass female archers), as well as the manly diversion of sheep anklebone shooting—a kind of aggressive dominoes, helpful for passing the long, drunken winter nights trapped in a *ger*—which took place in a nearby pavilion. We had bought the tourist-priced tickets to the opening ceremonies, held at the local ten-thousand-seat soccer stadium. Mongol flags, which looked like Muppet wigs on sticks, were marched in and set in stands, the symbolic equivalent of lighting the Olympic torch. The PA announcer had the guttural enthusiasm of a wrestling play-by-play man—appropriate, since the field was filled with giant, hairless Mongolian men wearing light blue Speedos and what I can only describe as a skin-tight shrug: lavender or red decorative arm coverings tied across their bare chests with a bit of string. (At one point in the past, wrestlers wore full shirts. After a woman was found to have competed in a match, the uniform was altered to expose the men's—in some cases still pretty womanly—chests.)

Mongolian wrestling is admirably simple. The unmasked luchadors approach, grapple, and spend most of their time trying to trip each other. Whoever hits the ground first loses. A handful of judges in robes and hats, looking like nickelodeon versions of Catholic bishops, milled and hovered and declared winners. The victors then performed a slow-motion, high-stepping victory dance, turning to face all 360 degrees of the crowd with hands held high. It had the lumbering grace and pathos of a dancing elephant in the center ring.

The bench seats of the stadium were packed, and there was an ugly tension in the crowd. We had already seen a man on the ground being kicked in the face and a cop sprinting by, and it wasn't even sundown. Maria and I sat in what had obviously been designated as the foreigners' section, squeezed between two French boys and a Canadian lady. It was while shifting from cheek to cheek to keep my ass from falling asleep that I almost missed the kid walking by in a full Nazi stormtrooper uniform.

He and his skinhead buddy were making a determined circuit of the whole stadium, glowering straight ahead and daring someone to object. He was in perfect blackshirt drag, cargo pants tucked into boots, red, white, and black swastika armband and all. His friend was a standard-issue boots-and-braces skinhead: red suspenders, white T-shirt, rolled blue jeans, Doc Marten boots.

"Did you see that?" said Maria.

Our neighbors stared straight ahead and ignored them.

Tania Branigan reported in *The Guardian* on the rise of Mongolian neo-Nazis in 2010, noting that "with their high cheekbones, dark eyes and brown skin, they are hardly the Third Reich's Aryan ideal. . . . It is, by any standards, an extraordinary choice. Under Hitler, Soviet prisoners of war who appeared Mongolian were singled out for execution. More recently, far-right groups in Europe have attacked Mongolian migrants." The article described a group of nationalists obsessed with defending the racial and sexual purity of the Mongols, particularly against the "imperialistic, evil" Chinese: "Some believe Beijing has a secret policy of encouraging men to have sex with Mongolian women," and transgender Mongolians have also been a target.

Jay, a gay European, managed an expat bar in Ulaanbaatar with the unlikely name of Satchmo's. It was there we played our one Mongolian show. (I'd gotten no response when I tried to book local pubs via e-mail and telephone, so I posted on the numerous expat forums until somebody put me in touch with somebody else who led me to Jay.) The bar was owned by two mining executives, an Australian and a New Zealander. Most of the bars in UB were expat bars.

"They're pubbing up around here for sure," said the Australian, a ruddy, sunburned man in an open shirt who had bought the place six months ago partly as an investment, mostly for something to do. "A lot of them [are] empty whenever you walk by and you wonder, what's going on? Then you realize, with all the money-laundering . . ." He gave me a meaningful look. "There have been a lot of changes over the last few years, for the better. It's not so dangerous, the corruption . . . is still there, but they're trying to keep a lid on it. Anyway, none of that here— we're trying to have a nice place, where you can bring your family. Here, take my card . . ."

His business partner had left New Zealand when he was "twenty-two, never been back. . . . Been here fifteen [years]. It was better before. The politics are so . . . sensitive."

Maria pointed out later that the nationalists may have a point about outsiders coming in and exploiting the country, but that they're wasting time being paranoid about the Chinese—it's these Western mining corporations that are tearing open the mountains, flooding the political system with money, and filling the Irish pubs that had opened just so politicians could launder their bribes.

Jay was a barrel-chested loudmouth of a kind of mongrel origin: "Bottom line is I'm Belgian. . . . Hey amigo!" he greeted a Mongolian busboy. He was born in Belgium but is part French, part Native American, part a long list of other things too. "I had a consulting job in Belgium making 12,000 euro a month, with a 7,000 [euro] expense account. I would walk into restaurants and the waiters would say, 'Oh, welcome, let me get you some champagne!' But [the firm] was bought by a company with ten thousand employees, and I thought, 'Who needs it!' I was working for British Telecom, vice president, flying to London for meetings. The first few times was great, like a movie! But then I thought, 'What a waste of money.' My father couldn't believe it" when he quit.

He met his current partner twelve years ago, a Mongolian from the Gobi Desert who moved to UB at eleven, became a ballet dancer at the State Theatre, and met Jay while on tour in Belgium.

"And then you decided to move here?" I asked.

"God, no! I hated it. You couldn't get good wine, you couldn't get toothpaste, you couldn't get Dove soap. People were always asking me, 'Can you bring soap?' . . . It was amazing for me, [coming] from Belgium, a country with 450 people to the square kilometer, to come here, which is completely deserted. I take these trips to the country, it is beautiful, sure, but five hours later it is the same mountain and the same valley! A huge country and it all looks the same. So the mining"—a boom that began in 2006—"they take two mountains, who cares! I say, we could have driven an hour and it would look the same."

Jay's second job was teaching English. "They've been taught by the Russian system: read this grammar, copy down everything, the teacher is up here like a god. I said, 'Put away your notebooks. We will talk.' They said nothing. So I provoked them: I said, 'Mongolians are corrupt.' They said, 'No!' I said, 'Oh yeah? Raise your hand if in the past four years you never gave your teacher a bottle of vodka for a grade.' And they got so mad—that got them talking! Ten minutes later I said, 'Listen to yourselves, you are talking English!'"

His partner, a slim, quiet waiter at Satchmo's—he had quit dancing after a knee injury—glided up and deposited our food: cheeseburgers with fries, a salad with blue cheese and cheddar. After a week of mutton and *airag*, American comfort food was more appealing than usual.

"Well, the *airag*," said Jay, ordering more vodka for the table. "You have to understand how it's done here. You are in a tent all winter, eating nothing but horsemeat, and it blocks you up. Then when the warm weather comes, you have nothing but *airag* for seven days, ten days . . . it cleans you out.

"It is very difficult to live my lifestyle here. Even the staff doesn't know. Two ultra-nationalists followed me into the office last week, they said, 'It is against nature, the way you live, if you stay here we will beat the shit out of you.' My friend, a Filipino who manages [a pizza place], he dates a Mongolian girl. They kidnapped him in a car and beat him up, stole his ATM card and PIN number. Another friend got a note pinned to his door saying, 'The elections are over, now it's time for foreigners to leave the country.' I come to work every day with a bodyguard—I don't need to be beat up and be in the hospital two weeks!"

He leapt up to supervise a table setting. His T-shirt said "I ♥ BJ" in giant letters.

Two weeks later, after a couple of shows in China, I flew from Beijing to London for the last leg of what had become a six-month worldwide tour. Maria continued east, to the Pacific Northwest, to teach accordion at a folk music camp. There were no newsstands in the Beijing airport. On my LOT flight via Warsaw, you could buy alcohol from the crotchety, elderly Polish staff only in złoty or dollars, not renminbi or pounds. I retraced in nine hours by air what had taken two months by land: northwest from Beijing over Mongolia, across Irkutsk and Novosibirsk, Yekaterinburg and Moscow, to Warsaw. The slow pace of land travel is frustrating or relaxing or simply literal, time to be passed. It has the smoky flavor of nostalgia. The train journeys were always over too soon—I always had another chapter to read, another chapter to write, another hour I wanted to sleep. The flight, though, felt endless. If the faster you travel, the slower time passes, perhaps the slower you move, the faster you find your way to the end of the line.

PART II

I.

~⚜~

Drunk Nihilists Make a Good Audience *(Croatia, Slovenia, Serbia)*

I spent my thirtieth birthday on a bus with the Russian national rugby team. The band I was in at the time, the Hold Steady, was on an overnight drive across the mountainous border between Slovenia and Croatia, and we wound up passing a bottle of duty-free Jameson's between ourselves while the athletes harassed a trio of unfortunate Russian girls. We should have been on a flight from London to Zagreb, but it was delayed so long that the Zagreb airport was closed by the time we left. The airline, a suspect budget option out of Hungary called W!zzAir (exclamation point and purple-and-fuchsia logo *sic*), flew us to Ljubljana—in Slovenia, an entirely different country—and loaded us onto cross-border buses. In the twelve-hour interregnum, it being my birthday and all, I'd had the chance to get drunk on Bloody Marys and sober up twice over. A couple of the Russians hadn't quite competed the cycle. Two of them, in fact, didn't make it on the plane at all. One was so drunk that his coach, a short but tough-looking man in his fifties, held him by the throat against the terminal wall, slapping him across the face and cursing.

"You're not letting him on the plane, are you?" I asked the stewardess as we boarded.

"Don't worry about that," she said. "Not a chance." An unlucky teammate drew a short straw and had to stay behind to babysit. He planted himself next to his slumped friend, plotting grim retribution.

Five years later, I left Padova, Italy, in the pouring rain and headed east again to Zagreb, on the way to shows in Serbia. It was early spring of 2013, and I was three weeks into a seven-week European tour.

Maria was pregnant, and I was ambivalent and worried. I don't think I ever affirmatively said I wanted children, but I had stopped saying I didn't, and I knew that it was a precondition for the future of our relationship. But I liked our life the way it was, and I didn't want it to change. It was insecure and unpredictable, sure, but I was my own boss, and I could travel wherever I wanted and get paid to do it. Maria had finished her PhD, and we were living an unsettled life, following her through a series of postdoctoral appointments or sojourns in Boston, New York, Toronto, Virginia. I was touring frantically—maybe I thought I needed to prove my earning power as we tried to figure out the shape of the rest of our lives, maybe I just wanted to get in as much travel as I could before the baby came and I'd be off the road, for all I knew, forever. So six weeks after I'd returned from our six-month tour, I was on the road again, for a disheartening monthlong circuit of the United States. Then, three months later, I headed back to Europe for seven weeks.

The tour started well. I was making money in Poland and Germany, and the weather was crisp and bright. I was playing French shows outside Paris for the first time, mostly successfully. I would head east after my French week, then south into Romania and Bulgaria for the first time.

Then the snow came, a series of spring storms that would chase me eastbound all the way to Serbia. I was about an hour from Paris on day three of the storm when the traffic stopped. The snow had begun to pile up against the guardrails, but at least the center lane was clear. I'm not surprised that there's been an accident, I thought. But they should have this cleared pretty quickly—an hour at most. Both lanes of traffic pulled to the side and a cop car and an ambulance made their way through the center.

An hour passed, then another. People got out, stretched, pissed in the snowbanks. Three hours passed. I hadn't had breakfast, but luckily I had bought groceries in Heidelberg. A man walked back with news: the big trucks were barred from driving, but there weren't police to organize them so that we smaller cars could pass. So, it seemed, we could be here all night, or at least until someone took charge.

My phone buzzed. "Are you on your way to Orleans?—Fabien."

"On my way," I texted.

"OK—the bar is open until midnight, so whenever you get here is fine."

Four hours had passed by the time the line of traffic finally began to crawl forward. Exhilarated, I took the first exit—it was westbound, toward Calais, but at least I was moving, and I could cut south shortly. It was cutting it close, though; the Orleans show was supposed to be from seven to nine, and my estimated arrival now was nine thirty and creeping toward ten. I texted Fabien.

"The bar says no one will stay after ten," he replied. "You can come here, but I think it is better if we cancel and you stay in Paris. Do you know someone there?"

I didn't, really. I called Maria. "Can you do me a favor? Can you book me a hotel in Paris and text me the address?"

In the meantime, I'd found another southbound highway. This would all be fine—I'd get to Paris in ninety minutes and have a nice night off. Maria texted back with a hotel: "It looks crappy, but I think it's the best bet."

When I saw the traffic begin to slow, then the red emergency lights start to blink ahead of me, and then realized that we were once again stopped and trapped, the despair set in. I cursed myself for changing highways. I cursed the French highway department for their incompetence. I cursed myself for my life choices and swore I would never do another tour, I would learn a trade and fly right. I read every publication on my phone and every scrap of paper in the car. I listened to five hours of the *History of England* podcast, from Alfred the Great through the Norman Conquest, and tried to identify the irony, if there were any, of being stranded so close to the Norman heartland. I heard a beep as my phone battery died and opened my laptop to find that it had too. I ate my provisions: five bananas, two yogurts, a package of Wasa sesame wafers, a whole packet of sliced herbed cheese, and a liter of multivitamin juice. I turned the car off and let the heat drain away, then turned it on full blast. A couple of cars went rogue, forming a third lane in the deeper snow, and I joined them for a glorious third of a mile or so. I pulled out my pillow, curled up, and decided to give up and sleep, but every time I did the line would move forward a hundred yards for no obvious reason.

It was nearly twelve thirty a.m. when the movement started in a sustained manner. I'd been trapped for seven hours, plus the four hours on the other highway. And I was still almost ninety miles from Paris.

We wove, single file, between and around the miles of hulking, cold trucks, which formed perfect bulwarks for banks of wind-blown snow. It took nearly an hour just to creep along the mile or so of trucks before we got to the open highway and rose to a cruising speed of thirty—or, when we were lucky, forty—miles an hour. I was looking at arriving in Paris at, optimistically, three—more than two more hours of white-knuckle driving. Neither plows nor highway patrol were anywhere to be found. The rest stops had Ibis hotels, but half the entrances were blocked by trucks or by snow; at the others the hotels were booked full of truckers. On one exit, even the off-ramp from the highway was closed and rerouted to an empty highway patrol building.

By this point I was nearly the only person on the highway. It was pushing three, and I was on my third bottle of Club-Mate soda, shivering with cold and caffeine in equal measure.

It was after four when I finally pulled into an arctic Belleville. The hotel, on a cobbled side street, was locked. I pounded on the door until a middle-aged Arab shuffled over and opened the door with a malevolent glare.

"Do you speak English?" I said, hopefully.

"*Non.*"

I handed him my passport, wordlessly, and he checked me in.

Not wanting to get up in five hours to check out, I asked, "*Deux nuits?*"

He shook his head. "Tomorrow," he said, indicating I should come and deal with that in the morning.

I'd logged onto the Wi-Fi while he was checking me in and ran back downstairs to quickly Skype Maria and let her know I was OK. He gave me a look as I passed the check-in desk. I logged onto Skype, hit call—and the Wi-Fi signal disappeared. I ran upstairs and grabbed my laptop. He saw me and said, "*Internet, n'est pas.*"

"What the hell? I saw it! I got my e-mail just now!"

"*Internet, n'est pas.*"

Motherfucker had turned it off so I'd leave his lobby.

I took a Xanax and waited for the nerves and the caffeine to let me sleep.

Then, at the legendary Miroiterie squat, I was robbed. My bag with my passport, laptop with all my new writing, my Rebecca West book, and all my tour cash (somewhere north of two thousand euros), was stolen from the backstage room. The soundman said he'd seen the tall, drunken guy who had been heckling the show—whose hand I'd even shaken from the stage—walk off with a black leather shoulder bag. But everyone else had already left, and he gave me the French equivalent of "Shit, sorry bro" and disappeared as well. I raced around the blocks, looking for the drunk, looking for my empty bag in the trash, looking for anything in the snowbound, deserted streets. The expat New Yorker with whom I was staying was kind to me while I cursed, cried, swigged from his bottle of Jack Daniel's, and vowed to head straight home and never tour again.

Touring musicians, of course, are vulnerable targets. We are usually carrying a significant amount of cash, sometimes have a language issue, and almost always have to be hundreds of miles away the next day. So this sort of thing is a kind of occupational hazard.

The next day was a throbbing mess of rage, despair, generosity, and clenched, shivering anxiety at the U.S. consulate, a locked-up La Miroiterie, and the local police station (where I managed, pointlessly, to file a report despite the lack of a common language with any of the officers), followed by a self-flagellating drive to the provincial town of Le Mans.

I called Maria. Having put some physical distance between myself and Paris, I was feeling a little less broken and violated. Maria, four thousand miles away, pregnant and staying with her mother in Virginia, was not. Why, she raged, was I even on tour? I wouldn't even be coming back with any money now. All the well-paying shows were behind me in Germany and Poland.

I wanted to come home too. I felt defeated. I loved touring, I truly did, but it wasn't like I was playing for rapturous crowds every night or making enough money to justify grinding it out. The idea of four more weeks alone in a car felt impossible. But if I quit now, I'd be returning with no money, still on the hook for the plane ticket, rental car, and merchandise. I had to keep going. The snow chased me through the Mont Blanc tunnel, down the serpentine roads of the Italian Alps and east to Zagreb.

The terrain was dull and flat until just before the Slovenian border, when it roughened and rose and lost the marks of cultivation. In Slovenia the rain turned inevitably back to snow, and the rural country was all white hills and powdered pine, its few villages dark and deserted.

Once in Croatia, the old capital glowed like a fairy tale. The snow had stopped, but it was too cold for it to start dripping, and the streetlights had the hazy amber aura of a Rembrandt. I parked my car in an underground lot. It wore an armor of ice scales, whipped backward and frozen by the wind.

But people were still out on this Sunday night. It wasn't too cold to visit the pubs, though the plastic outdoor chairs were stacked and stowed. The city was a layer cake, if not a soft-serve swirl, of histories. The wide central square and tram stop had the vastness and aggressive branding of a post-Soviet capital, but in the center stood a statue of Count Jelačić, a mustachioed horseman, that celebrates the Hapsburg defeat of the Hungarians, with whom the Croats had an uneasy relationship, not to say rivalry, from their twelfth-century union through the post-1867 dual monarchy, in which Croatia was placed under Hungarian authority by Maria Theresa. The statue was erected in 1866, controversially, by the Austrians, removed in 1947 by the Communists, and returned in the nationalist 1990s. The monumental buildings of the central square are not Communist; in Rebecca West's words, "those vast, toast-colored buildings, barracks, and law courts, and municipal offices . . . are an invariable sign of past occupancy by the Austro-Hungarian Empire." It was against the Hungarian national hero Kossuth that Count Jelačić rode.

Another layer, though, was not political but cultural. It was a distinctly Mediterranean place, though Zagreb is 160 kilometers from the sea. It was a town of cobblestones and cafés (which advertise, in bold letters, that smoking is permitted), steamy low bars, and pizzeria after pizzeria, offering a kind of uncut bowl of a pizza that manages to be both soupy on top and crusty beneath. Zagreb almost seemed more Italian, in its own relaxed way, than the raucous, frivolous Italians. This was a city built not for grandeur but for low-slung charm: "It has no grand river, it is built up to no climax," West wrote of Zagreb. It "marks from its featureless handsomeness something that pleases like a Schubert song, a delight that begins quietly and never definitely ends."

There were near-whiteout blizzard conditions when I left Zagreb in the morning, continuing east, and I nearly turned back. I'd be damned if I'd spend another night on the highway. But storms are slower than rental cars, even those without winter tires, and within two hours I'd gotten out ahead of the clouds, past lumber farms with square clear-cut acres and little hills with villages huddled at their humble feet. In the no-man's-land between the Croatian exit and Serbian entrance borders it began to sleet, but it was just a border chill.

"To change one's country is tantamount to changing one's century," Custine declared. Nowhere else—save, possibly, the contrast between Mongolia and China—did I feel this more literally than at the crossing between Croatia and Serbia, once partners in the Yugoslav federation. In the wake of the wars of the 1990s, Serbia, as the most recent loser of the Balkan musical chairs of local villains, became persona non grata on the international stage. Croatia, meanwhile, was in the process of accession to the European Union,[1] to be followed at some point by—against the vehement advice of the British and Polish—adoption of the euro.

---

1. The split between Western-facing Croats and Eastern-dominated Serbs goes back at least as far as the early Middle Ages, when the Croats allied with the Carolingian Franks as a bulwark against the expanding Bulgarian empire. The Serbs at the time, prior to their own imperial period, were ruled from Constantinople as Byzantine subjects.

The laments of the locals notwithstanding, by most appearances this was a modern and relatively developed place.

Not so Serbia. After a bad cop/bad cop routine from the skinhead thugs of the Serbian border patrol, who worked out of what would otherwise pass for an outhouse shack on the side of the road, I crossed into the country and might as well have passed back into the nineteenth century. I was now in a world of oxcarts (really just wooden platforms on truck tires) and conical haystacks, of old women in kerchiefs and old men in flat caps.

I experienced a psychological shiver during the crossing into Serbia. "Serbo-Croat speech has an expression," wrote Christopher Hitchens, "a *vukojebina*—employed to describe a remote or barren or arduous place—[which] means literally a 'wolf-fuck,' or more exactly the sort of place where wolves retire to copulate . . . easily adapted to encapsulate a place that is generally, so to say, fucked up. This is the commonest impression of the Balkans." For me, born in 1977, the beginnings of my consciousness of world events coincided with the Balkan wars, in which, Hitchens argued, "the greatest harm was arguably inflicted upon the Serbs themselves. . . . Serbia lost its national honor and became an international pariah." On some preteen synaptic level, for me, the Serbs have remained filed under "bad guys." It's the same frisson our grandparents' generation must have felt visiting Germany or Japan (for our parents, it was Russia) or what our younger cousins will feel if they go to Iraq or Afghanistan a decade from now. And so I stared southbound, trying to catch a glimpse of the Bosnian border that lay just a few miles outside the right-hand windows, and pondered the intensely local and bloody politics that, in Rebecca West's words, "grow on the basis of past injustice. A proud people acquire the habit of resistance to foreign oppression, and by the time they have driven out their oppressors they have forgotten that agreement [with each other] is a pleasure."

I was headed for Bačka Topola, a small town up by the Hungarian border, which is, and has been for centuries, majority ethnic Hungarian. The street signs were in both Hungarian and Serbian. The locals recalled the Communist years with something like active nostalgia. The Yugoslav era "was like Disneyland," said Nicola, the affable impresario of the café. He wore his long hair in a ponytail, like an Israeli backpacker or a Burning Man enthusiast. Bačka Topola had been an industrial town where everyone worked for one of four state-run corporations. They sent employees' families on vacations to the Croatian coast or skiing in Bosnia or Montenegro. Each company was privatized or closed by the post-Milošević democrats, and, not coincidentally and as part of a common regional trend, reactionary nationalists won the recent elections. The local public swimming pool and spa shut down for the want of municipal maintenance funds.

All of which added up to pretty depressing situation, and the near-universal chain-smoking lent a morbid pall. But Nicola, a printer by trade whose father was a local politician, was one of those congenital optimists you find from time to time returning to their troubled hometowns after a cosmopolitan youth with big ideas about making them off-the-beaten-track hipster destinations. He convinced the city council to let him use the lobby of the old unused theater to open a bar and café with a small stage. (The restaurant next door was named, without explanation, Poughkeepsie N.Y. 12601.) He planned to refurbish the ruins of the theater for bigger shows. Maybe he'd even put on a festival by the river. He had lived in London for five years, studying drums and touring with an American jazz bassist. He'd even had plans to tour the United States with a band, but his visa hadn't come through. Then his British visa expired, so he came home instead. "It's OK," he said. "The singer killed himself a week into the American tour anyway! . . . Have you met Miki?"

Miki was another small-town type: the solitary hipster. A lugubrious Harry Dean Stanton lookalike, he was proud of his two-thousand-item vinyl library, meticulously collected over thirty-five years of pre-Internet, cross–Iron Curtain mail order (although the Coltrane and others were Soviet pressings of dubious authorization). "I have four Velvet Underground original pressings!"

He lived in a farmhouse well outside town that he had inherited from his recently deceased mother. "He's like a forty-six-year-old baby," said another person at the café. "He always lived in that house with his mother, and she cooked for him and cleaned his clothes, and now he's there alone and he doesn't know how to do anything." Miki told me he was farming corn and herbs in the plot behind the house. "Just enough to survive." We stayed up late smoking weed and listening to the Incredible String Band.

Serbia has two major highways: a north–south road, the M5/E75, that runs from Budapest to the Greek coast at Thessaloníki, and an east–west road, the A3/E70, from Zagreb to Belgrade. I was only on the latter—no traffic but for a few trucks—for forty-five minutes before turning onto village roads. Like many structurally challenged areas, such as Mongolia and Siberian Russia, the trash-disposal protocol left something to be desired, at least from the standpoint of presenting the best face to the gaze of the passing traveler. The town dump was a half-acre pile by the road, and thus the surrounding farmland was littered with windblown plastic bags. The only town center en route to Novi Sad was something called Irig, whose sole distinguishing architectural feature was a brick structure buttressed in all directions by two-by-fours. Garish nouveaux riche mansions separated themselves from subsistence garden plots with prefab metal fences. Homemade signs advertised MED—VINO—RAKIJA (honey, wine, moonshine). The color palette, like much of rural Eastern Europe, was pastel wash: pink, lime, lavender, goldenrod, beige.

The GPS, for some geopolitical reason, knew only the two crosswise highways in Serbia, so I had to navigate the old-fashioned way—if by old-fashioned, we can agree to mean finding the route on my phone's Google Maps app, then taking screenshots of zoomed-in chunks. The road went up into Fruška Gora National Park. These are the Frankish Hills, "which are called by that name," said Rebecca West, "for a historical reason incapable of interesting anybody."

The Englishwoman West, described by Robert Kaplan as the "writer of twenty books, young mistress of H.G. Wells, social outcast, and sexual rebel," is the spiritual guide of any Westerner traveling through the south Slavic countries. Her massive *Black Lamb and Grey Falcon*, based on a six-week trip through the then Kingdom of Yugoslavia in the midwar interregnum of 1937, is like a nut of a travel book wrapped in layers of encyclopedia, mythology, and psychological and sociological history, spiced with shiv-sharp feminist commentary. Its steely and principled opposition to encroaching fascism is undercut only in retrospect by faintly erotic paeans to Serbian militarism and masculinity— then, of course, a celebration of an underdog nation long harried between the Hapsburg and Ottoman empires.

West repeatedly compared the Fruška Gora ("the jewel of Serbia") to Scotland, describing "the most entrancing rounded hills, clothed with woods now golden rather than green with springtime, which ran down to vast green and purple plains, patterned with shadows shed by a tremendous cloudscape." She made of the mountains, and the ancient monasteries within that held the relics and mummies of the medieval Serbian empire, a symbol for the masochism and nostalgia of Serbian nationalism.

It goes to show you the difference between seeing a place in the summer and the winter: I saw only low hills with sad, thin forests, like the Ozarks, without even a layer of underbrush. A line of trucks was doing about fifteen miles per hour, and cars began to pass them in the left lane, at first just one or two and then by the tens and dozens. As I joined them, I thought that everyone had just decided to cruise in the passing lane until they saw an oncoming car. In this part of the world, in which traffic laws are indistinguishable from anarchy, I wouldn't be surprised. (Eventually, within the forest, the highway divided into opposing lanes—not that the change was marked.)

On the far side of the mountains was the provincial center of Novi Sad, the longtime cultural center of Serbia. The club CK13 was a walled compound of progressive and activist sentiment. Like many similar institutions on the Danube periphery, it was quietly funded by virtuous German NGOs and foundations supporting antifascist organizations. It's a peculiar irony of postwar German liberalism that its NGOs (or perhaps GOs—the level of state subsidy is unclear) underwrite the antiglobalization, antistatist, anarcho-syndicalist activism of these sorts of youth centers. It's all in the name of combating bigotry—the rest just comes with the worldview of the young European left. In years of touring Germany, I've often bristled at the oppressive political consciousness and correctness of German punks.[2] One explained to me recently that "because of our past, we have to go out of our way to be the 'good' country, and to take the high moral ground on every issue, and it can make us seem humorless because we are trying to all the time be a kind of policeman of ourselves and everyone to do the right thing." (Former West German chancellor Willy Brandt said his country had to be "a nation of good neighbors, at home and abroad.") It plays like a cultural descendant of a particularly moralistic Protestantism, reminiscent of the righteous reaction of postwar children that also led to leftist terrorism in the 1970s, and becomes a kind of authoritarianism of progressive ideals.[3]

My mother hen here was a soft-spoken, dark-haired elf named Ozren. He warmed up soup and pasta in the communal kitchen, showed me the bedroom over the bar, and then took me on a quick walking tour of the center of town. We recapped the relatively short but eventful history of Novi Sad. The second city of Serbia and the capital of the northern, Hungarianized region of Vojvodina, it was founded late and destroyed repeatedly. Like many historical divides in the Balkans, this one has to do with the complex interactions between ethnic settlement and the shifting Hapsburg/Ottoman border. West explained that after

2. I remember being cornered, just before 9/11, by an intense German demanding the details of President Bush's policy on Macedonian border disputes. I could only respond that not only did I not know the president's position on that question, I was pretty sure the president didn't know it either.

3. I came to think of it as "Germansplaining": that moment when a German kid starts explaining to me how the American political system works.

an ill-fated Serbian revolt against the Turks in 1689, the reigning Austrian emperor "offered [the Serbs] asylum on his territories, with full rights of religious worship and a certain degree of self-government. . . . The [Serbian] Patriarch accepted the offer and led across the Danube thirty thousand Serbian families, from all parts of the land, as far south as Macedonia and Old Serbia," now known as Kosovo. This migration of refugees, combined with Serbs settled there in earlier times by the Ottomans, became the Vojvodina region and the city of Novi Sad. It was the largest Serbian city for the next two centuries, until it was decimated by the Hungarians in 1848.

"It's a complicated history," said Ozren. "Have you talked to anyone here about the bombing?" he asked me, referring to NATO's 1999 air campaign.

I hadn't.

"It was crazy. The bombs were so . . . accurate. They sent one to the parliament building and hit one specific office. The rest of the building was fine. . . . They would announce what they were targeting, so mostly people weren't killed."

In a moment of absentmindedness, he'd thought the show was scheduled for April 25, not March 25, until our mutual friend Dejan called two weeks earlier and reminded him. "We canceled the movie screening," he reassured me. I replied that I'd opened for stranger acts than a movie.

We met Dejan at a beer bar. A charismatic, hyperverbal, big-boned booking agent for hardcore bands, he had an intense manner that set Ozren's quiet and ironic demeanor in relief. I was under the impression that Dejan had put me in touch with some Bulgarian booking contacts and thanked him.

"No way," he said. "They have a real problem with right-wingers at hardcore shows in Bulgaria. People get their tires slashed and stuff, so I don't book there."[4]

It's the second most common complaint I hear, and they followed it, like a script, with the most common: that the punk scene in Novi Sad, they agree, is not what it was a few years ago. "These things come in cycles," said Dejan philosophically. "Five years on, and five years off."

I'd met Dejan the year before, when we stayed up drinking by the club's courtyard fire pit with an effusive Hold Steady superfan and his friend, the singer of the local punk band the Bayonets. They had strong opinions: about Gogol Bordello, who they condemned for doing a Coke commercial, and about the Serbian director and musician Emir Kusturica, whom they accused of being a radical Serbian nationalist in a progressive globalist's clothing. Kusturica converted from his Islamic roots to Orthodox Christianity, they said, and presents a face of inclusive "world music" while being a "state project" funded by the nationalist government. (Indeed, his film *Underground*, which won the Cannes Jury Prize, was partially funded by Yugoslav state-owned television, although that isn't necessarily an unusual arrangement.) "He showed his true face" while on tour with Manu Chao, they said—he objected to a Manu Chao T-shirt listing concert dates that included Kosovo as a non-Serbian city.

I'd fallen hard for the Kusturica mythos in the early 2000s, as did many in what became the New York "gypsy punk" scene. The colorful, gold-toothed Rabelasian fairy tales of his film

---

4. This wariness of Bulgarian touring was echoed by Sasha, my promoter in Kyiv: "I don't know any bands that go there. All the hardcore shows are full of Nazis."

Black Cat, White Cat and the Balkan rock of his band Zabranjeno Pušenje (later called the No Smoking Orchestra) fed a fac-
ile, romantic exoticism of a world of roguish present-day pirates
and clowns. Zabranjeno Pušenje ("No Smoking") was part of the
1980s generation of controversial, punk-influenced bands across
the communist sphere who became associated with a wry, surre-
alist version of anti-establishment commentary. The best-known
anecdote about the band involves a concert in Rijeka during
which a band member announced, "The Marshall is dead . . . I
mean, the amplifier." This was widely understood as a pun referring to the late Yugoslav strongman Marshal Tito, and the band
gained as much in countercultural credibility as they lost in the
official clampdown on their music—concerts canceled, records
banned from the radio—that followed.

Kusturica was a late, minor member of Zabranjeno Pušenje,
and the band broke up with the onset of the Yugoslav wars. After the war, Kusturica revived the name with a Belgrade-based
rump organization called Emir Kusturica & the No Smoking
Orchestra, with an "ethno-rock" sound barely related to that of
the original group. (A competing, Sarajevo-based group using
the name Zabranjeno Pušenje plays the original, garage-rock
style.) Kusturica's version of the group, while popular overseas,
is controversial in a wholly different and less sympathetic way
than the 1980s punk incarnation: he is widely seen as sympathetic to the violent Serbian nationalism of Slobodan Milošević;
is a supporter of Russian president Vladimir Putin (he was a
guest at Putin's third inauguration in 2012); and has written a
song ("Wanted Man") in support of the indicted war criminal
Radovan Karadžić, with lyrics including "If you don't like Dabic
Raso"—a nickname for Karadžić—"You can suck our dicks."

Tilman Zülch, the German president of the NGO Society for Threatened Peoples, published an impassioned anti-Kusturica letter in 2009 that began "Stop the propaganda for war criminal Karadzic on the Munich concert stage!" and ended "P.S. It is unbelievable that Emir Kusturica is still Serbia's UNICEF ambassador." Once again, as in the cases of Letov and Limonov, an artist associated with anticommunist rebellion in the 1970s and 1980s made a latter-day turn into strident, even xenophobic nationalism. As Nietzsche once said, "Extreme positions are not succeeded by moderate ones but by extreme positions of the opposite kind."

Both Ozren and Dejan were politely skeptical about the evening's show. There might have been six people in the room for my first visit last year, and we decided, at Ozren's strong suggestion, that I would perform acoustically on the floor. So when, back at the club, people started pouring in, I rushed to set up onstage. It was one of those shows that makes you think, against all evidence to the contrary, that sometimes the game still works like it's supposed to, that if you just *keep coming back* to a place eventually you'll break through. Drunk but articulate, the crowd was dominated by relentless, though good-natured, hecklers, and they kept me fresh and quick.

I slept in the guest room upstairs, under the warm gaze of gay-tolerance propaganda posters featuring stylish butch lesbians. The shower was awkwardly located down the hall, in the bathroom of an active office. I say "shower," but that's not quite right: there was a hose screwed onto the sink, and a cloth mop and bucket to dry the floor when you were done. A towel around my waist, I nodded good morning to the arriving office workers.

For three of the past four days, I had awoken to blizzard conditions, as the snow I outran the day before caught up with me in the morning. This morning, I pulled out my phone to call ahead and cancel the evening's concert, but some vestigial showbiz reflex made me pause and give the show a chance to go on. The streets of Novi Sad weren't, of course, plowed, but it was a heavy wet snow that turned quickly to slush and melted under my tires. I got out of the city, across the bridge over the Danube, and turned back up into the Fruška Gora hills, my wheels slipping ever so slightly.

At the park's entrance, two policemen were leaning into the window of a stopped car, and I thought the road was closed. They waved me through. I wound my way up to the ridge, crawling and slipping. At the peak sat a line of stopped cars. "Not again," I thought, with visions of another night spent becalmed on a snowy foreign road. I had the impulse to pull a U-turn, head back to the city, and take the longer highway route through Belgrade.

But Serbs are made of sterner stuff than the French—in West's words, "they were certain in any circumstances to act vigorously"—and not five minutes of fidgety inaction passed before a dump truck the size of a small house lumbered forward from the back of the line of traffic and nudged its way to the front, and we began to creep forward in its wake. Once the line was moving, restless drivers chafed at the slow speed and began to pass the plow truck on the snowy downhill, and in this way we put the storm behind us.

Assume what you might about potholed Serbian highways, but they had the benefit of being nearly deserted, and the gas stations had free Wi-Fi and toilets with proper seats, which is more than I can say for large portions of France. The road was steamy with fog and littered, on both sides of the Serbian–Croatian border, with the broken fluff of what must be the slowest, dumbest sparrows in creation. It's hard to imagine what the birds were eating on the roads—worms can hardly crawl through asphalt—but they didn't have the reflexes for such hazardous grazing. Every mile or two, another startled bird thudded off my front bumper. One was a direct, bloody hit in the center of my windshield. A stubborn feather stuck to the glass for hours.

I crossed the border alongside a convoy of vans and heavy machinery painted blue with a yellow stripe and labeled "Republika Slovenija Civilna Zaščita" (Republic of Slovenia Civil Defense). One flatbed hauled a four-wheel off-road vehicle; another was loaded with kayak paddles. As I passed Zagreb and approached the craggy Adriatic coast, the low hills and huddled hamlets gave way to frosted mountain tunnels and majestic elevated bridges over vast pine valleys. Some government organization had, for obscure reasons, erected bear silhouettes along the roadside, which caused me more than one adrenaline-shot double take.

Once through the final tunnels to the littoral, I might as well have been in a different country. The sun—the sun!—was shining in a clear sky, and the pine had given way to sweeping, sail-shaped mountain peaks covered in threadbare deciduous forest. The beauty of the Dalmatian coastline is matched only by the exploitation of same—once for natural resources, now for favorable exchange rates and Caligulan vacations taken by British lugs. "The human animal is not competent. That is the meaning of the naked Dalmatian hills," wrote West. Centuries of reckless logging, by Illyrians and Romans, Hungarians and Venetians, had treated the land with "the carelessness that egotistic people show in dealing with other people's property. . . . After this wholesale denudation it was not easy to grow the trees again." But over the hills is the blue vista of Rijeka and the sea, with accents of port crane. Like Dundee, or Duluth, the city climbs vertiginously from coast to cliff. Here the cliffs are scaled by weathered stone buildings and crumbling concrete housing projects, whose grotty and disintegrating functionalism stands in sharp contrast to the spectacular seaside.

From the sixteenth century well into the eighteenth, Rijeka (historically called "Fiume" in Italian—both names mean "river") was a free port city and a haven for a guerrilla group known as the Uskoks, who had a taste for piracy and a flair for the dramatic: adding their victims' blood to their bread and collecting bags of Turkish noses.[5] It had been a flashpoint border for centuries: militarily between the Austrians and Turks, and theologically between the Catholic and Orthodox worlds. Between the world wars, the city had a colorful and violent interregnum while Italy and the new Kingdom of Yugoslavia disputed its control. Into the vacuum swooped the Italian "poet warrior"—and proto-fascist—Gabriele D'Annunzio, who invaded with a private militia and introduced a kind of commune dominated by his own cult of personality.[6]

In the fallout after World War I, the expansionist Italian government, collecting on what West (referring to the 1915 Treaty

---

5. The Uskoks were finally suppressed by the Hapsburgs after they moved from helpfully harassing the Turks to annoyingly harassing the Venetians.

6. Unsurprisingly, D'Annunzio is something of a hero and role model for Eduard Limonov. D'Annunzio's vigilante freelancing in Fiume was an inspiration for Limonov's scheme to foment armed revolution in Central Asia with his National Bolshevik volunteers. The plan led to Limonov's imprisonment for two and a half years.

of London) calls "a bribe to induce the Italians to come into the war on the Allied side," made an attempt at the Paris Peace Conference to undermine the nascent Kingdom of Serbs, Slovenes, and Croats in order to claim regional hegemony and Adriatic control—specifically, over the port of Fiume. Italian prime minister Vittorio Orlando stoked the still-hot fires of Italian nationalism to pressure American president Woodrow Wilson to acquiesce to, or at least ignore, the move. Wilson, though, had developed a personal distaste for the Italian delegation that accentuated his political disagreement with their territorial demands.

Enter D'Annunzio. Short, bald, mustachioed, and flamboyant, he was a parody of the Byronic artist-provocateur—womanizing, free-spending, ludicrous, but memorable in wartime. In *The Balkans*, Misha Glenny described him "charging Austrian trenches in the middle of the night with pistols and knives, dressed in a flowing cape." Caught up in the paranoid nationalism of 1919 Italy, he and some units of the Arditi special forces decided that, rather than wait out the vacillations and negotiations of mere politicians, they would march on Fiume and solve the issue by force of arms, will, and the fate that favors the bold, naïve, and narcissistic.

For the next fourteen months, the Free State of Fiume became, depending on one's viewpoint, the "last of the pirate utopias," an aesthetocracy, a proto-fascist testing ground, an anarcho-syndicalist dictatorship, or an ongoing orgy. The constitution declared, in Hakim Bey's paraphrase, "music to be the central principle of the State." Leaders resurrected the Uskok pirate tradition to fund the never-ending party. Bey, who idealized the Free State as an anarchist utopia—"very nearly the first" of what he calls "temporary autonomous zones"—described it as a magnet for

> artists, bohemians, adventurers, anarchists . . . fugitives and stateless refugees, homosexuals, military dandies (the uniform was black with pirate skull & crossbones—later stolen by the S.S.), and crank reformers of every stripe. . . . Every morning D'Annunzio read poetry and manifestos from his balcony; every evening a concert, then fireworks. This made up the entire activity of the government. Eighteen months later, when the wine and money had run out and the Italian fleet[7] finally showed up and lobbed a few shells at the Municipal Palace, no one had the energy to resist.

Mussolini's Italy dismembered and swallowed much of Fiume. The border between the Kingdom of Yugoslavia and fascist Italy ran through the middle of the city—along the river, right behind the club I was playing, in fact.

While some contemporary anarchists, influenced by Bey, look to the Free State as a model of a temporary autonomous zone with what he called a "shared air of impermanence . . . [where] no-one was trying to impose yet another Revolutionary Dictatorship," the judgment of history has been more damning. Bey himself admits that "D'Annunzio, like many Italian anarchists, later veered toward fascism," but in fact Italian fascism took its

---

7. The Italian government had finally become wary of this charismatic rival power center.

aesthetic cues from D'Annunzio. Glenny quotes Michael Ledeen: "Virtually the entire ritual of Fascism came from the 'Free State of Fiume': the balcony addresses, the Roman salute, the cries of 'aia, aia, alala,' the dramatic dialogues with the crowd, the use of religious symbols in a new secular setting, the eulogies to 'martyrs' of the cause and the employment of these relics in political ceremonies." Mussolini, an early supporter of D'Annunzio, later came to see him as a threat. Il Duce was first implicated in an assassination attempt against the poet—he was pushed from a window—and then chose to bribe him into retiring from an active role in Italian politics. West, who has both a dog's nose for the barest whiff of fascism and a feminist distaste for its cult of male power, dismisses D'Annunzio with ad hominem contempt for his "singular example of male privilege . . . I will believe that the battle of feminism is over, and that the female has reached a position of equality with the male, when I hear that a country has allowed itself to be turned upside-down and led to the brink of war by its passion for a totally bald woman writer. . . . Here in Fiume the bald author had been allowed to ruin a city: a bald authoress would never be allowed to build one."

It wasn't until after World War II that Fiume, renamed Rijeka, finally passed from Italian control into that of nascent Yugoslavia,[8] but it retains a strong Italian influence. Cosmopolitan and relatively prosperous thanks to tourist money, it boasts a strong café culture, and "ciao" is heard everywhere.

"D'Annunzio was interesting," judged promoter Damir, who greeted me with a warm hug, "but ultimately he was a complete

---

8. In post–World War II Yugoslavia, the vast majority of its sizeable Italian population "self-deported" under pressure.

failure." He pointed out that the poet's grand vision, regardless of the riffraff who were drawn to it, had a strong component of ethnic nationalism. He compared it to the Republika Srpska in Bosnia, the northern province of ethnic Serbs who favor political integration with Belgrade. "He wanted to create an Italian state from Venice to Libya. It was a utopian idea, a free city of culture—there were concerts and shows every day—but only for Italians. Like Srpska, you can't ignore the other people around you without some kind of violent cleansing."

Damir was serious and full of idealistic energy—a college student studying cultural theory. When I first met him the year before, he had just returned from a weekend at a DIY festival—hardcore, postrock, krautrock—in Romania, by the Serbian border. He and an American girl had hitchhiked there from Zagreb—she was amazed, since hitchhiking isn't a thing that people do much in America anymore. He'd started booking shows back in 2003 because he "had friends who were into hardcore, and nothing was happening. We cleared out a basement, did fifty shows in the first two years. Then we saw there was another, bigger, empty room in the same building and expanded into there. Not many U.S. bands come because the currency is weak, and you can't make any money. Not like in Germany, where you can easily get three hundred euros a night."

He wore a black T-shirt with the illegible crust-punk font that looks like a hairy and poisonous centipede performing sex acts on itself. He had half-inch plugs in his earlobes and wore thin wire-rimmed glasses. He was concerned—unnecessarily—that his English was Russian-accented, and spoke in an intense flood of words, eyes scanning the walls.

"Jucifer"—an American guitar-and-drums duo notorious for

its wall of guitar amps—"is here next week. Last year they came and played a big room—four to seven hundred capacity—to seventy people. This year they'll come back, we'll have them in this small bar, they'll load in all those amps, and . . ." He mimed the roof exploding.

He lived in an apartment building that, like most of Rijeka, required a heart-racing uphill walk to get to, and he set a pace that left me breathless. The flat that he shared with his girlfriend Ray was divided by long, diaphanous curtains. The chandeliers were yellowed, and the wallpaper was peeling and archaic. *Ally McBeal*, subtitled in Croatian, played on their small television. (Many of his friends learned English from American television reruns, Damir told me.) There was no heat in the building. They had a couple of space heaters, but the electric bills made them prohibitive to use. "Next winter," Ray said, "we have to find a way to cut a hole in the wall and put in a woodstove."

"The landlord has announced his presence tomorrow," said Damir. "We are always running late with the rent. . . . He is a nice guy though."

"He must be," I said.

"He is always referring to himself in third person, like, 'Zdrako tell you last time . . .'"

Ray was from Šibenik, a seven-hour bus ride south down the coast toward Split. "Everybody's fucked up there. They are still fighting the war in their minds." She was tall and lanky, with a lip ring and black dreadlocks, sporting a red-and-black striped sweater. She struck me as the sort of heavy-hearted girl often drawn to vigorous, principled young men like Damir, for comfort and propulsive optimism.

"I must be honest," she said. "I don't like America."

She'd been kicked out of school and started working at a local indie rock club. She joined a collective: "It's very expensive" to live in Croatia "because we have to import everything," their friend Leo told me. "So we organize between each other and exchange what we can, use cash only when we have to." Their "infoshop"—the kind of leftist-activist organizing hub, marginally capitalist bookstore, zine-distribution center, patch and sticker vendor popular in Germany and the Pacific Northwest— and "riot folk collective," organized with someone named Ryan from Boston, eventually suffered the diminuendo common to collective activism: "People lost interest," Leo said.

Ray's real name is Ivana, said Damir, "but I think only her mother calls her that. Everyone calls her Ray, after a character in a manga book—not the porn kind, a dystopian story." She claimed to have not been able to find work in ten years and sighed. "When I look at a map, I think I've never been anywhere. Which is true."

Damir, by contrast, has lived in the United States and seemed to work at least three jobs amid countless other projects. He had been sent to Atlantic City on a work/travel program, first as a busboy, then as a dishwasher, then pushing wheelchairs on the boardwalk. He lodged in a house with a half-dozen other Croatians, and they sat up at night comparing notes on their experiences. One was working as a casino security guard and happened to be near a table where a man on a winning streak tipped any staff in sight with hundred-dollar chips. "He made as much in half an hour as I made all month. . . . I had to not think about it." In general, though, "when I travel, I want to travel; and when I work I want to work. But we'll see, after we join the EU—better a dishwasher in the U.S. than a bankrupt cultural theorist in Croatia."

Back in Rijeka, he did some manual labor for two euros an hour—not too bad, he said: "My friends in Macedonia are working eight-hour days for 150 euros a month." He ripped tickets at the local art house theater. He booked shows at a handful of local clubs and worked in a vague way for Radio Rijeka. We stopped by the radio station (which had a balcony where they hold annual concerts), located on the main pedestrian mall, so he could have a brief argument with a patron. He wore a pin bearing the image of a Molotov cocktail and the slogan "Keep warm: burn the rich."

He was thinking of moving to Zagreb to work at the squatter complex Medika. "Better to have a bad job in Zagreb than be out of work in Rijeka. Since I've been a student it's been OK—they have a student job office, they pay money to the university, and the university pays me. But when I'm not a student . . ." Croatia was set to enter the EU in June, and there was a general low-level panic about prices. "Everyone is worried. Prices are going to go up. Small farmers have to bring their operations to European standards, and they don't have the money to do it. Rijeka has one in four or five out of work already." The government was giving out money, a hundred fifty to three hundred euros a month, to blunt the effects of the unemployment. "Everyone is depending on the seasonal tourist work, when the drunk English people come."

There were some reasons for optimism, though. Damir and Ray's friends were planning a gay wedding after nine years together. "They are big metalheads, tattoos and everything. I am so happy about it," Damir said.

He took me to Tunel, the club I'd be playing that night. Tunel was just that: an arched stone tunnel under an active railroad bridge. It had been a jazz club for three years under previous owners, and then was taken over by the guy who runs the town's biggest rock club. The next show after mine was the Kilaueas, "the only surf band in Serbia, from Belgrade. A surf show is easy, like hardcore, people just like it and they will come." They did acoustic Tuesdays—"so that made sense, since you are an acoustic fellow." The bartendress, Zuna, poured shots of local *rakiya*. The first shot was flavored with olive and almond; the second, "made from red wine," tasted like port. Smoking is officially illegal in bars in Croatia but, Damir complained, everyone has found loopholes, and the smoke in the club was as fog-thick as in any Chinese or Serbian dive. It was another rowdy and superb show, and the black cowboy hat I passed returned loaded with coins, paper, and a couple of cough drops.

After the show, I met a bespectacled young man from the consonant-challenged island of Krk who was taking on the (perhaps fruitless) task of bringing punk shows to the island.[9] He'd just found out that Nikola Šarčević, the Serbian singer of the Swedish skate-punk band Millencolin, was vacationing on Krk for a month, and he was petitioning Šarčević's management to let him promote a Šarčević solo show there. But the price they quoted was prohibitive. "Maybe it's because he's Swedish," he speculated. Swedes, because of the strength of their currency, have a reputation around Europe for extravagance. "They expect

---

9. Maria and I once spent a day off in Krk (the name is from the Roman "Curicum") near the remains of a Soviet-era resort that had become a burnt-out and collapsed shell of 1970s tiles and insulation. Ivy had overtaken the out-buildings and moss the tennis and bocce courts, and you could just about read the remains of the sign "Please Help Us to Make This Park Even Nicer!" in three languages. The water was crystalline, impeccable, and impassive.

Krk is home to an odd style of a capella sung in two parts, following an un-tempered, six-note scale. Howled at top volume, in wavering pitch, it sounds like the improvisations of a pair of drunks.

big guarantees—they don't know" such amounts are impossible here.

It would be a short drive to Ljubljana the next day, and Damir and I went for a sightseeing hike in the morning. Easter was a few days away, and he pointed to a supermarket (this one operated under the Orwellian name Konzum) and said that it was "full of old people buying young onions" for Easter dinner. "You have this tradition in the U.S., the long, young onions?"

We climbed the 561-step path up the sheer cliffs behind the city to the restored ruins of Trsat Castle ("This is anti-Turk castle"). Damir had ambitions to mount an outdoor film festival there, under the aegis of the theater where he worked as a ticket taker. The castle, which West described as "a huddle of round and square towers, temples and dungeons and dwelling-houses," was the home of the Frankopan ruling family in the Middle Ages, though some of the fortifications are Roman. In West's time it was overgrown. Now it has been restored just to a state of picturesque disrepair, enough to hold a small restaurant, tourist barriers, and perhaps, if Damir's plans came through, films projected on the old walls. From the tower one, like West, could still see "Sushak"—now incorporated into Rijeka—"lying brown by the blue sea," and across "the dark ravine that runs up from the town to split a mountain range on the high skyline" were the bleached white tower housing projects of the suburbs. Damir pointed out a factory in the valley, beneath the suspended viaducts that ferry traffic to and from the inland, which in socialist times was the world's third-biggest producer of cigarette papers. Now it was fashionable, out of financial necessity, to buy loose homemade tobacco, in half-kilogram plastic bags, from old ladies in the market.

We left the castle grounds and climbed the next higher hill, to the south, along a path prowled by Franciscan monks that wound between statues marking the twelve stations of the cross. (Real pilgrims do the 561 steps on their knees.) West described a myth associated with this hill, that it was "the site where the Holy House, in which the Virgin Mary and Jesus and St. Joseph lived at Nazareth, rested for three years and seven months, from the year 1291 to 1294. . . . The picture of the little house floating through space is a lovely example of the nonsensical function of religion, of its power to cheer the soul by propounding that the universe is sometimes freed from the burden of necessity." Damir had never heard the story and shook his head in bemusement. "I used to smoke weed here," he says—it was cheap in the 1990s, smuggled in from Bosnia and Albania.

He wanted to show me his favorite spot in the city, the old cemetery. We crossed through the town center to the facing hills, past D'Annunzio's balcony and the home of the British industrialist Robert Whitehead. The latter's invention of the torpedo in the 1860s laid the economic foundation for the development of the city. Damir said it was "like [Moriarty] in the last Sherlock Holmes film": an independent fortune built by a private war profiteer, selling his proprietary technology to all comers. But Whitehead used his money to build the modern Rijeka (then still called Fiume), and the lawn around the city museum displayed the rusting husks of his torpedoes.

Damir liked wandering the cemetery because he could trace the city's complicated history in the mélange of names and dates and varied fashions of memorial design. Here were mausoleums that provided cover for junkies and crosses molded to look like they were made from chunks of firewood. Here were gravestones with black-and-white photo vignettes of the deceased, pressed behind ovals of glass for a hundred years. If the relatives of the long-dead, separated by decades of war, stopped paying rent on the plots, the remains were moved to the—"What do you call it? The skull chamber?"—ossuary. The exception was the Jewish section, whose gravestones lie flat to the ground, covered in piles of white pebbles. Their rent is waived in perpetuity as a kind of reparations. The families that might have paid for the upkeep had vanished in the wars.

Here was the plot of the evocatively named Famiglia Skull, and here a soldier whose name, Vincenzo Petrovich, perfectly encapsulated the Italo-Slav nature of Fiume-Rijeka. We skirted a funeral that spilled out from the main gate. Just uphill was an Art Deco church, in disrepair but still angular and surreal—dirty white stone with mauve and green oxidized-copper accents, featuring a memorial to dead Italian soldiers. This was a Fascist church—a combination not necessarily unique to Italy, a country where religion and authoritarianism had been synonymous for millennia, but still striking.

I asked Damir if he thought people were moving on from the wars of the 1990s.

"I don't think so. I was at home in 1991, and it was a trauma for me." Damir grew up in the suburbs of Rijeka. "There were no casualties in my family, but we didn't go to school for months, were in the apartment, eating German milk, and always hearing the bombing." He said that not long ago, "I went home and hung out with my friends from high school. I played them a band, a good band, from Belgrade, and they said, 'Of all the bands, you have to like a Serbian one?'" There was a Serbia-Croatia football game in Zagreb recently, and Croatians chanted slogans from the World War II–era Croat-led fascist puppet government. "In Zagreb!" he exclaimed, shaking his head. "Which is like a little Vienna!"

There was no one on the highway from Rijeka to Ljubljana, which was a bad sign—a slow crossing means bored guards. This was the EU border to boot,[10] and sure enough, they waved me over. I was to pull out and count the T-shirts and CDs (the trick to avoiding customs duties is usually to keep the count under a hundred). They opened the trunk compartments and asked if I was bringing in cheap cigarettes from Serbia; when I said no, they asked again. They brought me inside the shack and emptied my pockets.

"Where are drugs?"

"No drugs. I'm not stupid."

"No drugs? But you are musician!"

They called in the captain, and he asked again about smuggling cigarettes from Serbia—so this must be the real issue. Finally they waved me on, warning, "Probably they'll give you trouble" at the Slovenian entrance border a hundred meters away. They didn't.

So what do we know about Slovenia? And what do we think we know about Slovenia that is actually about Slovakia (also rural and forested) or Slavonia (the eastern wing of Croatia)? Even in books that are nominally concerned with the Slavs of Europe, you'll find nary a mention of the Slovenes. They are the mountain Slavs, tucked in between Italy, Austria, and Croatia,

---

10. In 2015, this border would be reinforced with razor wire to keep Syrian refugees from crossing.

who enjoyed an unusually uncomplicated relationship with the Austrian world. West mentions these forgotten central Slavs as "the unhappy Slovenes, who were incorporated into Italy" after World War I. "These six hundred thousand people are the worst-treated minority in Europe." In the 1930s, West reports, the fascist Italian newspaper *Popolo d'Italia* asked, "Have bugs a nationality when they infest a dwelling? That is the historical and moral position of the Slovenes living within our borders."

Slovenia didn't exist as a state until the 1918 founding of the federated Kingdom of Slovenes, Croats, and Serbs that predated Yugoslavia, and it didn't become an independent state until 1991. The Catholic Slovenes were something of an afterthought in the Kingdom, whose King Alexander I intended it more as a Greater Serbia of Orthodox Slavs than as an ethnic federation. "A sensible and unexcitable people," says West, who "had had better opportunities than their compatriots to live at peace," since the difference of their language from Serbo-Croatian encouraged officials in Belgrade to leave them to their own devices. Spared the history of Turkish battle and religious schism that had split their southern neighbors, they were "experienced in discomfort but not in tragedy."

Slovenia also avoided the melodrama of the post-Yugoslav wars and slipped comparatively peacefully into democracy, NATO, the EU, and the euro. Its only major city is Ljubljana, better known by its German name, Laibach (namesake of the infamous Slovenian band), and almost the entire rest of the country is thick-forested mountains. Virtually every kingdom and tribe in European history overran its territory, from the Celts and Illyrians to the Romans, Magyars, Franks, Hapsburgs, Napoleonic France, Turks, and fascist Italy. One theory for their isolation from the complexities of Yugoslav politics is that the Magyar invasions cut Slovenians off from their fellow South Slavs. There was a massive (one in six) emigration around the turn of the twentieth century. The impression is of an educated, marginal people with something of a historical inclination toward democratic governance and political stability, whose sense of nationality coalesced slowly and almost without their conscious attention.

"Slovenians are a different temperament than the rest of Balkans," Ray said. "Colder." Their revolution and independence predated the rest of Eastern Europe's, after a "Ten-Day War" with the Yugoslav army in 1991, but, Damir explained, "ultimately [the Yugoslavs] didn't care" if Slovenia left "because there weren't any Serbs there." How did they avoid the wars of the 1990s? I asked. "Maybe they are smarter than us," Ray replied with her usual glum cynicism. "They don't have the coastline"—like Croatia, she meant—"and that's what the Serbs wanted." Both claimed to find Slovenian, nominally related to Serbo-Croatian, unintelligible. Damir said, "If I concentrate, it's like the Zagreb dialect," while Ray simply said, "I find it hard to listen to."

The country has a population of only 2 million, a quarter of them in Ljubljana. Since its independence was relatively painless, industry remained socialized until recently. As a result, it didn't see the mass unemployment and societal upset that befell other postsocialist countries. When the last prime minister, a proponent of privatization and, it turned out, corruption, decided to sell off Slovenia's sole port, he was duly driven out by mass protests in Ljubljana—"five or ten thousand people every day in the square," Damir said.

The northbound road toward Ljubljana was at first lined with ads offering to change Croatian *kuna* to euros, and then passed through a series of farming hamlets and snowy mountains, each town capped by a single-spired church that was its tallest structure. It looked more like Austria than the Balkans. The only splash of color was a Roma caravan, painted in loud checkers, parked in a pull-off just past the border. Each highway sign was written in four languages.

Ljubljana is low and drab, except for two bizarre housing projects. One looks like it was designed by the architects of the Death Star, and the other might have been inspired by the mobile staircases used to board airplanes. It's basically Missoula, Montana—a nondescript city in picturesque natural surroundings—with a castle. The castle itself is heavily renovated, if not completely rebuilt: more like a museum in the shape of a castle than a vintage structure. From the top of the castle's watchtower, the pencil-yellow and umber color scheme of the old city is distinctive, and the greater urban area was bigger than I would have thought, but it seemed less a city than a swollen town.

The venue in Ljubljana was Metelkova, a self-proclaimed "autonomous zone" in a former Austro-Hungarian army barracks. Squatted since 1993, it is modeled on Copenhagen's infamous Christiana neighborhood. I thought I had been here with my old band World/Inferno in 2005, but to my surprise that was a different walled squat complex, in Nova Gorica, south of Ljubljana on the road toward Trieste. The European squat experience feels as formulaic at this point as the black-painted rock bars of America or the British toilet circuit: technically accomplished graffiti, welded-iron trash sculpture, banners with solidarity or antifascist slogans, surly and monosyllabic residents, brutal crust punk and metal playing on the PA. The little bar on premises did have a Christmas tree growing from the roof and a calming iron woodstove.

The night was an object lesson in how squats can be bullshit. No one was in charge or knew what they were doing, no one had communicated anything to anyone else, and nothing worked. The sound guy had one semifunctional mic, and took three hours to figure that out. (In the end, I abandoned the broken PA and played acoustic.) The hostel room cost thirty-five euros for what was essentially a frat house (drinks with curly straws in the lobby). My dinner was a "burrito" (grilled zucchini and cheese sauce in a tortilla) that cost six euros. The money? "We can't afford more to pay you more than fifty euros because we never charge entrance." Then, after two encores and "Man, you're a legend," five euros in merch sales. This was a Disneyland squat. It looked like a cynical and businesslike exploitation of an outlaw aura, but at the end of the day it was just an overpriced hostel with Axe in the showers and visitors who got to ignore the liquor laws.

As I packed the car, a guy with a skateboard, mismatched Converses, and wraparound sunglasses said, "You leaving?"

"Yup."

"Why? All weekend is going to be fucking awesome party."

"I . . . got stuff to do."

"OK." He shrugged—my loss, clearly. "Ciao."

I returned to Zagreb and saw a sign for the Museum of Broken Relationships—irresistible. On a hill, past a panoramic promenade where teenagers came to drink beer and straddle one another on park benches, was a small gallery with a unique collection: exhibits of the debris, some personal, some mundane, left behind by one person leaving another. There was a love letter written on glass, then shattered; an ax used to demolish shared furniture; a small deer woven from bamboo; and a breakup letter from the head of the Croatian Roma Forum to the prime minister. Their gift shop sold clever, if twee, items such as a "bad memories eraser" and T-shirts with a tear or a Band-Aid over the heart. Naturally, the Smiths were on the stereo.

The venue, Medika, was another cookie-cutter walled squat complex, cold, black, and covered in graffiti.

"You're staying there?" Damir had asked me.

"I don't think so."

"Good, I was there—I remember they don't have heat."

I huddled with some others around a woodstove while we waited for the venue to open. Medika had been in existence only five or six years, and so the punks running the place were still idealistic; cynicism was at a minimum.

"Do you live here?" I asked Josip, the promoter.

"No! I am, how do you call, bacteriaphobe."

We were waiting for the New York punk band Morning Glory. In a triumph of wrong-minded routing, they would arrive after an overnight drive from Berlin, which would take eleven hours under ideal circumstances. As it happens, they left Berlin at about five a.m., and arrived just as the show was starting, about nine that night. I didn't recognize anyone in the group besides the frontman, Ezra, from the last time I'd seen them, though I'd played a show with the rhythm section when they were in my ex-bandmate Lucky's short-lived thrash outfit Devastation Wagon.

Ezra sported a gentle beard and seemed shell-shocked by the drive. The band was tight but tired. My expectations were high: I'd seen a version of the band in 2005, at the Hook in Brooklyn, play what I still remember as one of the greatest punk sets I've ever seen, and Ezra is a kind of musical savant. This, though, was a sober, professional group with a testosterone vibe and branded thongs and panties (appropriately labeled "For Reals?!") on their merch table.

"My friend said he started reading your tour diary"—which I'd been posting on my website—"and fell asleep halfway through," a guy told me as he flipped through my records. "It was so long."

"Imagine how it felt to live it," I replied.

Among the axes and borders that define the Balkans, the historical gulf between Serbia and Croatia is particularly deep: Serbia was occupied by the Turks, while the Croats were enthusiastic Austrian allies. Like the Russians who paid tribute to the Mongols for five hundred years, the Serbs became tough and ruthless, and they ridiculed the Croats as effete lawyers and intellectuals. The Croats, in turn, found the Serbs brutish: in *Balkan Ghosts*, Robert Kaplan quoted a Croat calling Serbs "weird, irrational, like Gypsies. They actually liked the army. How can anyone like the army! . . . Belgrade's the Third World. I feel much closer to Vienna."

"There is a real imbalance in this country between Belgrade and the rest," Ozren from Novi Sad told me. "All the money goes to Belgrade."

"Do you know Rebecca West?" I asked. He didn't. "It's funny, people were making the same complaint in 1933, and probably 1333."

West sat with a table of Dalmatian Croatians who exclaimed, "Belgrade! The Government does nothing for us, but they take our taxes and spend them in Belgrade. . . . Is that fair, when down here we lack bread? It was a wretched little village before the [First World] war . . . a pig-town. . . . But now they are turning it into a place like Geneva, with public buildings six and seven stories high, all at our expense. I know there is corruption and graft in American politics, but you have no idea what it is like here. The trouble is not only that . . . the money goes to Belgrade, it's what happens to it when it gets there. It sticks to people's palms in the most disgusting way."

Belgrade happens abruptly: one minute I was driving through miles more of table-flat farmland and huddled village houses, then around the corner was a dystopian, double-barreled skyscraper and some irredentist socialist housing projects. The air conditioners and laundry hanging from half-open windows made the buildings look flaking and scaly.

I was almost immediately exhausted. There was a hectic, dangerous energy to the traffic, and the city was dirty, loud, frantic, and disreputable. Belgrade has been completely destroyed and rebuilt innumerable times, and perhaps it has acquired the habit of building quickly, without the expectation that the buildings will enjoy a long lifespan. Eventually I found the venue, down by the rubble-strewn bank of the Danube on the way out of town. It was another cold, graffiti-plastered squat of what looked like an old public school. The doors were open, but no one was around. I headed back toward the town center.

What Belgrade doesn't have is the acres-wide plaza that I expect from a postsocialist capital, the kind usually named "Revolution Square" or "Plaza of the Heroes" and ringed with columns and concrete. Belgrade's "Park of the Pioneers" is cramped and grassy, flanked by two unprepossessing palaces and a rather attractive (if judged on a sliding scale) parliament building. It does have a truly monumental post office (which also houses the Ministry of the Economy, and probably more) that would be right at home in Moscow and a lovely legal-pad-yellow train station.

It was when I stepped inside the rebuilt, beehive-like St. Mark's Church, though, that I felt true relief. The stench of diesel was replaced by incense; the frantic activity of the city center gave way to a pair of old ladies in headscarves praying and lighting candles. The stone floor was covered in a thick carpet. The tiny tomb of the fourteenth-century tsar Stefan Dušan, whose reign marked the high-water mark of the medieval Serbian empire, had a single candle burning before it. I just wanted to sit there for a while and give myself over to the velvet comforts of an Orthodox church.

Tonight's squat had an unusual pedigree. It had housed some sort of film production company, then was bought as an investment property by a "tycoon"—that's what the promoter, Nikolai, called him—who used the property as bank collateral for another loan and so wouldn't be developing it while it was thus engaged. The squatter collective went to the "tycoon" and asked if they could use it in the meantime, and he said, "Why not?"

Fresh and legitimized, these were the happiest squatters in Europe, thrilled to be alive. They were serving a godless concoction of vodka, soy milk, and peach juice, shaken in a plastic sandwich bag tied around a straw. Just a bunch of cool kids who wanted to get drunk in a freezing hovel. Nothing wrong with that.

"The country is all fucked up," said one. "But so you can do whatever you want."

"You playing Budapest?" said another. "A lot of Americans are living in Budapest."

"And Belgrade," a friend added.

"Well, in Belgrade it's cheap to live."

"And cheap to die."

Drunk nihilists make a good audience, and this was my biggest of the tour. Exhausted and cold, I let one of the organizers know that I was ready to leave whenever she was, but my show, it was clear, was just the beginning of the party. This was a Belgrade squat on a Friday night, and no one had any plans to wrap it up. I found a back room and fell asleep by the woodstove. At some point, a kind woman with bleached hair covered me with quilts. Around four in the morning, Nikolai and his girlfriend roused me and filled me in on what I'd missed.

"While you were asleep at the show, somebody broke a window from outside. And we thought it might be Nazis, so we got in two cars and chased them, and we caught them! They were so scared, they didn't think anyone would chase them. So we didn't beat them."

I got in my car and followed them for twenty minutes to the city's outskirts and to their surprisingly nice apartment.

"Hey, Nicolay," said Nikolai, "I'm going to the store in the morning, you need anything?"

"Oh no, I'm OK."

"He is shoplifting," added his girlfriend. "So it's no problem to tell him what you want. That's why the vodka was so cheap tonight."

The Kalemegdan, the fortress of Belgrade, sits atop the overlook above the river Sava and the bend in the Danube, facing an island that's been given over to nature in memory of the Great

War. This prow of land has been fought over by every tribe, petty king, and emperor since before the dawn of European history. It is the place where the two great marauding tribes of the region, the Turks and the Magyars, faced off. The first shots of World War I were fired from the north shore floodplain up into the fortifications. Its very name is drawn from the Turkish words for "battlefield" and "fortress." "The old fortress of Belgrade," wrote West, "till the end of the Great War knew peace only as a dream. . . . Ever since there were men in this region this promontory must have meant life to those that held it, death to those that lost it."

First among the shadowy, purgatorial ranks of great forgotten battles, World War I itself has more memorials here in this city of its nascency than perhaps any other place in old Europe. Atop a tall pillar, facing the former Hungarian lands, stands a slim nude man molded in tarnished copper, erected in 1928 to commemorate the tenth anniversary of something called the Breach of Thessaloníki. West records that since the statue was "recognizably male," the townspeople refused to erect it (so to speak) in the city proper and placed it atop the pillar, nearly hidden by the height, his offending parts facing the enemy.

The Kalemegdan is a castle of labyrinthine fortifications, brick walls, and ditches, and a rare haven of quiet in all of Belgrade. I found four busts and tombstones of antifascist partisan heroes, a socialist realist statue in honor of a fourteenth-century despot, and a bench painted to look like a watermelon slice. Medieval tombstones with Old Slavonic inscriptions lay in the grass. The capstone of the park is, fittingly, a military museum, surrounded by tanks, howitzers, and heavy artillery going back hundreds of years. One may be forgiven a twinge of Ozymandian despair

that the centerpiece of this harried, desperate city is the remains
of the armies that made it that way.

After last night's rain, though, summer had finally arrived. It
was sweaty and hazy and I was northbound to Budapest.

II.

❧

A Fur Coat with Morsels
(Hungary, Poland)

The Pannonian plain, with its poplar farms and stacked rolls of hay, is about as interesting to drive across as Kansas. The old imperial capital was more prosaic, more bourgeois, and altogether less interesting than the provincial cities that made up the rest of my week. It might as well be Berlin or Paris—though it is calmer and more monumental than either, a Berlin or Paris of the romantic imagination rather than the hectic, expat-and-immigrant hives of the two western capitals. Both Eva Hoffman and Rebecca West, visiting Budapest fifty years and a world apart, describe a city of commerce and extravagance that is somewhat devoid of the exotic Eastern *je ne sais quoi* they are looking for, a city of what West calls "dazzling," "staring" lights ("In no Balkan town are there such lights," she wrote, keen to underscore the imperial imbalance). Hungary in 1989, said

Hoffman, was "at a very different point of evolution" in private enterprise than its neighbors, "and the distance [it] has to travel to become a 'normal' country is visibly shorter."

In contrast to the Serbian entrance, the Hungarian border guards were nonchalant, even negligent, waving me through with barely a glance at my passport. The Serb province north of the Danube known as Vojvodina (including both Novi Sad and Bačka Topola), long the subject of dispute between Serbia and Hungary, also constituted an anxious border between the Hapsburgs and the Ottomans. Until the establishment of Serbian autonomy in the early nineteenth century, Vojvodina held the only population of Serbs outside Ottoman territory.[1] So in the course of a barely six-hundred-kilometer journey, one crosses not only the historical north–south fault line between Catholic Croatia and Orthodox Serbia but also the east–west line between the Islamic Ottomans and the Christian Hapsburgs (which itself succeeded the Danube frontier between Rome and barbarism). In that crossroads is the heart of the conflicts of a thousand years.

Szentes is a sleepy country town with a wide central square punctuated by statues of Kossuth and more obscure heroes with pigeons for headdresses. I spent the afternoon at the old municipal "medicinal" baths, a shabby thermal affair of piss-yellow bricks and a Turkish-style (after all, Hungary was Ottoman territory for a century and a half, and the bathing habit stuck) central bath decorated in a mosaic style I would call mod-Etruscan. There was a closet-sized sauna in the basement, off of a 1970s rec room complete with wood paneling.

---

1. As an example of the complicated nature of borderland identity, Serbians in Vojvodina made a good living selling pork to the Islamic Ottomans.

Hungary is a place of singular language difficulties. In general, most of the kids in the worldwide DIY scene speak decent English, and Maria's Ukrainian spills over into Russian and Polish. But Hungarian is an impenetrable language: Paul Theroux, in *Ghost Train to the Eastern Star*, quipped, "When you don't understand a single word, it's usually Hungarian," though Eva Hoffman found it "enchanting and utterly perplexing, [with] Bartokian syncopations and sensuousness." (If you can reliably pronounce Hódmezővásárhely, the name of a town between Szentes and Szeged meaning "beaver field marketplace," you may have powers of enunciation strong enough to overcome a mouthful of marbles.) In this smallish town, though, no one seemed interested in offering a helping linguistic hand. We couldn't find the club, and Maggie—the GPS (or, if you prefer, satnav), whose authoritative voice I'd anthropomorphized with a conflation of the brand name Magellan and Mrs. Thatcher—directed us to a residential neighborhood that hardly seemed likely to contain a venue for a punk show. The old men in the square refused even to look us in the eye as we asked for directions to what turned out to be "Tisza Beach," the waterfront of a wide, slow river, sluggish and shaggy, that outlined the town. We pulled the car up over a high levee, down a cobbled and then unpaved road, into a collection of battered trailers and houses on twenty-foot stilts, rattletrap and insectoid, something like the Mississippi Gulf Coast but with shacks instead of McMansions. If it weren't for the odd expensive-looking car, I'd have taken it for a Roma camp.

In fact it was a fishing village, located next to a river that has long flooded the Hungarian plains. The Tisza River (there is some confusion whether the "Tibiscus" that features in classical Greek and Latin literature refers to the Tisza or to the Timiş, which runs more or less parallel and to the west; Gibbon conflates the two) springs from the Carpathian Mountains near Rakhiv, in Ukraine. Attila the Hun is said to have been buried under a section that was thereafter rerouted so his tomb would never be disturbed. In antiquity the region's inhabitants were the Dacians, "who subsisted," according to Gibbon, "by fishing on the banks of the river Teyss"—from the German *Theiss*—"or Tibiscus." An invasion by the Sarmatians, steppe nomads from what is now Ukraine and southwestern Russia, drove the Dacians into the Carpathian Mountains. The Sarmatians were themselves later victims of a servile revolt, Gibbon wrote, and forced to cede the "marshy banks which lay between [the Teyss and the Danube, which] were often covered by their inundations, [and] formed an intricate wilderness, pervious only to their inhabitants, who were acquainted with its secret paths and inaccessible fortresses," to their former slaves, who called themselves the Limigantes. The latter were later defeated by Constantine's son Constantius, who exposed the Limigantes' camps by setting fire to the forest. The emperor was on the verge of generously allowing them to resettle as a Roman colony near modern Budapest, when, as he addressed them, they treacherously attacked his person. The result was "the extinction of the name and nation of the Limigantes" in reprisal, and the Sarmatians returned to the region.

The empty concrete foundations in some of the plots where houses had once stood attested to the functionality of the stilts that gave the whole place the quality of a Baba Yaga fairy tale. The venue itself, called Tiszavirág Büfé, was a fishing bar that looked as if it had been airlifted from a Key West backwater: the name was spray-painted on an old surfboard, and a rope fishing net, a life preserver, and an anchor hung from the balcony. It was run by an amiable snaggletooth who had been a water polo player in Serbia for eight years. Now he refereed polo matches at the local water park in his spare time. "Serbia is the most beautiful country," he said. "So stupid. Ten years of war, and they have nothing." He boiled a stew of rice, tomato sauce, and soy protein on a welded, wood-burning stove standing in the dirt in front of the bar, which did nothing to detract from the sense that we were camping on a beach. We would be playing next to the stove, on the concrete patio outside the front door.

The opening act was a hapless group of teenage folk-punks. We were remanded into the care of one of them, a passive bon-bon named Martin, who lived with his willowy sister in a small student apartment in Szeged, the nearest city. Szeged is ancient, near the former seat of Attila's empire, and yet almost nothing there is more than 140 or so years old: a massive flood swept away virtually every building in 1879, and it was rebuilt in a classic pastel Hapsburg style. We had all day to sightsee and were hoping Martin, who had contacted me on Facebook months before offering to host, could show us the sights.

"So what do you want to do?" he asked softly. Hoffman wrote, "Even when they speak English, Hungarians manage to transport some of the off-rhythms and softness of their language [and] give it strange, lunar resonances." I'd describe Martin, less generously, as a mumbler, and we quickly got the impression that he didn't understand quite as much English as we'd originally thought.

"Um . . . I'm not sure. What's interesting to see?"

Martin shrugged.

"I guess we're hungry—shall we go get some food?" we offered.

"OK . . . what do you want to eat?"

"What's good?"

He shrugged.

"Something vegetarian?" I suggested.

"OK..."

He led us to a cafeteria-style lunch counter and gestured at the menu, written on a whiteboard above the counter, entirely in Hungarian. "So what do you want?"

I don't mean to sound ungrateful. It is a thankless task, escorting foreigners around your city, and the onus is on me as the one who doesn't speak the language. But I was frustrated nonetheless. There is a passivity to traveling, especially touring—not the heroic romantic engagement with the foreign but a radical withdrawal in which you engage only on specific and circumscribed terms: food, timetables, logistics. For anything beyond that, the impulse is to let the person operating on their home turf dictate your fate.

"Can you tell me, maybe," I asked, "if there are any vegetarian options?"

"Hm," he said doubtfully. "Mostly it is chicken."

"Just point at something," said Maria. "I think there's pasta."

"In my view," wrote Hoffman, Czech and Hungarian food "are close competitors for awfulness, but . . . Hungarian cooking could well take the prize. What's happened to the famed Hungarian cuisine of yesteryear?" Peter, the promoter in Szeged, simply said, "Hungarians put sour cream on everything. And a lot of it." Lunch in Szentes two days earlier had been cold peach soup topped with whipped cream, accompanied by fried croquettes of breaded mushroom wrapped around soft cheese with dill. In Budapest, a dish advertised as "Mexican chicken" bore the description "Paprikash chicken meat was frying in a fur coat with morsels." Szeged is the home of spicy Hungarian paprika, yet I ended up with a plate of cold white pasta, topped first with a giant tablespoon of sour cream, and then shredded white cheese on top of that. I was hungry, but I made it through only a few bites.

The opening act that night was an enthusiastic duo, both named Peter, who had organized the show. After soundcheck, said the Peters, talk to the bartender; he'll hook you up with dinner.

"You are vegetarian, I heard," said the bartender. "I think we can prepare for you . . . pasta with cheese and sour cream."

There are physical markers I've come to associate with particular countries: the Serbian horse carts and trilingual signs (Latin, Cyrillic, and Hungarian), the light-pastel housing projects (a color scheme borrowed from the pastel wash of the Hapsburg buildings?) silhouetted against the outer hills of the minor Eastern European cities. In Hungary, it's giant concrete cones bristling with the entire telecommunications infrastructure of each small town, looming on the outskirts like the water towers of middle America. We were on our way to an "acoustic punk picnic" in Veszprém, ninety kilometers outside Budapest, where we'd play an afternoon set before heading to the capital for the evening show. Veszprém is a small town, and the picnic was near a zoo clogged by Sunday parkgoers, up a gravel road, on a grassy hill overlooking a bright valley. It may have been lovely, but a certain kind of situation can make "anarcho-punk" a synonym for "lazy and disorganized," and a free-beer picnic with an iron cauldron of stew on a fire is one of them: no one in charge, no master plan. At least we hadn't taken a bus overnight from Vienna just to play, like Jack, the friendly Brit in whose filthy student apartment we'd stayed a few weeks before.

Budapest is the second city of an old world. The Compromise of 1867 made the Hungarian capital the nominal equal of Vienna as an imperial city, and "much of Budapest's design and architecture dates from this period of national ascendancy," Hoffman writes. "The central avenues are as wide as the Haussmann boulevards in Paris." We arrived at dusk. These days, the other invariable sign of past Austro-Hungarian glories are backpacker hostels housing drunk twenty-two-year-olds, and we played a show in a bunker below one. After the show we stayed with Eliot and Laci, who run a hardcore label; Maya, a social worker; and their grouchy Boston Terrier. Maya helped Afghan refugees who had been told by their traffickers, "This is Norway," and dumped in Hungary to fend for themselves.

Returning to Budapest the next year on my own, a perfect storm of small things added up to a bad show. I was worn out by Belgrade and the boredom of the drive, and the café, though staffed by stunning, feline Hungarian women with Central Asian eyes, had no place for me to curl up and nap. I had outrun the summer again, and the city was cold and wet. The stage was by the door. When that happens, the people who are there to see the show are already seated and settled, so what one notices from the stage are either those leaving or those entering—and their attempt to suppress a look of dismay when they see that there's live music. It was a pass-the-hat deal, which I know from experience averages about two euros a head regardless of the general enthusiasm level. And Hungary is a place where my conversational stage shtick just doesn't work. The language barrier, even for people with decent conversational English, is just too great.

That said, I ended up pocketing more on this disappointing show than at Belgrade's fantastic one, so there was no actionable lesson besides a macroeconomic one about comparative currency valuation and free trade zones.

"I just want to let you know," said the man who was putting me up, "I had a band staying over last night, and I haven't had a chance to clean up."

"It's OK—I want to go straight to bed."

"I understand. The guys last night were in a drinking mood. We stayed at the club for a long time, then when we came home we played *Passion of the Christ* with these." He held up a pair of pink furry handcuffs. "So I am still hungover."

The previous year, Maria and I had a two-day drive through the Czech Republic to Poland. We stopped in Brno for lunch (after the bland Central European cuisine, we sought out what we figured must be the only vindaloo for miles around) and spent the night in Olomouc, a half-deserted college town with dark, baroque sculptures, a spectacular astronomical clock, and automatons in the town square. Something of a Peter Lorre horror movie atmosphere prevailed in this cobblestoned Moravian backwater. Passing us as we strolled were identical twins with waist-length straight blonde hair, walking arm in arm and wearing identical outfits: denim shirts tied up to bare their midriffs, white belts, black skirts, dark eyeshadow. As they glided by, a capella choir music spilled like a sudden rain shower from an alley window.

When I first started coming to Germany to tour around the turn of the century, people told horror stories about terrifying, drunken Polish punks. But a decade later little seemed to differentiate Polish touring from German. In Poland the young, hip crowds were even more stylish, more self-consciously curated, less bar and more coffee shop, less infoshop and more gallery. One of the great ironies of international prejudice is the stubborn survival of the "Polish joke" in America, premised on the Pole as the incorrigible dullard. I haven't read any study of the chronologies of immigration and assimilation that explains its tenacity. Maybe German Americans were well enough ingrained in American society that when working-class Poles began to emigrate, the old European stereotypes already had a foothold. But the Poles see themselves, not without reason, as the cosmopolitan, artistic elite of Eastern Europe and their country as the home of serious film and literature, with a long, aristocratic history. And the anti-Communist resistance was more sustained and more class-integrated than in much of the rest of Eastern Europe, priming it for the easy emergence of the kind of civil society often declared a necessity for countries emerging from totalitarian government.

There was one major difference when I first visited in 2012, however: in Germany, with its wide autobahn and lenient speed limits, there are virtually no two cities between which the drive takes more than seven hours. In Poland, a country nearly the same size, there were only divided highways with limited passing opportunities. This is a country with a huge business in trucking (and a correspondingly huge business in incongruously glamorous roadside prostitutes, standing alone, checking their cell phones, in the pull-off rest areas every few miles). So any Polish drive, as we crisscrossed the country from Kraków to Szczecin and Gdańsk, south to Wrocław, back north to Poznań and Łódź, south again to Kraków, became an exercise in tense frustration. For thirty miles, we would crawl behind a couple of tractor-trailers, before exploding into a five-hundred-foot drag race past six cars into a half-mile of glorious open-road speed, only to stop dead against the next convoy. Poland and Ukraine were then in a mad race to build infrastructure for the Euro 2012 soccer tournament starting in a matter of weeks, so what few highways there were tended to be under construction or closed for expansion, sending a flummoxed Maggie into a frenzy of back-roads recalculation. We almost missed the show in Poznań, racing on foot across the central square, loaded down with instruments, arriving directly onto the stage at set time, in front of an already seated crowd of two hundred.

Maria has a distantly related but beloved aunt in Łódź who is an excellent example of the Polish intelligentsia of the Solidarity era—someone who, in Hoffman's words, "got to live out something that for Western intellectuals of that generation was the great, unlived romance: they made a revolution, or at least were at its vanguard." Her friends are painters and writers, and her apartment, inside the usual gray and peeling post-Soviet building, was as pristine and meticulously decorated as any Manhattan studio. She has a smooth, bowling-ball bob and is from a small town outside Łódź. She was sent to the city in 1971 to live with her grandmother in order to attend a better secondary school. Her parents wanted to join her, but "it was a closed city after World War II, and they couldn't get a 'reason' or an apartment trade to live there."

She made us a lunch of spinach pie, cranberry cheese, and asparagus with béchamel. She set out a pitcher of water with lemon and mint and reminisced about the nationwide general strikes of 1980–81.

"We all went on strike. It was funny because we were government workers, a different union than the factories, so we would strike in shifts—one hour this room would strike, then the other room would strike. I was on vacation with my young son and pregnant with my daughter. My husband Igor was a judge, and because of the times he was called to Warsaw" while they were away. "The whole country shut down and we didn't know [where he was]. We went to the store one day and all they had was vinegar! We went to the train station every day" in case her husband returned. "I was listening to Radio Free Europe for news, and now I am an expert about the Israeli kibbutzes since that was the story on the radio." She laughed. "Everything we learned about the strikes we knew from word of mouth, from other people, from ten million people realizing we all thought the same way."

The name "Łódź" means "boat," and the city flag is literally an image of a boat slapped over a Polish flag. It's an artificial city, in a way: for hundreds of years it was a hamlet of fewer than three hundred people, until in 1815 the tsar decided it should be an industrial center. Seventy-five years later, seven hundred thousand people lived there.

We were playing a coffee shop in a renovated deli (very hipster New York, like Arlene's Grocery), still named Owoce i Warzywa ("Fruits and Vegetables") in order to save on a new awning. The sound engineer was a hobbyist who used to work at the radio station but was now a civil engineer; after work, he helped out his friends who run the club. He was working on a municipal plan to tear up the railroad station and relocate it underground. The European Union was promoting a plan to run a high-speed train underground from Estonia to Germany, but there was widespread skepticism. The planners had only part of the money, he said, "and people around here are pragmatic. Maybe in twenty years we can sell newspapers and coffee to travelers, but for now? . . . The worst thing they could do is start digging. They would run out of money and it would paralyze the city."

III.

Poor, but They Have Style
(Romania)

While Poland is the poster child for post-1991 integration and success, Romania and Bulgaria are the bêtes noires of Western European protectionists and EU skeptics. At the same time, of course, they are equally the most exoticized and the most romanticized: there is a fantastic idea of Romania as colorfully downtrodden, a nation of (if I may quote the renowned Balkan historian Cher) gypsies, tramps, and thieves, with a history of picturesque corruption and genteel untrustworthiness. As Josip in Zagreb put it, "Bulgarians, they have it really poor. Romanians, they are poor, but they have style."

Having retraced my steps from Poland back to Hungary, the road to Romania was eastbound from Budapest, past simple farmland, flooded fields, a pair of mule deer, and a giant concrete soccer ball by the side of the road marking nothing obvious. The village houses were made of thatch with mossy tile in the centers, and all faced the main road. They were accessible by little one-car concrete bridges over thin drainage ditches. I passed a police car with one working headlight and arrived at the Romanian border.

Crossing the border, I lost one hour to daylight savings time and another to the time zone. "It's a rental car?" asked the border police, examining my documents—in this part of the world, that includes your "green card," the car registration. "They are OK with you coming to Romania?"

"Yes," I lied, and pulled over to buy the necessary highway vignette, as European countries call the little windshield sticker some of them use to indicate you've paid the highway toll. In fact I'd been repeatedly and explicitly warned not to take the rental car into Romania or Bulgaria. "There are gangs stealing German cars and taking them to Albania" I was told, though it was a Vauxhall and surely not one of the more desirable models. But there was no way around it: I couldn't afford to leave this car in Vienna and rent another, Balkan-cleared junker. I'd just have to be vigilant about the legal details of tolls and speed limits and leave the rest to hope and fate.

As I exited the shack with my sticker and a handful of slippery, plastic-feeling Romanian currency, I saw a slick-haired, potbellied hustler in a leather jacket eyeing my license plate. "Samsung Galaxy?" he offered, brandishing a phone.

As an instructive tableau of the spectacular failure of industrial gigantism imposed on an agrarian culture ("the corpses of empire, they stink as nothing else," says West), the road to Cluj does not disappoint. Herds of long-haired, thus filthy, sheep—this shaggy variety is distinctive to Romania—clustered by a

trucking warehouse. The rusted remains of an abandoned nuclear plant, one dirty smokestack still belching, were the stuff of
postapocalyptic nightmares. In Romania and Bulgaria, the biggest structures standing are usually the most decrepit. Farther
down the road, a demonic blackened dam held back a reservoir.
Robert Kaplan noted that while heavy industry created "cruel,
ugly things throughout the communist world, factories in Romania seemed to belong to a deeper circle of hell." The successive
Communist regimes of Gheorghe Gheorghiu-Dej and Nicolae
Ceauşescu were infamous, among many other things, for monstrous red-herring projects—dams, canals, plants—begun not
so much in the interest of national development as to provide
an object for hard labor. Stalin is said to have casually advised
Gheorghiu-Dej to "keep the masses occupied. Give them a big
project to do. Have them build a canal or something."

The traffic on this pitted two-lane road was clogged and
Hobbesian. Cars drafting off one another, bumpers mere feet
apart, executed suicidal passing maneuvers past the trucks.
I braked abruptly as a horse-drawn cart pulled into my lane.
There were pedestrians on the side of the road, too: a man carrying an ax, a grimy pair with bushy black mustaches. A small
orange car passed, a decal reading "Street Pirate" pasted in its
rear window. One yard was full of shrink-wrapped toilets. The
low hills were scarred with ancient, overgrown terraces, the road
lined on both sides by flags—the Romanian tricolor and the blue
of the European Union.

Like northern Serbia, this part of Transylvania was controlled
by Hungary for many years, and ethnic Hungarians remain a
significant population bloc. After World War I and the fall of the
Austro-Hungarian Empire, the memory of a feudal arrangement

in which Romanian peasants worked for German and Hungarian landlords led to a nationalist reaction bordering on ethnic cleansing. Ceauşescu had, Kaplan reported, "outlaw[ed] abortions and birth-control devices so the Romanians could outbreed the hated Hungarians" and "forbade Hungarians from giving their children Hungarian names at baptism." Cluj's far-right 1990s mayor Gheorghe Funar mandated the exclusive use of the Romanian national colors in such civic improvements as park benches and Christmas lights, and he worked to scrub the Hungarian history of the region from municipal monuments. (He was eventually ousted for allegedly running a massive Ponzi scheme.) Kaplan called the Hungarian–Romanian border, despite lying between nominal allies, "for decades the meanest frontier crossing in Europe . . . scarier than the Berlin Wall." Eva Hoffman, traveling the same route in the early 1990s, was warned not to enter Romania in a car with Hungarian plates.

Along the road from the border to Cluj, I saw just one Hungarian flag, but that was outside a unique town. Most Romanian villages followed a pattern: at the town line stood a naïve painting of a crucifix on wood (Polish villages had Virgin Marys), and a ring of fields and ten-foot cones of hay circled a town center. Driveway bridges crossed the drainage ditches that ran parallel to the road on both sides and led to one- or two-story houses. The houses are decorated with the most distinctive, and stylish, feature of the Romanian countryside: their street-facing fronts are covered in prefab plastic tiles, about the size of a brick, with four diagonal lines rising from the corners to form a slight relief peak. These tiles are arranged in colorful, geometric mosaics and give the main town streets the look of a glossy but homemade quilt.

The one "Hungarian" town was made up of a string of half-built nouveau mansions with triple-canopied roofs and gaudy turrets in the baroque Hungarian style. Some, still without a finished exterior, were visibly built in layers—a few feet of concrete blocks, followed by a few feet of bricks, as if the contractor had bought as many materials as he could while he had the money, then left off work until he could come up with some more cash. Some of the cupolas, also triple-lobed, were covered in shiny aluminum. One was topped, like a kind of minaret or weathervane, with a silver BMW hood ornament. I saw more of these insta-villages of Hungarian-style McMansions farther south, on the way back to Szeged. I wondered—and was unable to find anyone to confirm or deny this—if these are settlement attempts by rich Hungarians, flush with EU money, to push back against anti-Hungarian sentiment with flashy displays of means, if not taste.

In any case, the dull Pannonian plain mercifully ended as the road followed a river and a train up into the hills. I abandoned notions of a trackless Transylvanian woods: these hills have been deforested for some time. Elderly people sat outside the gates of their houses, canes akimbo. The older generation was picturesque and well-dressed—the women in black kerchiefs and wide skirts, the men in suit jackets over cardigans and flat leather caps. Those under forty tended more toward the ubiquitous Adidas tracksuit (for the men) and tight, pre-ripped jeans and puffy white parkas (for the women). Teenage boys seemed to have a taste for the shaved-on-the-sides pompadour.

I was mildly surprised to find Cluj a lovely, prosperous-looking city, a university town with a familiar, British-style high street—there was a Vodafone shop what seemed like every hundred yards, a string of cafés, a KPMG office, takeout coffee, joggers. Hoffman exulted that it was "unmistakably European in a way that surprises me—recognizable, beautiful Europe, in this far region of the world!" The buildings in the colorful "little Vienna" style surrounded a small central square dominated by a Hungarian-Gothic sculpture of the fifteenth-century king Matthias Corvinus. (The pedestal used to include "of Hungary" after the king's name, but those two words were removed by Funar.) Transylvania and western Ukraine were the easternmost outposts of Western European culture for much of the last millennium, with all the shared artistic and intellectual experience that implies.

Cluj also constituted the northeastern frontier of the Roman Empire at its greatest extent, after the Dacian conquest by Trajan. (It was officially renamed "Cluj-Napoca" in the 1970s to accentuate the connection to Napoca, the Roman town which once stood there.) When, in the 270s A.D., as Gibbon relates, Aurelian withdrew Roman forces from Dacia to the old boundary on the south bank of the Danube, he brought most of the Romanized Dacians with him to the denuded but still fertile region and left the north bank to the Goths and Vandals. He renamed the south bank "Dacia" to soften the loss of territory. Some, though, stayed behind: "The old country of that name detained, however, a considerable number of its inhabitants, who dreaded exile more than a Gothic master. These degenerate Romans continued to serve the empire, whose allegiance they had renounced by introducing among their conquerors the first notions of agriculture, the useful arts, and the conveniences of civilised life. An intercourse of commerce and language was gradually established between the opposite banks of the Danube; and after Dacia became an independent state, it often proved the firmest barrier of empire against the invasion of the savages of the North." In a note, Gibbon added, "The Walachians[1] still preserve many traces of the Latin language, and have boasted, in every age, of their Roman descent."

Though the area was Roman for less than two centuries, the heritage is cherished—not least in the blessedly comprehensible Romanian language, a familiar Romance relative of Italian, with some Slavic borrowings. With a couple of semesters of college Italian and some pan-Slavic pidgin, I could read a menu on day one. In addition, Romania, like Russia, was historically Francophile, and "*mersi*" is widely used in both Romania and Bulgaria for "thanks." But so are some archaic Latinisms, like "*servus*"— essentially, "at your service." (Latin remained the administrative lingua franca for the Kingdom of Hungary, including parts of modern Romania, until 1844.) A stylized statue of a wolf suckling Romulus and Remus stands atop a short pillar in the pedestrian mall. Similar statues, wrote Simon Winder, were gifted to Romanian cities by Mussolini to solicit a potential alliance based on notional historic ties. "A Latin island in a Slavic sea" goes the nationalist trope.[2]

The territory converted to the Eastern rite church in the ninth century, while a part of the Bulgarian empire under Boris I. It was Easter Sunday in the Roman Catholic world, so I'd been unable to book a show in Catholic Hungary. In Cluj, as people were eager to clarify, "we're Orthodox," and Orthodox Easter, following

---

1. A term for the people living north of the Danube and south of the Carpathians. The name itself confirms this history, deriving from *walha*, which was used by Germanic peoples to refer to Romance-speaking neighbors (see also Wales and Cornwall).

2. Historian John Lukacs said that Romanians "have something mock Latin about them . . . reminiscent of the mock-European quality of the Argentinians."

the Julian calendar, fell later in the month. The churches were nonetheless full—of Hungarians, I suppose. I entered one that was dark and draped with chandeliers, and decorated with carved filigree (and, for some reason, a painted Masonic Eye of Providence). A men's choir sang in low harmony.

Alex and Alex met me at the bar where I'd be performing, just off Piața Unirii (Unification Square, renamed by Funar as a pointed reminder of the unification of the region with Romania). The Alexes were part of a small group of college-age guys who had taken over management of the bar a little over a year earlier, with the idea of building a punk scene. Alex One, dark and sharp-featured, was a junior in college. In addition to bartending at the club, he had moved into an apartment upstairs two months ago. He wasn't entirely thrilled with the arrangement, though. When you live above the bar where you work, sometimes it's hard to get, let's say, breadth and depth in your life. "Some days," he said, "I'm never leaving this building." The flat was secured with a small padlock. The kitchen faucet had stopped working after he broke off the handle. I asked him if I could use the washer. Sure, he said, though he didn't have laundry detergent and didn't know how it worked—he'd never used it. (Dish soap, I discovered, is an acceptable alternative in a pinch.)

It's a charming town, I told him.

"Well, I could show you the bad neighborhoods," he said. "But this part of town, yes. Cluj and Timișoara are probably the more beautiful Romanian cities. Their old towns were preserved. Not like Bucharest, which was completely leveled and rebuilt." Alex Two had been a work/travel lifeguard in Ohio. "People there were Catholic and conservative," he said approvingly. "They respect authority. It was great!" Paul, who booked the place, doubled as a tour manager, and we compared notes on border crossings. His bands don't even bother with Croatia, he said; the border guards are sticklers for what is called the "ATA paper," the equivalent of a work permit, which costs about a hundred euros.

The soundman Sergio was Catholic, thus missing his Easter "vacation" and not a little resentful about it. He played cajón, of all things, with the opening act, alongside an acoustic guitarist and a singer in a Wasted Youth T-shirt. By showtime, he'd relaxed a little and told me he worked as a geologist for building and roads projects. A civil engineer, I clarified. "Yes, a civil engineer. Five years ago, we were turning down work in Bucharest because there was so much here. Now we would go anywhere!"

It was a late club. Maybe it was a late town. Sergio's opening act was due to go on at eleven p.m. on this Easter Sunday, and Alex One worried aloud whether people would know the show was starting so early.

The next day I headed south into the Romanian heartland, over a ridge through a thick, obliterating cloud, then down into a wide valley walled with hills denuded by and speckled with sheep. Roadside vendors in one village sold blown glass on folding tables set up every hundred yards, like a head shop's display of distended bongs. These were dirt-road towns where old men stood around, shadowed by stray dogs ranging in temperament from wolfish to craven. Between villages, hitchhikers and police traded stations beneath the ubiquitous storks' nests. One village had a brilliant church shining in brass, brick, and copper. Outside the next, a monstrous doughnut of trash, tended by a bulldozer, slumped slovenly around a central fire. As I turned west,

I began to pass castle ruins of medieval Hungarian provenance, a fortress church, fuchsia and lime houses tucked in between irregular mountains. A donkey cart slouched past men dismantling a roof. Driving conditions, I pondered while stuck behind trucks and flinching at kamikaze passing maneuvers, go a long way toward determining my opinion of a country. Traffic manners have emotional consequences.

I was on my way, at the suggestion of my uncle, to a village called Maşloc. It is located in the historically, if not presently, polyglot and multicultural western Banat (named for the Persian word for a Turkish military governor) region of Transylvania and was the ancestral homeland of my maternal great-grandmother and her sisters. I'd known one of the sisters, Sophie, as a feisty ninety-year-old living in a Jersey City walkup. Their father had been a tobacco farmer in what was then, in the pre–World War I twilight of the Austro-Hungarian Empire, a farming village with the German name of Blumenthal. The young girls helped smuggle tobacco across the border and snuck out of the house to party in the provincial capitals of Timişoara (then known by the Hungarian name Temesh) and Arad. They were, I believe, part of that German diaspora known to West as the Swabians[3] or Banat Deutscher, "which is to say," to quote West, "a German belonging to one of those families which were settled by Maria Theresa on the lands round the Danube between Budapest and Belgrade, because they had gone out of cultivation during the Turkish occupation and had to be recolonized."

---

3. Swabia is a region in southwestern Germany. Since many of the German migrants to Eastern Europe were from that area, the term was used to refer to Germans in general.

There are several stories about the scattered German communities in the east. Some German colonists were resettled in former church lands after the dissolution of Catholic monasteries by the Hapsburg emperor Joseph II. Some moved to lands left vacant after Tatar raids. Kaplan tells a different, and older, story of the larger "Saxon" community in western Transylvania. He says it was the twelfth-century Hungarian king Géza II who "recruited the Saxons to settle in what was then medieval Hungary's eastern flank against the Byzantine Empire. There, the Saxons founded seven fortified cities . . . [and] entrusted themselves to nobody, building tight and efficient communities behind their fortress walls. . . . They became, in historian Lukacs's view, 'the grimmest Lutherans in all of Christendom.'" It was this isolated community of Saxons, claims Kaplan, that gave rise to the tale of the Pied Piper of Hamelin (a town in lower Saxony), who enchants and steals German children, as gypsies—long associated with Romania—were reputed to do, away to his homeland in these Transylvanian mountains. What better way to explain a community of Germans, isolated both from the larger Germanic world and from their Romanian neighbors, speaking an archaic dialect, tucked away in a European backwater?

My great-grandmother and her family emigrated to the United States in the years before World War I. In retrospect this might be considered "getting out while the getting was good." In the wake of the war, the region was quickly annexed by Romania, which made the Saxon community first a target of Volksdeutsch reabsorption by Hitler, and then a target for expulsion by and retribution from Romanian Communists and their Soviet allies. The bulk of the community, Kaplan wrote, was exiled to coal mines in eastern Ukraine and Siberia or "sold . . . for hard currency, as visa hostages to West Germany" by Ceaușescu. Most of the few "Germans" remaining by the time of the fall of the regime in 1989 wasted no time self-deporting (to borrow a phrase) to Germany.[4]

When imagining the home of this line of my family, I pictured the kind of bucolic villages I passed during the bulk of the day's drive: pastel-washed cottages, tin-roofed churches, and donkey carts, hidden in the foggy Chinese-tapestry mountains and little round turtle hills along the Mures River, by the castle ruins of Lipova.

But once I passed another husk of a nuclear plant, the foothills melted back into the familiar tedium of the Hungarian plain and the serpentine alpine byways turned into new highway laid over dull fields. The rich purple and loamy brown landscape gave way to dusty tan. Without the slopes to confine them, the villages became indifferent sprawl, like used cardboard thrown in a ditch. I left the highway for a series of unnamed asphalt roads ridden with potholes, sometimes stripped to their cobblestones, then down to what West called "a casual assembly of ruts." Squat concrete mile markers, like miniature postboxes, counted off the distance between the passing towns and the regional centers of Timișoara and Arad. It was flat, soggy, uninspired land. One farm complex looked abandoned, until a barking dog alerted me that at least one of the buildings was still occupied. Demonic black chickens picked over its yard of mud.

Past a filthy hamlet with the telltale German name of Neudorf, the road improved a little as I crossed the Timiș county

---

4. Yet some did remain. In November 2014, Romania elected as their president Klaus Iohannis, a Transylvanian German Saxon and the first member of one of Romania's ethic minorities to attain the presidency.

line. The mile markers at least had a fresh coat of blue and white paint, but the concrete pillar that once read "Timiş" had been stripped of the letters. Someone had spray-painted a red heart around the scar where the "ş" had been ripped out.

Maşloc, when it finally appeared, had a long, low central street of cracked asphalt and a few dirt side lanes where chickens pricked mud puddles. A general store sold a Romanian pilsner called Neumarkt. Two churches faced off across the main street: one, beige on tan, bore the inscription "Bete! Rette Deine Seele! Arbeite!" ("Pray! Save Your Soul! Work!") carved in old German script over the lintel. A fuchsia primary school that looked like a barracks faced a crumbling, white-plaster monument to five local Germans who had died in World War I. A banner over the playground urged the case of two regional politicians.

The bourgeois main drag, smelling of wood smoke, belied the muddy farm life in evidence off the side streets. Barbed wire strung between trees passed for fencing. A man in dirty purple track pants whipping a horse with a stick gave me a dirty look. Someone was building a small, round chapel out of brick, but the rest of the houses and barns were gray and weathered wood. There weren't many people in evidence, but I had the distinct sense I was arousing suspicion in the few that were, as I circled this town of horse carts in a new rental car with German plates. I was looking for the cemetery; I thought perhaps I could find a familiar name or two. It took a good fifteen minutes of driving up and down this not-large town before I found it, tucked in a back corner and fenced with barbed wire and bramble. I realized that the entrance was through some private backyards, and while pondering my next move I was approached by a toothless shepherd in a conical black fur cap. He shook my hand, grinned—I'd been unfair, he did have one yellow incisor—said something, and gestured toward the cemetery fence. Following his hand, I noticed the fresh corpse of a vulpine feral dog, sodden from the day's rain, hanging upside down from the barbed wire. I decided I'd seen as much as I needed to of this godforsaken hole. I mentally thanked my great-aunt Sophie and her sisters for leaving a century ago and headed back to the relative comfort of Hungary.

It was still a holiday when I got to Szeged: Easter Monday, when, according to promoter Peter, "You water the girls. All the guys go to all the girls they know and—it used to be they would dump water on them, with a bucket, but now it's eau de cologne, perfume. Sometimes they get chocolates or cash too, but it's mostly about the watering with perfume."

"Mostly it's fun when you're younger," his friend says.

"I don't know—I watered my girlfriend today!" says Peter. "It's like a fertility ritual, and the coming of spring. And it's like a popularity contest for the girls—who has the most guys watering them. And the guys get drinks and food when they go around, so you can get pretty wasted. So that's why the cops are out today."

"That's a crazy tradition," I said.

"I think only three countries are doing it—Hungary, Slovakia, and maybe Czech Republic." Anyway, he said, I shouldn't have any drinks if I'm driving to his house after the show, lest I get caught in the girl-watering dragnet.

Southbound the length of Serbia toward Bulgaria, I am traveling all week the route of a major Roman and Ottoman military road: Istanbul to Belgrade, and on to Buda, via Plovdiv, Sofia, and Niš. This stretch more or less follows the Velika Morava River, whose

Wikipedia entry deems it "a textbook example of a meandering river." The river carried barges of gravel past colorful riverside fishing cottages. The highway developed that phantom third lane you find in countries with lax policing and indiscriminate passing standards. South of Belgrade alleviated the tedium of the flat farmland and industrial trucking infrastructure of the north. The land blistered into low, green mountains reminiscent of Ireland, and the road slung viaducts over paved ditches, railroad tracks, and valleys of trash. It was wine country, though some of the vineyards had gone to seed and were grazed by storks. The graveyards had unfenced black tombstones, not the manicured and colorful plots of Croatia, and the mountain tunnels were eerily lightless. Once through, I was almost the only vehicle on the road to Niš in the rain.

The ancient town of Niš, birthplace of Constantine the Great and the site where the Roman emperors Valentinian and Valens met to split the empire, was a low city spread like a quilt over a gently sloping valley. As I approached it, the traffic coalesced into a dual stream of speeding BMWs and Audis on one side and putt-putt Yugos and Zastavas on the other. A hitchhiker with a birthmark covering half his face waited by a tollbooth.

I passed through the city as quickly and fluidly as through a one-crossroads village. Its southern end, through the suburb of Prosek, was a slim fortress of a mountain pass flanked by hundred-foot gas tanks painted to look like huge vodka labels. The lumpy and irregular mountainside villages became increasingly ramshackle, their shack walls stripped of plaster exposing wooden slats, and then petered out into forest.

IV.

You Are an Asshole Big Time
(Bulgaria)

It felt like a literal gateway, this pass. The road is ancient: it was the Roman Via Militaris and the medieval Constantinople Road, the route from the fantastical Illyria to the truly eerie, tribal, ineffable Thrace. And the country opens wide on the far side, from the claustrophobic Serbian mélange of huddled village and heavy industry to wide, fertile vistas, forested, not cultivated, with pine and even a little birch. There was wood smoke from beyond a dry, umber-and-sienna hill, some Turkish flags, and the white peak of Vitosha, the snowy sentry of Sofia, in the distance. The skeletons of a couple of factories, which looked like they had been shelled, simply served as the contrast underlining the Montanan beauty. In fact, the visual resonance with the American West is well known: the Italian directors of the 1960s filmed their spaghetti Westerns here as an inexpensive stand-in for cowboy country.

I had a pocketful of Serbian dinars and, worried about highway tolls up until the moment I crossed the border, hadn't changed them while still in Serbia. On the far side, to my dismay, the usual string of low-rent money-changing shacks was deserted, except for one manned by a teenage girl who proved unable to do the simple conversion math. When I took the calculator and showed her the figures, she shrugged and showed me that she had only the equivalent of a little under thirty euros worth of Bulgarian leva. I'd have to figure it out in Sofia. Luckily, I found, this was a nation of petty hustlers and ad hoc dealers.

The approach to the capital was like the outskirts of a Chinese or African city, with corrugated tin shacks overseeing construction supplies and auto parts, though far less populated and hectic. Stray dogs barked at hobos with shopping carts. The city itself was in the shadow of a tall, snowy ridge, the Srednogorie. With the wide boulevards of a planned city and the odd neon-lit casino storefront, it gave the impression of a frontier center— Salt Lake City or Bozeman—gone to seed.

The city center was a different animal altogether. The "crossroads of culture" trope is hackneyed, but in the moment it was hard to resist: the cobblestoned streets and monumental parliaments of a European capital around the corner from the rotting public housing of the postcommunist East, a shockingly colorful onion-dome cathedral, Turkish music from a cab window, an alley market of corrugated tin booths.

I picked Cvetan up from his job at the national radio station, and he snorted a pinch of snuff off the back of his hand.

"I haven't been sleeping much," he explained. He had been on the road for four days with a former Bad Seeds guitarist and up late the night before on a strange errand. "This is going to sound especially weird to an American, but it is time to register kids for school. They are required to go, but in some neighborhoods there is not enough room in the good schools for all the kids." So parents began lining up outside the schools at one a.m. and formed informal cartels to register one another's kids until the classes were full. "They are calling names at one a.m., two a.m., until six thirty in the morning, like it's a concentration camp." He was a serious fellow, baby-faced, with a soul patch and wide-set, catlike but earnest eyes, cuffed jeans and Doc Marten boots. His passion was the avant-jazz of the original Knitting Factory and the scene associated with John Zorn, Eugene Chadbourne (whom he'd recently booked), and the avant-garde accordionist Guy Klucevsek.

The booking process for all the Balkan shows had been haphazard: I'd get a few e-mail addresses from someone in Romania who knew someone in Serbia who might know someone in Bulgaria, who couldn't do it himself but here were his friends in Sofia. I'd first talked to a Nikolai who directed me to Kostya, who worked with Cvetan.

There had been some unpleasantness before I'd left the United States. Kostya had passed me off to Cvetan with an exchange in the morning of February 18:

"Hi Franz, my colleague Cvetan shall be in contact with you regarding the sofia(and probably ruse) booking. see u in sofia. cheers"

"Cool," I replied, "I've been talking to Cvetan already. Thanks!"

"ok, no probs, we work together so everything is fine. cheers"

Then, time-stamped 4:37 a.m., this:

"Franz,

you are an asshole big time.

The reason I think so is that when Nikolay asked me to help with promotion I said OK. While I was waiting for your promo material (you never send me one) I have booked you for a venue in Sofia for the 6th april.

Yesterday I understood that you are booking yourself with my colleague Cvetan, who has your contact from ME. I was the person to let him know about you and show him your website. So while I am working on your dates I understood you have been already dealing with someone else. So the result is that there is a double booking for the same date in Sofia in two different venues.

And you owe us (Nikolay and ME) 100 euros for that booking you have done through our contacts. And if you don't pay us I will bring the finance police to your gigs and you have to spend at least 10 hours in the police station explaining in writing why are you working in Bulgaria and not paying taxes on your earnings. Then you will be charge with tax fraud, not only in Bulgaria, but in the states.

I am serious."

"I think there has been a big misunderstanding," I replied. "You said yesterday you and Cvetan are colleagues, right? So what is the problem?"

9:46 a.m.:

"Franz,

Don't worry. I like you. I work together with Cvetan. No problems. He will organize everything. I apologize for my email, but I was pissed because we (me and nikolay) to promote you on Nikolay's condition. Nikolay made me problems last night that we (me and Cvetan) are booking the same artists for the same date in two different venues. So, please don't worry. Cvetan will take care of everything regarding your gigs.

cheers"

"Drunk," I said to Maria, relieved.

"You're gonna stay with my friend," said Cvetan. "Normally you could stay with me, but I'm having a divorce. I just finally found a new place, but it's pretty dirty now. . . . I was living the last six months at the radio station; I had a couch there."

We arrived at a bar and approached a slight, dark, bearded hustler with thin eyes and a permanently raised brow. He was chain-smoking slim Russian cigarettes.

"This is Kostya," Cvetan said. "He's the best unsuccessful promoter in Bulgaria."

(*"You are an asshole big time,"* I flashed.)

"It's true!" Kostya grinned. "I was the first to bring American wrestling to Bulgaria" (professional wrestling, that is). "And the last. Then I did a tour of thirty-five tango dancers from Argentina. But they wouldn't pay me presales, so I had to cancel. Do you know Fucking Hell beer? Here, have one. What do you think?"

In addition to being Bulgaria's best unsuccessful concert promoter, Kostya Todorov—"like told-her-off," he said—had recently purchased the exclusive rights to distribute an undistinguished pilsner associated, for marketing purposes, with the Austrian town of Fucking.

"First my friend and I rented a warehouse. We were going to make [it into] a venue, and rehearsal spaces, and so on. But I walked away." He bought a truckload of Fucking Hell and

stashed it in the empty warehouse, hawking it case by case to local bars and party promoters.

"The problem is, Bulgarians don't have any taste. They don't
know about brands. The bar owners, they say, 'I can get Corona
for seventy euro cents,' trying to [bring] me down. Well, OK,
then kids are going to the corner store and buying Corona even
cheaper and drink them at your place. I have a warehouse full of
this beer, I'd rather just go and drink it myself for the next ten
years than give you that price, I tell them. Bulgaria is entering
the Schengen zone, free-trade zone, and then all the prices are
going to double. Heineken price is going to double. This price I
will lock in now, then in two years it'll be cheap" by comparison.

He can, he offered, get me the fake EU passport, for five hundred euros, that I'd need to avoid the FBI background checks
required to live and work in Europe. He outlined a conspiracy
theory that Justin Bieber, Celine Dion, Nickelback, Avril Lavi-
gne, and Bryan Adams are the work of an elaborate Canadian-
based plot to destroy the U.S. music industry. It took me longer
than it should have to realize that he was pulling my leg.

I was reminded of Kaplan's description of one of his Balkan
contacts: "A classic hustler and survivor . . . a type who never
starts revolutions but who always figures out how to benefit
from . . . whatever the new order is." Or, per West, "one of those
strange polyglots who seem to have been brought up in some alley where several civilizations put out their ash-cans, since only
bits and pieces have come their way, never the real meat."

Kostya interrupted my thoughts. "We need you for an actor
tomorrow!" He and Cvetan were collaborating on a Web series
centered on a vampire character they call "Zozulka," which is
Czech and Ukrainian for "cuckoo" but also related to the Serbian

zezenye (meaning "joking")—and a little like a Bulgarian term for which the American equivalent would be "a mooch."

Some years ago he was living in London, working as a tour manager (he'd been tour-managing the Seattle gypsy-rock band Kultur Shock when I saw them in Zagreb in 2007) and festival promoter. He was married to an Italian architect. "But our schedules were never the same, and I thought, I need to go live in Bulgaria, since after all I am Bulgarian. She said, 'If you go, just leave me the keys.' So I bought the tickets at two a.m. and left at six a.m. I left everything—a [Hammond] C3 [organ] with a Leslie, a DX7 [synthesizer], some expensive guitars. . . . We divorced over the Internet. You can do that in UK."

Once back in Bulgaria, he promoted big arena shows, he claimed: the Scorpions, Jennifer Lopez, a guy detoxing from a coke habit who'd been in Poison and Mr. Big. A dispute with ticket middlemen of dubious provenance led to his blacklist from that business, he said. "I was having dreams about taking a Kalashnikov and killing them. I got a Facebook message from them saying, 'You're insane.' I replied, 'I am killing you—in my dreams.' You understand the difference? Not 'I'm gonna kill you.' That would be a threat."

"You're staying in my bed," he added, as we prepared to leave. "I only have sex with young boys there. Under eleven, it's not illegal. Over eleven, they're minors, it's illegal. Same with old people: necrophilia, there is no law against it." He gave me a poker-faced look to see how I'd react to the joke.

"Here"—we arrived at his building, and he opened the door to his walkup. He was solicitous, even excessively so, about my comfort, airing out the room, opening a jar of soap by the bed for fragrance, insisting on digging out a night-light from the other room so I had a reading lamp, asking if two towels was enough. "When you're here, you're like my child."

He gestured at the kitchen, and we opened a couple of Fucking Hells from a case in the corner. "It is better than a squat but worse than an apartment. I have the lease, but I'm not living here. I live with my family, but I keep this place, for when my girlfriend is here from Plovdiv. In the meantime some students are living there. I say it's like a squat because they haven't paid rent in months. They left a receipt for an electric bill they paid, and I was shocked. They are always on amphetamines, and meth, and you know. . . . Just don't open those doors, they're broken. I had a fit and broke everything in the room."

He knocked on the bedroom door in the morning. "Your car had—how do you say—the boot on it. I was five minutes late to text the parking payment. I took care of it."

While Cvetan prerecorded an episode of his radio show, set to air while we were in Plovdiv, Kostya took me on my errands: get a Bulgarian SIM card for my phone, patch a hole I'd worn through the right knee of my suit pants, change that stack of Serbian dinars. Bank after bank turned us down, saying curtly, "We don't deal with Serbia." Kostya maintained a ceaseless, exhausting stream of opinion about the beer promotion business, the greatness of U2's *Achtung Baby* and early Pearl Jam, the triad of music promoters that divided up the Bulgarian territory to the exclusion of independents like himself. He and Cvetan operated through proxies: specifically, the national radio station, which gave them the cover to avoid being targeted by the cartels. "You know," he said, "I don't listen to music. I don't care about music. I support the underground scene."

I told him I didn't believe him.

You're right, he said. "They call me B with a capital B, because I am always talking bullshit."

As another Western Union turned us down, he told me about his background. "My parents were living in Turkey, in Adrianople. It was one-third Greek, one-third Turk, one-third Bulgarian. Then after the 1912 Balkan war, the border moved, and they decided to move to Bulgaria, and because of this I'm screwed. My life would be easier if I was a Bulgarian in Turkey! I am stuck with this Bulgarian passport!"

"Will it be easier for you after Bulgaria joins the Schengen zone?" I asked.

"I have a UK passport. I am speaking metaphorically.... I just feel oppressed by the way things are done here. Under forty-five years of communism, people learned to be cheaters—everyone had a job, but they had after-hours jobs too. Because you made the same as a street sweeper as you did as a writer. Now it is vile capitalism, but the habits are the same.... There are no societal classes here. No one has any respect. They talk the same to a professor as they would to a streetwalker.

"There is one good thing about Bulgaria," he conceded when I told him about getting robbed in France. "No one would steal your things. Because of communism, we have a respect for possessions."

We found an off-brand exchange kiosk and joined the scrum. "Give me the cash," said Kostya and stuffed it in his pocket. We had to duck to speak to the woman behind the scratched and opaque Plexiglas, and she and Kostya exchanged a complicated combination of dinars, euros, and leva. "Here," he said, handing me a pile. Then he thought better of it and took thirty euros for himself. "Remind me to pay you that back."

We ran into a friend of his who played in a popular "Balkan beat" band and realized we had some mutual friends—the DJ Joro-Boro, the band Balkan Beat Box, and Eugene Hutz of Gogol Bordello, for whom he used to promote shows. One of my favorite musicians is the Bulgarian clarinetist Ivo Papasov. When I was just out of college, I had a cubicle job at a failing advertising concern working with my college friend Eric, of the avant-jazz band Gutbucket. Their drummer had come across a bootleg cassette of Papasov in the course of his job at the public radio station WNYC. We dubbed the cassette onto CD on the agency machines and passed it around like samizdat, trying to count the time-signature changes.

"I did a show for him once," said Kostya. "I saw him smoke an entire pack of cigarettes in ten minutes after he got offstage. He has gotten a big beer belly. It's like a table—when he sits down, he can arrange all his supplies, ashtray, drink, papers for rolling a joint, on the belly."

We stopped into a tailor shop with my ripped pants. A half-dozen older women were seated behind sewing machines. The first we approached, white-haired with irregular swatches of henna, said she couldn't do the repair before tomorrow. OK, we said, we'll go elsewhere. She yelled across the room. Another woman waved us over, grabbed the pants, and told us to go get a coffee.

We took a walk around the market: three or four blocks of tarps and tin with merchants hawking vegetables, dried fruits and nuts, plumbing supplies, used cassette boom boxes twenty-five years old, chainsaws, and a dangerous contraption for heating water that involved a coil of electrified wire you drop in the tank and plug in.

"These are all gypsies, you see, with the . . . chocolate faces and Indian hair. Everyone is renting the stall by the month, and everyone is trying to cheat each other." We crossed a street. "This is the 'hygienic' side of the market. Look at that." Kostya pointed at a pile of severed pigs' ears the size of baseball gloves. "I love to come here and watch the faces." Hoffman quoted one of her interviewees on the subject of Sofia: "Sofia is in the middle of the world, and of the wonderful faces one sees here, created by centuries of cultural intermingling . . . you can trace the continuity of culture from India to here in the various shades of blue along the old silk road."

I asked Kostya about the ongoing, sometimes quite heated, debate about the use of the term "gypsy," as opposed to the more politically correct "Roma."

"Well, there are seventeen tribes of them in Bulgaria. Some of them, the ones that are baptized and they want to live partly in society, they call themselves 'Roma' and they think 'gypsy' is offensive. But other tribes, they say, 'We are gypsies, we are not Roma.'"

The pants were done and cost three leva, or about a dollar and a half. It was raining, and we both had soaked feet. Kostya texted payment for another hour of parking and suggested we retire to the apartment for a nap.

"I was up until three talking to people in Canada. I am making a deal to import iPhones, you know, from China, with the iPhone certificate, but not real iPhones, you know? At a tenth of the price. There is a market for them here. . . . It is just a problem because we don't have all the money right now, because people owe us money."

While we were walking around the town center ("walking" is a relative term; objectively we were moving at a near run),

Kostya was making me see Sofia through his conspiratorial eyes: everyone began to look like a huckster or a thief or on the make, engaged in some sort of low-stakes but high-stress single combat of wits, chicken, and street-level capitalism.

He stopped in a storefront for coffee, and, when I didn't have the coins, got the hostess's assent to pay her later. "I have, like, credit there. I'm always coming in, and tipping a lot. I have paid for this coffee five times over. . . . You see those guys sitting in front?" He gestured to a handful of overweight men sitting around a plastic table. "They are the Black Lottery mafia. You know this? They run the gambling on sports. They sit there all day and figure out their schemes."

We crossed a square and found ourselves in the path of a black-robed priest with a large silver cross around his neck who was a dead ringer for Seth Rogen. "See that statue?" said Kostya. It showed six figures with their hands crossed in front of their waists and celebrated the 1,300th anniversary of the Bulgar conquest of the region from the Slavs. "It's called the six angels and the six wankers."

"You're a good driver," he offered after our respective naptimes, as I ferried him to some sort of business lunch/coffee/hand-to-hand combat.

I should be, I said. I'm doing it five or six hours a day on tour.

"I see—so you're a professional driver and part-time musician. You should be picking up hitchhikers and asking them for money too."

I'm not really supposed to have taken the rental car to Bulgaria, I said, so I can't afford to have anything unexpected happen.

"Ah," he said dismissively. "You can just tell them you were kidnapped."

I picked up Cvetan at the radio station. He had edited a phone interview I'd done with him from Berlin for air the next day. We headed south to Plovdiv. There was just one road, so it was easy to find. In Russia, people giving directions like this always said "*priamo, priamo, priamo*" ("straight, straight, straight")— a word that, in Bulgarian, Cvetan says, means "honest," in the sense, I suppose, of a straight shooter.

It was a relief to have a sense of breathing space in the land-scape again and to see forested land. Croatia, Serbia, and Hungary were either flat farmland or denuded hills. Here we had true peaks, fuzzy with pine, then a wide valley in green and purple, and the blue-gray thrust of the Balkan Mountains themselves. Once again, it reminded me of Montana. In fact Montana was a nearby place-name (as of 1993, after spending a few decades named Mihaylovgrad for the communist insurgent Hristo Mihaylov), and Cvetan said that a village near his hometown shares the name too. "There was a Roman town called Monta-nesium. I don't know why they just didn't call it that. I guess in the nineties an American name sounded cooler."

He grew up in the Danube flatlands east of Ruse. "I was a shy kid, antisocial, just reading and writing short stories." His grandfather was "Afro-Bulgarian—he had the African face and round eyes and curly hair. My mother had African straightened hair too. In the old [Ottoman] days, you know, they were using Egyptian, Somali, soldiers to guard this frontier."

Shy he may have been, but one day, as a teen, he took some of his stories to the local newspaper office. He rang the wrong button, though, and ended up in a radio station owned by the same guy. "Hey kid," they more or less said, "you talk pretty well. This guy just quit his radio show, you want to take over?"

"Yeah," he said. "Right now or next week?"

"Right now."

He had ended up on national radio, which in his telling was about as formal in its hiring and budgetary practices as American college radio. By then he had moved to Sofia. "I didn't have a phone or anything, and I was at a friend's house, and someone called her phone and asked for me. I don't know how he knew I was there. He said, 'Get down to the radio station right now.' They wanted someone to do little spots, analytical things, like five minutes about New Model Army, or West African songs post-revolution, and he knew I knew about music." He has had a regular gig ever since.

I asked him about Papasov. "Ivo Papasov is a real, tortured artist—he's calm, you know, and he's good at the fast stuff. But then I heard him play a slow song, and I was like, wow! Like Charlie Parker. . . . Some of the other guys in his band, they are . . . not so subtle."

One side of the southbound road from Sofia (the accent is on the first syllable if you mean the city, on the second syllable for the woman's name) featured a combination of hulking and abandoned communist buildings ("publishing, mostly," said Cvetan) and new, half-built, and glass-fronted office blocks and luxury hotels, none in working order.

I commented on the confused state of the architecture in the Sofian sprawl. "Have you been to Skopje?" Cvetan asked. "Their new ultra-nationalist government decided to build, like, two hundred monuments, but right next to each other, and all in different heights and sizes. Like, you have a forty-meter statue of one shared hero, and then a five-meter statue of someone from a different era completely, and so close you can't walk between them! It's pure kitsch. Like a Serbian guy who moves to the U.S. and becomes a mafia boss and buys all this stuff for his house."

Skopje was hit with a devastating earthquake in 1963 that destroyed 80 percent of the city, which meant that, like in Normandy after World War II, there was a near-blank slate for architecturally adventurous local pols. Ever since the earthquake, Cvetan said, Macedonians have felt a special kinship with the seismic travails of Japan and send aid after every Japanese earthquake. But, he added, Skopje was the most vibrant place for the arts in the Balkans.

"Often," I said, "places that are in economic or political turmoil are good for the arts."

"Yes, but here it's not happening. Bulgarians are not curious about the larger cultural world. It used to be even under censorship, there was some great novels, cinema, even poets—now, very little." Like Kostya, he spoke in terms of trying to educate or lead the country to the cutting edge of global culture.

The Balkan Mountains receded to the east, and we passed through rocky, dry, scrubby hills, descending into a wide and colorful plain and thus into Plovdiv. It was a small Mediterranean city. The venue was a basement bar on a quiet residential street. A loud and tight Balkan heavy rock band was rehearsing as we loaded in. Cvetan took my leopard-print merch suitcase. It had been drawing comments and derisive laughter all tour long, but, as Maria pointed out, with a black suitcase, you can leave it in any corner of any club and forget it—this one, I would never leave behind.

"What do people think of this design in America? Like, what associations?" he asked.

"Probably sexy underwear or strippers."

"Here we associate it with a particularly cheesy kind of turbo-folk. With, you know, big-breasted women singing and wearing dresses with this print."

A pair of teenage girls, hippiefied in not-quite plaid, striped hoodies, and bandannas, giggled over my merch table. A thin and sensitive-looking twenty-three-year-old with a *Don't Look Back* thatch of black hair sat in the corner of the club, wearing faux Ray-Bans and brooding self-consciously. He was the opening act and got the assignment to take me out for Italian food.

His English was superb—he was raised in Vancouver from age two to twelve, before his parents moved back to Plovdiv. He taught English, of course, but to one- and two-year-olds. "Their parents are maybe too ambitious for them," he said. "One of [the children] is there every day, four hours."

As someone with a functional, if shallow, comprehension of Ukrainian, I found the Bulgarian language reassuringly familiar. "I think the pronunciation is similar," said Cvetan. "All the Ukrainians who live here, unlike the Russians, they speak perfect Bulgarian, with no accent." It was here that the Cyrillic alphabet was developed in the ninth century and from here it was spread, "making Bulgaria, more than any other land," wrote Kaplan, "the birthplace of Slavonic languages and culture. To this day, Bulgarians consider their native tongue the Latin of Slavic languages."

After dinner, the Dylan-manqué gave me walking directions to the town's sights—the oldest mosque in Europe, a Roman amphitheater, the "old town"—and we headed back to the club.

"There's the post office," he pointed out as we crossed the square. "The old communist building. They only use about 15 percent of it. The rest is just—empty. I talked to a really old lady, like ninety-seven, who said they used to use the basement for torturing people."

The other opening act was Cvetan's uncle Neven, a stocky, gregarious middle-aged man with a shaved head, a goatee, and a shiny lavender headscarf. As a matter of fact, he was playing all my Bulgarian shows. "Man, I'm shutting down my festival," Cvetan had told him. "This is your last chance to play your nephew's thing."

I met Nikolai—Nicky—the local rock booker, the first guy I had e-mailed looking for Bulgarian dates. He and his girlfriend were drunk and cheerful and poured us a round of shots.

"Are you going to Greece on this tour?" he asked.

"I think they don't have any money."

"Man, we don't have any money! Greeks are always complaining about not having any money, but they are putting on big bands on a Tuesday." He shook his head. Macroeconomics is best judged in one's own sphere. "Where were good shows for you?"

"Well, the best guarantees were in Poland."

"Yes, the Polish played their entry into the EU the best. All the young people are getting money from the government, and the Germans and the British. They are smart, Poles. . . . Have you heard the one, what is the biggest Polish city? Chicago! Ha ha ha ha. . . ."

The Dylan-looking kid was playing, seated, with his shades on, singing with a high tenor. "It's not easy doing shows in Plovdiv," said Nicky, sounding the universal refrain. "Because we have Sofia right here, an artificial city, and if you don't have shows Friday or Saturday you don't get the people who work in Sofia. But still, shows in Plovdiv are better."

The uncle was surprisingly good at scatting ("I told you I had some gypsy in me!" said Cvetan) and, drunk, wanted to accompany me on cajón, which he did from the floor with mixed results. While the closing band ran through ska punk versions of "Land Down Under" and "Too Drunk to Fuck," he held court at a private table with a rowdy crew of middle-aged women, passing around bottles of homemade liquor—one *rakiya*, one *belin*. "Two kinds of wine and twenty herbs," he explained. "Good for . . . everything!"

"Good for human soul," said Cvetan.

The next morning Cvetan was hungover, and in no mood to get up early to join my Plovdiv sightseeing. We'd spent the night at a small, three-unit hotel. The owner-proprietor watched black-and-white television in the tiny lobby.

"Is the hotel owner a friend?" I asked. It wasn't as if the place, nestled in the warren of the Old Town, were the closest to the venue, the most comfortable, or the easiest to find.

"He's good at making the receipts a little extra," Cvetan said, so that when Cvetan got reimbursed by the radio station, he could use the extra money.

The Bulgarian ethnicity—part Turkic steppe people, part Slav—is a striking one and produces men with the handsome combination of worn-leather skin and silver hair and women who are slim and tall with jet-black curls and favor tight pants and high boots. Their features range from the Persian to the practically Bangladeshi, and they age pale and dramatically, faces stretched taut and slashed with Cruella De Vil lipstick.

Plovdiv is one of the world's oldest cities—and, Kostya added, "the most relaxed city in Bulgaria. Lazy!" Named Philippopolis by Philip II of Macedon, the father of Alexander the Great, and known by that name into the twentieth century, it was a place where one glance encompassed the communist post office surrounded by the ruins of the Roman odeon and the modern-day street grid, the Thracian fortress, the Roman amphitheater, and the fourteenth-century mosque with a striking pattern of red brick framing stone masonry. A black-robed monk in a stovepipe hat strolled past a sixteenth-century bathhouse, and there was incense in the crisp mountain air. Two gypsy (for lack of a better word) musicians, old men in flat caps and long woolen coats, sat down on a corner of the mosque, then thought better of it and moved along, an uncased accordion on one man's shoulder, a fiddle case with an improvised strap on the other's.

"Plovdiv has a problem," Cvetan said. "It has all these beautiful old buildings, and they are falling apart because no one takes care of them." This reminded me of the Tomsk arsonists, and Cvetan said that would probably happen here if the buildings were made of wood. The old town is a warren of cobblestones atop one of the small, steep hills that outline the city. The second stories of the houses are wider than the bases, supported by reverse-buttresses of curved wood. This is, Hoffman explained, "what is known as the National Revival style of architecture. This aesthetic was a rather self-conscious child of the late eighteenth and early nineteenth centuries and the reawakening of Bulgarian identity, after its long dormancy. And since Bulgarian identity didn't have many avenues of expression aside from the arts, these became infused with all kinds of folk-national implications. The National Revival houses, usually built by wealthy merchants, tried to synthesize various elements of native arts and crafts," and now they were alternately renovated or repurposed as museums and tourist attractions.

One was now a small museum of icons in tempera and gold leaf on wood, some with hammered-silver headdresses bolted in the appropriate place, whose style changed not at all from the fifteenth century to the nineteenth. A "Jerusalemiad," according to the museum labels a kind of guidebook writ large and for the illiterate, indicated holy sites for pilgrims to visit in Jerusalem. A St. George demonstrated some exotic ordeals, like "the torture of the ox tendons" and "the torture of the glowing boot."[1]

Orthodox churches are by no means as grand in scale as Western cathedrals and are in fact often quite humble in size, but it's easy to forget that when faced with the overwhelming density of their interior decoration. West observed, "The Orthodox Church conceived that its chief business is magic, the evocation by ritual of the spiritual experiences most necessary to man . . . the Christians liked their churches dark, as good hatching-places for magic." The effect, emotionally, is as large as any Polish cathedral: the incense and the glittering iconostasis, the fruit left in front of the icon, still in its plastic mesh straight from the grocery.

Children scrambled over the ruins of the Nebet Tepe, the Thracian fortress that constitutes the high point of the town. It gave a panoramic view of tiled-roof houses, the minaret of

---

1. Philippopolis was for some time in the tenth centuries the center of a proto-Protestant sect called the Paulicians, who, among other beliefs, rejected transubstantiation, the virgin birth, relics, icons, saints, angels, and the Old Testament. Originally from Armenia, the Paulicians were eventually scattered throughout Europe, where for some time "Bulgarian" was used as an epithet for followers of variations of their heresy.

the mosque, the three rocky hills on one side of the river and housing projects and glass skyscrapers on the other, the Rhodope Mountains behind, and the silhouette of the Roman amphitheater. "It is one of the disharmonies of history," said West, "that there is nothing that a Roman poet would have enjoyed more than a Roman ruin, with its obvious picturesqueness and the cue it gives for moralizing."

It was a charming city, and no small part of my excitement stemmed from the fact that summer seemed finally to have arrived.

"Maybe here," said Cvetan. "Through the tunnels"—that is, on the Sofia side of the mountains—"it's always different." (Indeed, no sooner had we crossed back than it started to rain.)

When I got back to the hotel a little after noon, I found Cvetan sitting in the lobby hitting the half-bottle of wine I had left over from the night before. As we drove, he cradled the bottle in his lap in the passenger seat. He had polished it off by the time we arrived in Sofia.

Cvetan was deaf in his left ear after a childhood flu complication. Since I was driving, his bad ear faced me, so our car conversation was stilted by repetition. He'd been a Zappa fan as a child, which led him to Eugene Chadbourne via Jimmy Carl Black, and thence to Tzadik Records and the late 1980s Knitting Factory world. He told me a story of journeying via four bus transfers to see John Zorn in Slovenia. His radio show airs twice a week, nine thirty to eleven p.m., "but there are five guys, and some of them don't want to do it every week, so if I need more money I can be in every night."

After tomorrow's show in Ruse, not far from his hometown, he would take the train back to Sofia. "It's cheap, seven euros, and sometimes it is totally empty" except in the summer, since it's the route from Sofia to the Black Sea beaches. "And a lot of Romanians—it is still cheaper for them to come here" instead of their own Black Sea coast.

What did I think of Romania? he asked. I mentioned the abandoned nuclear plants in the Romanian north, and he told me about Pernik, a former mining town west of Sofia that has become a byword for hulking, rotting postindustrial buildings.

"The people from there, there are lots of jokes and stories about them, that they are really rude and rough." A common rural regional dish is meat and rice wrapped in a cabbage leaf, "and the joke goes, what is Pernik sushi? Canned fish in a cabbage leaf."

Sofia was the westernmost station on the massive Soviet train maps that still dominated the central station halls in places like Saint Petersburg. "Now they are a real tragedy," Cvetan said. "There used to be fifteen trains a day to where I grew up; now there are two or three. They are a state business, and every person who is put in charge of the trains is busy with a private business, and [the trains] are rotting from the inside. You know what is worse is the Greek trains. They think they are in a crisis, so they sold the trains to a private company. They are going to fix them up, they say, but it's going to take five or six years, and cost twice as much, and in the meantime there are no trains from here to Greece. And especially in southern Bulgaria a lot of people were going to Greece to work.

"Now we're at the city limits, so watch out for police. If the signs says eighty and you're going eighty-two, they gonna pull you over for sure, 'cause they'll see you're a foreign car and want to get some money."

For the first time in the five weeks I've been in Europe, I stayed at a genuinely nice hotel, a multistory cylinder in Sofia's ambitious outskirts. Bulgarian National Radio had a deal to put up artists there, and I was giddy with gratitude as the concierge ran down his checklist. "Sir, so you know, the minibar is complimentary."

"I put a Mexican hardcore band in there once," Cvetan said with pride. "They couldn't believe it."

"Plovdiv is usually the first hitchhike of the year for people from Sofia," said Yana, a radio colleague of Cvetan's. "Spring comes there sooner, and winter later." A pixie with one long dreadlock, Yana was born and raised in Sofia, a city girl—"a downtown girl," she emphasized. "Living in Sofia, you know everyone. You're always saying hello." She proved the point as we went for dinner.

Ready-to-eat soup restaurants were all the rage in Sofia, and maybe Plovdiv too—the Dylan kid had been keen to take me for soup the night before. Yana lived around the corner from the place we went. "It's cool because when there are protests, I can hear them from my window and go downstairs and join in!"

There had been massive protests a month ago. They had in fact toppled the government, though it happened only a month before the already scheduled election. Electricity prices went up drastically in midwinter, and people took to the streets against the trio of companies that control the market. "Actually," Yana explained, "the money doesn't even go to them, it goes to the state electric company, which is not the state company anymore. . . . Anyway, we actually toppled the government . . . or did we? All of our last five governments were obvious criminals, but this one was also. Rednecks. You know, I am university-educated, and I want a government who is smarter than me. We had a minister of culture—actually, he is a very popular sculptor—but he can't speak! It's more than a dialect, he doesn't know how to talk. . . . Anyway, the protests were good, just we had those right-wing assholes who always want to show up at the protests so they can throw rocks. And of course they are the ones who end up on the TV."

She asked me about my vegetarianism and whether I was going to raise my kid vegetarian. I said we hadn't actually discussed it yet, but maybe.

"What about in kindergarten, when everyone is getting the same lunch, and they are forced to eat it?"

"We can give them a bag lunch. Don't you do that here?"

She shook her head. "I think every Bulgarian has a shared trauma of being forced to clean their plate. Everyone has one food" to which they have an irrational reaction. "They held my nose closed so I'd open my mouth."

The show in Sofia was at a metal (in both senses) bar decorated in gleaming chrome, and it would be broadcast live on national radio. Kostya had been dismissive of my attempts to see the Sofia sites, so I grabbed a tourist map from the hotel and snuck out after soundcheck for a rapid-fire circuit of the churches of the city center. The club itself was across from the beautiful-outside, dingy-inside Russian Orthodox church, with the inevitable bust of Pushkin in the park behind. At the nearby and majestic Nevsky Cathedral, built by the Bulgarians in gratitude for the role of the Russians in their liberation from Ottoman rule, a trio of men sang Mass, in what West rhapsodized as "the gentle lion roar of hymns sung by men of a faith which has never exacted celibacy from its priests nor pacifism from its congregations."

One church had been blown apart in 1925 by communists trying to kill the king. Another was an eleventh-century den tucked in the middle of a subway station entrance, near excavations of historical Roman streets, and full of junk like a walk-in closet (West described "the Serbo-Byzantine architecture which burrows to find its God . . . small, it might be the lair of a few great beasts"). Then the relatively humble red-brick St. Sophia, for which the city is named. It was founded in the fourth century in what was then Roman Serdica, where in 311 Galerius issued the Edict of Toleration, which decriminalized Christianity, in advance of Constantine's legalization two years later. Tucked around back were three stele memorializing the regionally unique Bulgarian state and episcopal role in rescuing the country's Jews in World War II: Kaplan called it "the cleanest Holocaust record of any nation in Nazi-occupied Europe—at least within its own borders." While Misha Glenny noted that "admiration for Bulgaria's record should be tempered" by the acknowledgment that King Boris of Bulgaria was using the issue as a piece in a complex game of international relations, the deportation of Jews was vehemently rejected by partisans and elites, marked by "an absence of popular anti-Semitism, and defiance among the Jews." The three marble stele are unequivocal, trilingual (Bulgarian, English, and Hebrew), and have the stony permanence of historical, if ungrammatical, judgment: "In the year 1943, while the Holocaust of Europe's Jews was reaching its peak, a unique phenomenon occurred in Bulgaria. Eminent leaders of the Bulgarian people, the heads of the church, enlightened public servants, writers, doctors, lawyers, workers, ordinary citizens and the royal family. They all stood together and succeeded to rescue all of the Bulgaria's 49,000 Jews from deportation to the death camps. The great majority of Bulgaria's Jews immigrated to Israel in the years 1948–1950 and took an active part in the rebirth of the Jewish state."

As I walked back from my mini-tour of the spiritual centers of the city, a slim man in a business suit and wire-rimmed glasses, carrying a briefcase, asked me the time. I told him and walked on. A minute later, he eased up behind me, smiling and proffering a business card. "Excuse me—I thought you might be interested in this: we have nice girls, they will come to your hotel room." He gave me an ingratiating smile, and, not sure where to go with the conversation, I crossed the street. I looked at the card. "Perfect: The most beautiful girls in Sofia!" it said. "Would you like a pretty girl for pleasure at a place convenient for you? The Best Service!" One side quoted 50 euros for an hour and 190 for the night; the prices on the other side, offering, "If you would like a beautiful top model at a place of your convenience," were 80 and 290. Sofia is for hustlers.

Back at the venue, Uncle Neven had again set up a station with his herbal wine concoction and started jamming along with my set on his cajón. He missed my suggestion that maybe his contribution was misplaced tonight, and Cvetan eased him back to his booth. His guitar had an unusually thick neck. At first, I thought it was a twelve-string with every other string skipped. As it turned out, it was a homemade six-string with a twelve-string neck, because "I am carpenter, and my fingers are too thick!"

Kostya came to lurk around the merch desk. "How about that thirty euros you owe me?" I asked him.

He grinned. "I don't have it right now. I gotta go out and . . . meet up with some people. I'll have it for you later." He disappeared for the rest of the night.

The road to Ruse runs through the Stara Planina ("Old Mountain") or Balkan (Turkish for "mountain") Mountains, historically the home of the peninsula's *haidouks*—outlaws, brigands, and guerrillas. Once again I went to pick up Cvetan at the radio station. As I pulled up to the curb in traffic, he hopped the fence. Instead of getting in himself, he shoved into the car a thin metalhead with a disappearing chin, a waist-length ponytail, and a leather motorcycle jacket covered in pins: AC/DC, Black Sabbath, a Confederate flag guitar, a bottle of whiskey. He was sweating cigarettes and carrying an open beer.

"I'll ride with my uncle," Cvetan yelled through the window. "This is Cvelin. He's playing tonight as well."

A bass player (seven-string fretless, as it turned out), Cvelin had cut his teeth on Metallica but had branched out since then. His current project was a "punk jazz" band with bass, sax, violin, and a female singer.

"That's a lot of melody instruments," I observed.

"Yes," he said. "We had a piano player, but he quit when I told him not to use his left hand."

After the mountain passes, there was a new and distinctive kind of tree—dogwood?—covered with small, white blooms. On the highways, outside the mountain tunnels, crashed cars were mounted on concrete pedestals as a kind of memento mori and cautionary example. I mentioned to Cvelin that the mountains reminded me of the American West. He told me that the Bulgarian president, giving a kind of state-of-the-union televised speech, projected photos behind him. As he waxed poetic about "our beautiful mountains," they clicked to a stock photo of a snowcapped range—in Colorado. "It was a scandal."

We passed roadside donkeys, a goat, some fruit stands, a town that seemed to specialize in selling bits of gnarled stone, and several of those generic communist monuments to workers and World War II that have surely aged as quickly and dramatically as any monumental art in history. Once we descended into the farming plains, there were a few miles of roadside prostitutes, pacing the truck pull-offs in tight jeans, heeled boots, and puffy parkas, shivering and pecking at their cellphones.

Cvelin was not much of a talker, and I put on a *Fresh Air* podcast in which Terry Gross interviewed a former Mormon missionary. Mormons were ubiquitous in Siberia and Mongolia, and I asked him if they showed up in Bulgaria.

"Not really," he said. "Who is everywhere is the Hare Krishnas. I played a festival last year, and like eighty percent of the people were Krishnas. They were running classes. We said, next year we're going to run a class on how to cook meat."

When I'd asked Yana for directions to the tourist sites of central Sofia, she said, "If you want my real opinion, leave early tomorrow and do tourism in Ruse." Ruse too claims the title "Little Vienna," for its architecture and wide central square. As the last Danube city before the river empties into the Black Sea, it is here that the epithet most overstates its case.

The outskirts were a mess of empty industrial buildings, remnants of the communist industry that had made Ruse one of Europe's most polluted cities by the end of the 1980s. The central square was alive with all the vital activities of a provincial city on a Friday night on the verge of spring: cackling old men with Jimmy Durante noses; worn-out old ladies with troubled dye jobs; an amplified Peruvian pan piper straight from the New

York City subways; young couples snuggling on park benches; young men in threes and fours drinking beer, trying to make eye contact, and then trouble. There was a political rally of some sort in the corner of the park. On the edge of the gathering, one teenage boy with jeans tucked into his combat boots and his skinhead friend waved a purple-and-black flag advertising the nationalist Bulgarian National Movement. This was a right-wing party claiming descent from the infamous revolutionary terrorist organization IMRO (Internal Macedonian Revolutionary Organization), which in the late nineteenth century fought for independence from Turkey, then pivoted to anti-Yugoslav terrorism aimed at uniting Macedonia with Bulgaria. They became, according to West, the Fascist Party of Bulgaria, a paid-for proxy front for Italian fascist meddling in the region, and finally a kind of mafia whose "chief resource was its ruthlessness, which . . . made Bulgarian political life a shambles."

My Ruse host Elisa was from Florence, tall, high-cheekboned, and stylish with short, curly hair. She left Italy and lived in Berlin for nearly a decade, then got a master's degree in Sofia and a job in Ruse running arts and cultural activities for the Elias Canetti Centre, named for the writer, Nobel laureate, and Ruse native. (Canetti's best-known work, *Crowds and Power*, was an investigation of mob psychology and its uses and abuses by populists and demagogues.) Ruse, which the Turks called "*Ruschuk*," or "little Russia," was, Elisa explained, arguably the most important Bulgarian city after its independence from Turkey in the late 1800s. Just downstream from Vienna and the other Danube capitals, it was a major trading center and the site of many Bulgarian firsts: the first bank, the first railway line, the first movie theater. The town center, of course, was built in a miniature imitation of the ornate Viennese style. But after the fall of the Hapsburgs, the two Balkan Wars, and two World Wars, the merchants left and the once-elegant houses fell into decay, their pastel facades peeling and gray.

I walked up to the Pantheon of National Revival Heroes, a blocky 1970s monument and ossuary for which a church was bulldozed. Thirty years later, a cross was apologetically added. Teens sat and drank beer, and a dad and a handful of kids played soccer on the small plaza. I walked over to the river as the sun set, past a store called Al Bundy Shoes and something designated on the map, with admirable literal-mindedness, as "Profit-Yielding Building." Aside from a graveyard of rusting propellers and a few cargo boats, both the Bulgarian and Romanian riverbanks were mercifully undeveloped. I got the impression of a nation in the wake of empires, still awash in the detritus and seaweed left after the tide goes out, the sediment left by the waves as they crash.

"I hope you brought warm clothes," said Elisa. The show was in the stripped interior of the house where Canetti's uncle had run his business. Across the street stood a statue of a man holding a handgun in a dueling stance—an anti-Turk revolutionary named Angel Kanchev. Renovations had been put on hold for years while Canetti's daughter and the municipality fought for ownership of this house and Canetti's birthplace. It was a bare brick and concrete warehouse that felt like a refrigerator, some fifteen degrees colder inside than it was on the sidewalk. Usually when the crowd at a show streams onto the street between sets, it's because the atmosphere is so stifling inside. Here they went outside to try to warm up.

"Making culture here is more like social work than presenting big exhibitions," said Elisa. There was money coming into Ruse for renovations of the downtown and for cultural revival, German and Austrian money flowing downstream in service of a concept of the shared cultural heritage of the community of Danube cities. The Goethe Institute funded both her position and the Canetti Centre itself. She'd had a lunch meeting the day before with German developers looking to invest in Ruse. "It's a little like colonialism," she said, "but it's the only way, I think."

Elisa spoke at least four languages—Italian, German, English, and Bulgarian—and seemed so foreign to this part of the world, a representative of a pan-European, cosmopolitan cultural elite, that I wondered aloud what was in it for her, wet-nursing the cultural infancy of a provincial city. "Bulgaria teaches you to be more relaxed than in Italy," she replied.

"Italy is pretty damn relaxed," I offered.

"Well, I was living in Germany for twelve years."

Cvetan was harried and late ("When I first met him," Elisa said, "I thought he was on coke"), arriving with some members of the opening act a half hour after their scheduled set time. The police pulled up not long afterward, during Cvelin's duo drone-jam set. Elisa went to palaver with them, and I prepared to pack up and make a run for it.

"The police are here," she told me when she returned. "They want to know if you need any help."

At the end of the night, I realized I would be crossing back into Romania the next morning, and that Kostya had predictably disappeared into the Sofia night without giving me my goddamned thirty euros. I generally attempt a performative geniality with the people who pass through my life intensely, daily, and ephemerally on tour, to the point where I've acquired a not entirely deserved reputation as a friendly guy. But I can be roused to what is certainly disproportionate anger by two things: first, imposition on my alone time; and second, those who try and hustle me for what are invariably minuscule amounts of money, be it fifty bucks off the guarantee or half off the merch. It is enough merely to recall the persons or the setting—details that never leave me—for my blood to rise. In the absence of Kostya himself, I took it out on the nearest available bystander.

"What the fuck," I raged at Cvetan, "with your fucking hustler buddy?"

"Can I PayPal you the money?" he offered.

"The number of times in my life," I replied, "in which a promoter has said they'll PayPal me the money later and has done so is zero."

"Maybe you want beers instead?" He gestured lamely at the case of—naturally—Fucking Hell beer he was selling off the folding table.

"The one thing I never have to worry about on tour," I snarled, "is free beer."

He turned to Elisa. "Can I borrow thirty euros?" he pleaded. "I'll send it to you later."

She nodded, and the deal was done.

"Good-bye, in case I don't see you again," said Cvetan. "I'm never gonna promote shows again. It's not 'cause of you, just the end of a long story . . ."

It wasn't the end of my currency troubles, but it was the end of my self-righteousness. The Bulgarian leva is pegged to the euro, but it is nonconvertible outside the country, and I had a stack equivalent to several hundred U.S. dollars. I hadn't exchanged it the day before because I had been waiting for the last night of merch sales and show pay. But I was leaving Bulgaria at seven a.m. on a Saturday morning, when neither banks nor gray marketeers keep hours.

Elisa asked how much I had and produced enough euros from her purse to cover the exchange. When I found another wad in a different pocket, though, I had no choice but to leave it all with her, secured only by an e-mail address, a brief introduction to PayPal, and the memory of my rant against faithless PayPalers.

It was a foggy morning by the pipelines over a particularly patchy stretch of the Danube. A horse and some goats grazed on rubble, and gnome-like ladies in kerchiefs passed in and out of the mist on their bikes. Three crows built a nest over a roadside meat stand. I could do a steady fifteen miles per hour amid the trucks, diesel fumes, stray dogs, and potholes. I dodged a horse cart as a man ran across the highway clutching a chainsaw. I stopped at a light across from a storefront with the intriguing sign "Totalcrap.ro" (I checked, it's defunct) and caught a glimpse of a squeegee man. There was a bridge without grace, over a river without beauty, into a city without charm.

Bucharest was not even appealing as a grotesque, neither especially dirty nor rundown. Much of the old city was bulldozed under Ceaușescu, and the modern city has a functional, rather than aesthetic, energy. I had a nine-hour drive to Timişoara, but I wanted to see the Palace of the Parliament, otherwise known as the Ceaușescu Palace. It remains the largest and most expensive administrative building in the world and one of the great wonders of contemporary folly. It stands in a country which, according to a 2010 *Economist* summation of a University of Pennsylvania study based on the ratio of life satisfaction to per capita income, was "the saddest place in the world."

Once a cautionary tale, the palace was now simply a fact. An auto show filled its plaza with pounding dance music. The complex, with its facing buildings topped with faux-Roman arches, couldn't be more removed from the picturesque and colorful clutter of Romanian village life. They looked like nothing so much as pretentious, tacky, and cheap shopping malls. There was no sign of pedestrian traffic: the area, as befitted its inhuman aura, was neither secured nor populated.

V.

⁘

Don't Bring Your Beer in Church
(Bucharest to Vienna)

My impression of a country's economic development is heavily influenced by whether they have divided highways (and whether the town dumps are located on the hillsides facing the roads that they do have). By that metric, Bulgaria (highways, if unevenly maintained) trumps Romania (few highways, all heavily potholed). That said, Poland, widely considered the most cosmopolitan of the Eastern European region and having "played the game well" vis-à-vis EU funding ("Well, they are right next to Germany," said one Bulgarian), didn't have highways until the rush to prepare for the Euro 2012 soccer tournament.

I had hours of driving to get to the western Romania city of Timişoara, through baking farmland, rust-roofed villages, and painted gates. The village houses in this stretch of southern Romania were one-story instead of the Bulgarian standard two. In the center of one village was mounted an army-green fighter plane with a bull's-eye painted on the tail in the Romanian tricolor. Outside another, Dolj, were parked a handful of decommissioned biplanes. A scooped horse cart sat on car wheels, next to a pair of dead dogs and a string of fish hung to dry.

I saw a church with its frescoes on the outside walls, facing the cluttered graveyard, and brash with the national blues, reds, and yellows. The "painted monastery" was a style native to the medieval Moldavian state, which comprised a region covering what is now Bucovina and eastern Romania, Moldova, and southwestern Ukraine. Robert Kaplan wrote that the fifteenth-century Moldavian king Stephen the Great had churches decorated with paintings of didactic and moral fables, saints and prophets, clad and painted in the local styles, to teach religion to the illiterate locals.

In a town called Balş, I passed two overloaded gypsy carts, and then in Craiova a nuclear plant that was actually open and functioning. A woman knelt to light a candle in a roadside shrine in front of an acres-wide abandoned industrial site, across from a mile of rusting railway cars.

I entered a wide, flooded valley where the Motru River was dammed, and drove past a small field of blue and white oil derricks and through a village with triple-gabled pagoda roofs and pink and aqua gates. Old couples sat and watched traffic while a young boy filled plastic bottles of drinking water at the town pump. Passing through Orşova, on the eastern Serbian border, I followed the Danube for a few last miles, where a small bay was clogged with barges loaded with scrap iron.

I turned north, back into the hills and the Timiş region. Any central authority was represented alternately by omnipresent speed traps and the ambulances that necessarily roam the roads in anticipation of frequent car accidents.

Somehow, I was not surprised to find Timişoara also claims the title "Little Vienna." It once adjoined, and was named for, the Timiş River (the name means "fortress of Timiş), which runs south from the Banat region to meet the Danube in Serbia. Due to various engineering projects over the centuries, though, the river now runs some miles away from the city. The urban center of western Romania, it has a legitimate reputation as the country's original revolutionary town, the place where, in the wake of the internal exile of an antigovernment Hungarian preacher named László Tőkés, protests led quickly and bloodily to the end of the Ceauşescu regime.

The city's name became a watchword and chant during the eight days between the beginning of the protests and the execution of Ceauşescu and his wife. It is also, deservedly, considered the capital of Romanian punk—they claim the first Romanian punk band, Chaos.

"I know those guys," said Casian. "But the singer, he has a kid now, and they don't have a drummer, so you know . . ."

Casian had a seven- and a four-year-old himself and was winding down his career as a promoter (with a special passion for psychobilly). A dark-featured, heavy-browed man, he worked for the local waste-treatment company, a public-private partnership that I'm now not surprised to learn involved a German investor. "I used to be at the sorting plant, but now I'm in the office doing contracts. It's a boring job."

One of the other promoters on this swing had mentioned that he knew Casian—Paul from Cluj, maybe?

"Well—we are like enemies, or competitors," Casian corrected me. No country is too big or too small to avoid the dreaded "scene beef." "He wanted to have a monopoly of promoting in Romania, and I was doing these psychobilly shows. He was yelling at me—well, not yelling, on the Internet. Anyway, it's his problem, not me."

Atelier DIY was in an industrial park, on the second floor of a warehouse, above a front-end loader and pallets of what felt like cat litter. The room looked and smelled like a basement rehearsal space. The walls were covered with 4" x 6" snapshots of hardcore shows and old posters for the same. I'd played a similar venue in Caen, France, but in place of that show's arty hipsters, the scene tonight was a small crew of middle-aged rockabilly fanatics. The opening band was called Graves for Sale, billed as "Romania's first surf band." (As it turned out, they were the Joe Meeks of space-age surf, with a guy twiddling electronics and cueing sound effects and clips of film dialogue.)

I shared a dirty couch with a hyperactive and hyperverbal man, tall and broad. He had a soul patch and a hand-rolled cigarette clenched between his teeth. His name was Marco: "Like Marco Polo! Half Serb, half Hungarian." He asked after my own roots, and when I told him I had family from the region, he exclaimed and threw an arm around me. "Ah! You are Banatian! Not American! You are one of us!"

His bandmate offered me a clear liquid in a plastic water bottle. "*Belenka!*" he said, with enthusiasm. "It is plum brandy, or apricot, or cherry. But always *belenka!*"

"I love ska, I love psychobilly, I love stoner rock," said Marco. "The cat has nine lives, but I do not have enough lives to listen to all the music I love!" His legs fell asleep under him while we talked. "Aah! I feel the termites!" He shook his legs. "It's like Tom and Jerry. You remember Tom and Jerry? Not like cartoons now. They are trying to imbecile our kids! Not like the Road Runner and the Willy the Coyote! I have a disk of fifty episodes of Willy Coyote. Not this Bob the Sponge, Bob the Fuck, Bob the blah blah blah."

They were another crowd of friendly hecklers: when I sang the line in the coda of my song "The Hearts of Boston" that quotes Cole Porter—"Which is the right life, the quiet life or the night life?"—someone yelled, "How about a quiet nightlife?"

"You must stay and drink!" said a five-foot lady with a red streak in her hair. "Romanians become more affectionate when we drink."

The after-party was a jam session that featured the knob-twiddler from the surf band freestyling in English. I was staying with Noemi, the lady with the red streak, and her partner Tibi, the drummer from Graves for Sale. Noemi had a classic Romanian face—high, soft cheekbones and jet-black hair—and sported a classic goth-punk style: a Cobra Skulls T-shirt, skull earrings, a hoodie, and a motorcycle jacket. Tibi had a gray pompadour and a coffin belt buckle. They, like their friends, were crazy about psychobilly, and we sat up in their kitchen drinking and watching YouTube videos. I showed them Speed Crazy and Bob Log III. They showed me a laughable redneck named Bob Wayne, whom they'd befriended at a festival in the Czech Republic. Noemi's thirteen-year-old son from an earlier marriage was asleep in the next room. Tibi was also divorced—he had a fourteen-year-old daughter who lived with her mother—and there was a carefree hedonism to their relationship. Tibi started the next morning by pouring *belenka* shots for both of us, and then, as I drove us to the center for some sightseeing, offered me one of the beers he'd brought.

"Here is multicultural square," he said. "Here is Catholic Church, service in German; there is Serbian; and on the other square is Romanian cathedral."

"Don't bring your beer in church!" Noemi scolded him, and he left the can on the steps as we peeked in the door.

Tibi was in the army during the revolution, doing mandatory service "just guarding a building." He and Casian go to the Czech Republic for festivals. "They are the most relaxed country in Eastern Europe. Everyone is smoking marijuana. The laws there now are more relaxed than the Netherlands." And, he added, it's less hassle than going to Western Europe. "Romanians have a problem in Europe: the gypsies go there, and they murder and steal, and they have Romanian passports, not because they are Romanian, but then the news says 'Romanians are criminals.'"

We met up with Casian and headed to the local brewery for eggs and beers. "A lot of Italians are coming here," Tibi added. "Because the language is similar, and because the women are beautiful, and Italian men are"—he mimicked a Tex Avery tongue hanging out—"about women. I think the biggest centers in the world for beautiful women are Romania-Hungary-Ukraine region. Maybe Brazil-Venezuela-Colombia."

The young Hungarian border guards had some civilian friends in sweat suits hanging out with them at the border station.

"You were in Bulgaria?" a guard asked me, studying my sweat-wrinkled temporary passport. "Why?"

"Playing concerts."

"You are musician? What kind? . . . You have a CD we can have?"

I keep one in the door pocket for situations just like this and handed it through the window.

"*Do the Struggle*, what does it mean?"

I tried to explain.

"It's the kind of music you can listen to in the gym?"

It took hours to wash the sour, stale cigarette smoke out of my clothes after I left the Balkans. The smell had permeated my suitcase, and the washing proved to be in vain. I spent the night with my friend Thomas, a graphic designer and indie publisher, who has always lived in the same neighborhood on the outskirts of Vienna (he inherited his apartment from his mother). He even met his wife, then a student from Bucharest, across the street. Hungover on a Friday morning, he went to the supermarket and she complimented his T-shirt, a homemade Black Flag parody that read "Black Coffee." He replied ("and I never do anything like this"), "'I have black coffee in my apartment across the street.' And she stayed until Monday."

I entered the German-speaking world feeling relief at the smoke-free bars and the wide, fast, unutterably dull, robotically policed highways but chafing at the merciless enforcement, flashing speed cameras, and iron parking regime. Today Europe is divided not on the east–west axis internalized by those of us raised in the twentieth century, but on an older north–south divide: on one side, the prosperous and legalistic Scandinavian, German, Lowlands, and Polish social democracies, with their high culture and ostentatious self-control; on the other, the South Slavs, Romanians, and Bulgars, but also the Mediterraneans, Spanish, and maybe the French—heterogeneous, anarchic, troubled, and vital.

"'Til recently," George Orwell once wrote, "it was thought proper to pretend that all human beings are very much alike, but in fact anyone able to use his eyes knows that the average of human behavior differs enormously from country to country. Things that could happen in one country could not happen in another." The idea of a national personality has become unfashionable, and the idea that one might prefer one national personality to another archaic, even taboo. (So too, writers like West and philosophical historians like Gibbon comfortable with offering their opinions and judgment have come to seem outdated.) Yet somehow I prefer, when traveling, the company of the Slavs and their neighbors, their pessimistic humor and their tribal pride and defensiveness, their preference for the possible over the permitted: that it is only natural and rational to cross the street if it's empty, to park on the sidewalk or median, to have a drink if having one will not adversely affect your neighbor, to pull the car into a river for a bath instead of wasting water from a hose or an artificial car wash, to free domestic animals to graze and fornicate and excrete in the commons, all of us being children of nature, and nature famously harder to tame than to indulge. (I won't get too romantic about it: poverty and necessity, of course, play the major role in these attitudes.) Perhaps Americans, committed in theory to an ideology of reinvention—Americans have no shortage of myths about themselves—reject the idea that a sensibility can be inherent, that you can't just pack off to the city or to another country and become a fundamentally different human. Perhaps some Americans raised with this ideology, believing in the essential disposability of things like family ties, religious tradition, and shared community experience, nonetheless feel the lack of a deep-rooted identity—unable or unwilling to register the inescapable hegemony of their actual American culture because of its sheer ubiquity. They may, West suggested, adopt a pet or favorite in the Old World, regardless of sense or genetic attachment or moral worth but out of an emotional and irrational reaction. I can't help but choose the places where I'm vulnerable, responsible, and engaged over the ones where I'm corralled and protected.

"Travel writing is a minor form of autobiography," Theroux wrote. After two years of nearly constant travel to and beyond the edges of the established touring map, I was heading home, packing up my Brooklyn apartment, and waiting for my first child, leaving the life of months-long touring behind. I didn't know exactly how to define myself if the answer was no longer "traveling musician." The caesura, when we lose the plot of the narrative we tell about ourselves, can be protracted and distressing, and linger. On the one hand, if these were my last major tours and the end of a fifteen-year chapter of my life, then to write about it was to validate and fix its memory in the evanescent world of popular music and live performance.

On the other hand, if I were to continue, how could I, as a husband and father, rationalize a low-paying, unstable, sometimes dangerous job that takes me thousands of miles away from my family on a regular basis? The justification must lie less in the petty vacillations of the ego and the pocketbook that come with playing the shows and more in bearing witness to the big characters and the little communities that dot the punk rock archipelago and the wider, wickeder world that surrounds it.

I remembered a conversation I had with Ed Hamell, a bull-necked and gentle-hearted bouncer of a man who tours as Hamell on Trial. Since Ed got divorced, his twelve-year-old son

Detroit travels with him on tour. Hamell told me about a conversation he had with his label boss, Ani DiFranco. He was worried about what kind of an example the life of a marginal songwriter and performer sets for a child.

"What's it going to look like," asked Hamell, "when I'm sixty years old and changing for the show in a beer cooler in the back of a shitty bar?"

She gave him a scornful look and laughed. "It's gonna look fucking cool."

PART III

I.

Changing the Country, We Apologize for the Inconvenience *(Ukraine After the Flood)*

"Don't watch something inappropriate," the small boy in front of me on the plane to Kyiv counseled his mother, with the pedantic moralism of the prepubescent. He dialed up *Despicable Me* for himself.[1] Two severe old women in black hijabs sat impassively in the front row, wearing laminated signs around their necks: "My name is *******. I want to go to Erbil Airport in Iraq. I only speak Arabic. I do not speak English."

"I wonder what their story is," said Maria.

"Probably nothing good."

---

1. Airplane viewing can indeed be tricky, as I found once when I decided a transcontinental seat-back might be the right time to check out the concupiscent cable TV show *Californication*.

We were returning—Maria to follow up on her research, I to concertize—to a Ukraine at war, a strange new kind of war of unmarked soldiers and undeclared objectives. In the months prior, Ukraine had seen a harmless-seeming student protest and a ham-handed government crackdown spiral into its second popular revolution in ten years. The euphoria quickly curdled as a stung Vladimir Putin launched a sub rosa invasion that the new Ukrainian government and the remains of the popular movement were in no position to rebuff. It was the dumbest and most pointless war in recent memory, one that it sometimes seemed Russia only started out of embarrassment after their man in Kyiv, Viktor Yanukovych, was run out of town with a dog, a cat, his mistress, a parrot, and, with the disingenuous or affected piety of a mafia don, a few well-worn religious icons.

We had already postponed the trip once, calculating that after the Ukrainian presidential election in late May we would have a better sense of whether the tensions with Russia would escalate. "Are you sure you want to go to Ukraine right now?" asked anxious, not to say disapproving, friends and family. "And with a one-year-old?"

"We're not going any farther east than Kyiv," I would say. "At most, it'll be like being in New York if there was a war on in Cleveland."

Lesia was born two months after I'd returned from Bulgaria the previous summer. We were living in a small apartment in the back of Maria's mother's house in suburban Virginia. Maria was applying for academic jobs. I was realizing that after seven years on the road, the hole in my résumé was growing unbridgeable. I learned how to tune pianos. Maria got a one-year fellowship in Toronto, a de facto maternity leave. We moved to Canada, where going to city hall to get a parking permit was like visiting a Montessori school. I tuned the dusty, rusted, and half-wrecked spinets of the spinsters and schoolchildren of Toronto, and I apprenticed with a genially irascible accordion repairman of Scotch descent in his storefront shop. I took long walks on the waterfront with the baby strapped to my chest and adjusted to a nine o'clock bedtime. I followed the news from Ukraine: thousands had taken to the subfreezing streets to protest the government's turn away from a European trade deal toward closer dependence on Russia. There were inspiring moments, and then ugly moments, and then more and more helpless moments, and then I had to stop reading the news from Ukraine.

I wrote a handful of new songs. The thought of making a new record and all that entailed—humiliating fund-raising, rejection e-mails from labels, paying a publicist to solicit half-literate blog reviews, months-long haggling over artwork—made me depressed. I'd been off the road for almost a year, and the world didn't seem to have missed me. Still, I had these songs, and it seemed a shame to leave them in a drawer. I made the record as quickly and cheaply as I could and called it *To Us, the Beautiful!* after a Ukrainian toast I'd heard: "To us the beautiful—and to those who disagree, may their eyes fall out." If this was going to be my last record—and I wasn't going to grind myself down to make sure it wasn't—that felt like a suitable valediction.

Maria got a job at a small liberal arts college in the Hudson Valley, and we bought a small house in the adjoining town, a one-crossroads hamlet that was a delicate mix of grouchy townies, oblivious college kids, and a handful of multimillionaires sequestered in mansions on the riverfront. I got a couple of shifts bartending at the local upscale hotel, stirring martinis for weekending gallerists. My commute was a ninety-second walk. We got to know the neighbors. It was comfortable. Then we left for Ukraine.

Kyiv in July was, on the face of it, a city going about its summer business, if somewhat depopulated by vacationers headed to country dachas or the beaches of Odessa. A young brass band by the Golden Gate played Herb Alpert–style arrangements of Abba, "Can't Buy Me Love," "Smoke on the Water," "Guantanamera," and other international classics. If I didn't hear "Hotel California" or the *Godfather* theme, I'm sure it was just because I missed that part of their set. The coffee trucks set up alongside the park for the men in anonymous-brand polo shirts or short-sleeved button-downs tucked into tight jeans, with, often, a kind of armpit-purse.

A city going about its summer business, but with a creepy sore at its heart. The Maidan Nezalezhnosti, Kyiv's central square, and the surrounding streets remained blocked off by a dirty tent city, makeshift memorials to the "Heavenly Hundred" shot by government snipers at the climax of the protests, and the rotting remains of the barricades. What had begun, just a year before, as an Occupy-style student protest against the scrapping of a vague agreement of "cooperation" with the European Union had curdled into a quasi-military camp for lean, dirty men in camouflage pants, shady and borderline homeless. (And a man in a Darth Vader costume, possibly the same one who had attempted to run for the presidency.) Bums and drunks were part of the Maidan from the beginning, one member of the self-appointed "Maidan Self-Defense" militia told me, riffraff brought in by the government to discredit the protests. But those protesters who had homes and jobs to return to had done so by now. The rump stayed, with nowhere or nowhere better to go, living a paramilitary fantasy surrounded by the relics of the winter's heroics, neat piles of cobblestones and tires, pop-up cafés for beer, and souvenir stands hawking anti-Putin propaganda: the Russian leader with a Hitler moustache ("Putler"), doormats and toilet paper printed with his face or that of ousted Ukrainian president Yanukovych. "EuroMaidan turns into a shady place," reported a headline in the English-language *Kyiv Post*, the site of "robberies, assaults, and beatings," as the remaining occupants ignored Mayor Vitali Klitschko's increasingly direct hints that it was time for them to leave.

On our first night there, I picked up pizzas. A half hour later and about two hundred yards away, a group of men in balaclavas and brass knuckles attacked the Maidan tents, reportedly looking for people "who didn't look Slavic." A gun battle ensued and they were driven off, with three believed killed. After the initial report the next day, the story disappeared from the news.

The Kraina Mriy ("Land of Dreams") Festival was taking place that weekend in a park on Kyiv's outskirts, and, befitting a festival conceived as a celebration of "ethnic music," national spirit ran high. The festival's bands adhered largely to the sunglasses-and-funny-hats version of "cool" and sounded like franchises of the Manu Chao/Gogol Bordello "ethno rock" empires. The band Koralli—at whose hostel in the Carpathians we'd stayed a few years before—accessorized its sopilka (a simple wood flute) with a headset mic. A Crimean hard-rock band joined forces with a traditional Tatar ensemble, and during their set someone in the crowd hoisted a Crimean flag. A young man hawked rides on off-brand Segways next to the amateur archery booth (an attraction that would never pass muster with the insurance underwriters at Bonnaroo). A few people passed out flyers with instructions on how to identify and boycott Russian goods: look for "46" at the beginning of the UPC code.

The Ukrainian version of festival wear for women was a floral head wreath and an embroidered blouse or dress. This managed to come across as simultaneously village virginal and, because not a few of the dresses were translucent, urban slutty. Meanwhile, the local variant of "barefoot hippie in a filthy sleeping bag" was "shirtless faux-Cossack in baggy pants with a shaved head and a topknot." For example, the cook at the food tent run by the Kyiv restaurant Cult Ra, who accessorized his bare chest with a swastika necklace.

This was not the statement it might seem. Cult Ra Rusyn Club was a New Age–y theme restaurant, proclaiming itself "the most original ethnic restaurant in Kyiv . . . where you can feel the world of Arya culture [and] pagan symbols re-create the sunny magic of the Cosmos." It was the local outpost of a trendy neo-paganism centered on the prehistoric Trypillian culture, which flourished on the territory of western Ukraine, Moldova, and Romania five thousand to seven thousand years ago. Among the decorative elements adorning the archaeological fragments of the Trypillians (and several other ancient Indo-European societies) was the swastika, and some adherents of the "Native Faith" movement have adopted it.

In a liminal country like Ukraine, national identity has been, in the 750 years between the Mongol invasion of Kyiv and the fall of the Soviet Union, alternately erased, denied, elided, and divided. Its historical zenith, the Kievan Rus', has been colonized by Russian revisionists claiming the Rus as proto-Russians, not Ukrainian forefathers. It was perhaps not unexpected, then, that young Ukrainians in search of a "true" native identity would reach toward prehistory for nationalist inspiration, going beyond the competing claims of still-extant politics or religion toward pastoral, Neolithic goddess fetishism and cosplay dabbling in archery and weaving. They seemed harmless, if preachy—the menu at Cult Ra lectured about the health effects of alcohol, excepting the natural and healthy honey wine and wine from the "temporarily occupied Crimea region" that they offer. But the "traditional" swastikas that decorate the napkin holders were, given Russian propaganda claiming that Ukraine is run by fascist putschists, unfortunate visuals at best.

We took the overnight train to the western city of L'viv. The old folks in the courtyard outside our apartment (where apartment numbers were chalked on the doors, as if the building, and presumably the same doors, hadn't been there for a hundred years) hollered between balconies about the end of the world. "It feels like it's already started," one said. But this was merely the kvetching of pensioners and daytime drunks who sit on folding chairs in the shade. Meanwhile, the rest of the city was out on the cobblestone promenade. L'viv felt like any small former Hapsburg city in high tourist season, though most of the tourists seemed to be from elsewhere in Ukraine. Cafés were open and spilling into the streets, their tables de facto common property. Teenagers held an impromptu jam session on an upright piano, painted the cyan and yellow of the Ukrainian flag, as a crowd clapped along. A gang of crusty punks with, improbably, a mariachi bass, attempted a klezmer song on accordion. An eight-year-old girl in a skinned-Muppet vest sawed on a violin. From a distance, she sounded like a prodigy. Up close, I realized she had simply been handed an instrument and told, "Just move your fingers as fast as you can." In the market, vendors hawked the ubiquitous Putin doormats, and boxer briefs printed to look like jean shorts with a $100 bill stuffed in the pocket. Women in short skirts and vertiginous, architectural heels were out on peacocking parade. The pops I heard at midnight were fireworks, not gunshots.

But we weren't staying in L'viv, not yet. We rented a car and headed south toward the Carpathian Mountains and the long-running ArtPole Festival. After several years in the small town of Sheshory, the festival had been shunted by noise-and-nuisance complaints into a river canyon by the flyspeck hamlet of Unizh. It couldn't be found on the road map, but we had some rudimentary verbal directions.

The road from L'viv was lined with billboards rented for birthday wishes, thanks to the Ukrainian people from the new president Petro Poroshenko, ads for the unfortunately named Brokbusinessbank, and solicitations from the government: "Support the Army." Corruption and inattention had depleted the Ukrainian army from its Soviet-era heights to as few, by some reports, as six thousand battle-ready troops. The military raised the age for mobilization to sixty and now seemed to be running a kind of Kickstarter war.

Individual cities, mostly in the west, were sending local militias, outfitted by private donations, to the front. Handfuls of men, fired with patriotism, piled into old Ladas with some food and a few shotguns and headed east. Refugees from the besieged eastern cities, sheltered in hotels in the safely nationalist west, came under increasing criticism if the able-bodied men in their ranks, having secured their families for the time being, didn't turn back and return to the front.

The danger, of course, of a war plan based in part on volunteer initiative is that the DIY soldiers coalesce into independent militias outside direct government control. Then, if the official government strategy is perceived to be ineffective, the obvious alternative for frustrated patriots is tough-talking paramilitaries—at which point Russian propaganda about a Ukraine controlled by an armed right wing indirectly fulfills itself. Indeed, the summer of 2015 saw skirmishes in western Ukraine between government forces and nationalist Pravy Sektor units. The latter had been allegedly funding their activities by smuggling cheap cigarettes into the EU with remote-controlled drones.

We passed the university town of Ivano-Frankivs'k, and the land widened into farming villages and then low, forested hills. The walls around a schoolyard were embedded with old wagon wheels. A policeman waved us down, but only to ask if we could give his buddy ten miles down the road a ride.

We stopped for dinner at a Bavarian-style roadside tavern. The blonde barmaid and waitress were silent. "These people are creepy," said Maria.

"They run an empty restaurant in the middle of nowhere," I said. "I'd get creepy too."

She looked me over. "I believe that."

"The bridge over the Dniester is in a catastrophic state," announced a sign. It proved accurate. The bridge's roadbed was made of loose wood planks that rattled and creaked as we drove over them into the town of Luka, a mix of hulking wrecks of old buildings and fresh construction, chickens and cornfields. A gigantic harvesting tractor, painted in bright colors, sat parked halfway through a gate. The road forked.

"Excuse me, which way to Unizh?" Maria asked a farmer. He waved to the right.

The road faded into dirt, then narrowed to a single lane, then disintegrated into potholes so deep we might as well have been driving down a dry riverbed. We slowed to a crawl and battered the rental car's undercarriage. The fields disappeared behind a kind of fence of Queen Anne's lace and tall pines, followed by a dense forest broken only by an occasional logging trail.

"Are we still on the map?" asked Maria.

After about a half hour, a jeep appeared from the opposite direction and waved us down. Four men, young and festival-bound, were equally lost. A Hitchcockian cloud of mosquitos swarmed the open windows. We decided to caravan a bit farther on. The forest cleared, and eventually we came to the depopulated festival gates.

The grounds were spectacular: a sprawling farm on a river canyon, the cliff walls a backdrop for the main stage. "It's the Grand Canyon of the Dniester," said our friend Ostap, whose group, Baj, had just played. A campground had sprung up behind the stage, and village women set out tarps covered with fried bread and fruit in between the mushrooming tents.

The attendees, though, were underwhelming and underwhelmed. There was a grouchiness in the air, that kind of sour-faced solipsism that can affect nouveau hippies and travelers (or hipsters of any persuasion) when, after days and weeks of anticipation of an obscure pleasure, they arrive and find only more of their own kind, everyone looking around, waiting for someone else to manifest the extraordinary happening they all came to experience.

The festival had been kept deliberately small; the organizers

felt that during wartime it was appropriate to prioritize community over raucous concerts. People from the east, where a cor-
responding festival had been held earlier in the summer, were
admitted free. But you need people for a community, however
small, and music for a festival, and the two hundred or so who
had found their way to the remote location were wet and tired,
and they needed someone (someone else, that is), to kick off the
community-building—or, at least, the fun.

And yet. The crusties I'd seen in L'viv showed up and turned
out to be Americans who went by the name Rail Yard Ghosts[2]
(the owner of the mariachi bass an acquaintance from years before, when he was in the New York gypsy-punk trio Luminescent
Orchestrii), and they took it upon themselves to lift the collective
torpor. They began to play under the bar pavilion. They were out
of tune and pleased with themselves, and the pockets of crowd
began to gather and to cheer. The band closed with a rousing
rendition of a song called "Shoplift from Tesco."

Across the dirt path, a Hutsul (a Carpathian mountain people) ensemble in embroidered shirts began to play a frantic,
four-on-the-floor, fiddle and flute stomp, and the crowd, ener-
gized and chattering, flowed to the plank benches.

Not two songs into their set, the band and crowd were driven
indoors by rain, into the cement-floored barn that had been
serving as a makeshift camera obscura, but they simply picked
up, mid-song, where they had left off. The rainy humidity mixed
with the sweat of a hundred people, now concentrated under a

---

2. They explained they were "a fifteen- or sixteen-person collective; we're trying to raise money to bring everyone over here to bring American folk-punk to
Europe."

low ceiling instead of dissipating in the river valley, and a circle dance broke out. A local *baba* stepped up to the band and sang along, then grabbed Lesia and brought her to join the circle. It had become a proper basement-show party.

Outside, the rain cleared and the moon rose. A Crimean Tatar trio set up on a low stage in the foundation of a collapsed barn. A bank of fog rolled down the river, and someone fixed a spotlight on it. Dancers climbed the roofless parapets of the barn in the moonlight, and a pair in the crowd raised the Tatar flag.[3] The band played to the hipster nationalist crowd—Ukrainian trident tattoos and horn-rimmed glasses, red-and-black nationalist flag patches—closing with an impassioned sing-along of the Ukrainian national anthem[4] ("Ukraine is not dead yet," goes the rousing chorus). The organizer of the festival, a young woman sitting cross-legged on a speaker, wept.

It is a lie that the rooster crows at sunrise. The rooster crows when he pleases—in this case four a.m., which woke me in time to hear the telltale trickle of a man urinating against the side of the building beneath my window.

Feeling ourselves a bit too old and weighed down for festival camping, we had arranged to stay in the village of Unizh proper, a hamlet with a church and a small slab of a war memorial whose population numbered in the low dozens. The few houses had snub-nosed gables, the endpoints of their roofs chopped off at

---

3. Crimea, of course, had been annexed by Russia months before with the kind of peremptory petulance that made one suspect Putin had a nagging aunt with a bungalow in Kerch.

4. It's the anthem, I will always think, that sounds like the "field and fountain" bit in the carol "We Three Kings."

forty-five degrees for some obscure architectural purpose. Rotting picket fences flanked ornate and freshly painted metal gates. The houses huddled along a rutted lane hugged by the riverside greenery, lush with an unbounded, over-full fertility.

Our muddy compound—two houses, a pigsty, a shed for the cows, a roost for the chickens, shoebox-sized rabbit cages, an outhouse—was ruled by a toothless old woman in wool stockings and a kerchief who wielded power with a long wooden stick. Everyone called her *babusya*—"Grandma"—as if it were an honorific, which it was. Rural Ukraine, where men are ranked more by degree of alcoholism than by relative distance from the poles of sobriety and drunkenness, is truly a matriarchy. The baba stomped around the compound in purple slippers, scattering cornmeal for the chickens, bent at the waist grating green apples for the pigs, or gathering a wheelbarrow full of beet greens for the chickens and guinea hens. Her bottom jaw was a meaty ribbon of unbroken gumline, and she stuffed a ball of fried dough in her cheek like a chaw. She grabbed the cat by its jawbone in her wide, rough paw, swatting it as she threw it out of the house. Her husband, grizzled and skeletal, was terminally ill and confined to the house.

Lesia took to her like calf to cow and ran to her, arms stretched wide. "A gypsy girl," the baba boomed, "she'll go to anyone!" She smacked the rooster out of the way with her stick and grabbed a fat rabbit by the ears to show the fascinated toddler.

The baba's daughter-in-law Olya was our hostess. She, her husband, and their nine-year-old son were staying in the village for the summer. The dark-featured man I'd taken for a Romanian farmhand was the baba's other son—"a disappointment," she said, loud and firm—a drunk who slept in a makeshift bed outdoors under a beer garden tent. Olya, who called me "Ferencz" (a Hungarianized version of my name), had a sun-ravaged back and a neutral, sexless fleshiness; she wore rubber shoes and a housedress. Her parents, only in their fifties, had been crippled in a car accident after a young man tried to pass three cars and a bus simultaneously. He was left with only an elbow injury; they would never walk again. Olya told me she had been struck dumb for three months afterward.

This village has everything, said Maria: the ebullient baba; the dying grandfather; the sullen drunk; the hot young thing—a cousin—in incongruously fashionable and revealing outfits, who spent most of her time on her phone. Our room was hers, with bubblegum-pink walls and a choking smell of mold. Next to a noseless stuffed dog, someone else's wedding picture, blown up to poster dimensions, leaned against the wall.

Slumming young Westerners assume uncleanliness must be a marker of poverty, and thus represent some kind of authentic existence. But the poor, in the absence of generative conditions such as mental illness or congenital drunkenness, are reliably neat and meticulous, sweeping loose dirt from a packed-dirt floor or painting a corrugated tin roof in geometric, quilted patterns. So here the outhouse, the last stop past the pigpen on the way uphill to the fields, locked with hammered iron hooks; was lined with vinyl wallpaper; had a clean, cushioned seat; and was as ventilated and odorless as any such building whose central receptacle was a white, thirty-gallon bucket full of human waste could reasonably be expected to be.

A filthy white duck, its feathers soggy and fouled with muck, squeaked its frustration as the gate closed before it and squirted a stream from its cloaca like tobacco juice. One of its feet was deformed, and the baba had wrapped a rag around it to soften its limp. The river was tropically ponderous with effluent run-off after the previous day's storm. Maria and Lesia had gone to bed, but I was stopped on the steps by Olya's husband, the baba's less-disappointing son. He was my age and installed radiators in Ivano-Frankivs'k. He seemed to be the one who had been struck dumb, in contrast to his wife's fluty chatter. After the women went to bed, though, he felt comfortable enough to approach, brandishing a liter of beer and an unmarked flask of *samohon*: moonshine.

"Are you good?" Maria asked through the door, in English, after the husband and I had spent some time compensating for our lack of a shared language with shared drinks. "Or do you need me to rescue you?"

"Rescue, please," I said. The steps had begun to spin. She played the spoilsport wife and called me to bed.

"It's nice," she said when I was safely tucked in. "He finally cornered you to do man stuff"—drink heavily—"with him."

It was a full moon. The village dogs didn't bark.

I woke early, choking on the moldy air, and went to sit outside and read as the sun, and the drunk son, rose. He stumbled over and leaned in, closer and closer, repeating a word I didn't know. (I later learned it was for "cigarette.") Lesia woke up grouchy, rubbing her ears. The baba prescribed oil of onion for earache: shaved raw onion, squeezed through a bolus of cheesecloth, warmed in a bowl of hot water, then soaked in cotton batting and shoved in the ear canal. The asphalt yard soon smelled of onion.

The road out of town climbed the cliff to the field of cornflower on the heights of the river's west bank. A nearly blind old woman, dressed in layers of dark gray and black wool despite the heat, cornered passing festivalgoers and harangued them with a megaphone squawk. As three German-looking men in sandals freed themselves from her attention, she turned her monologue and her stick toward the birds circling the cliff across the river.

As we drove back through Luka that morning, we saw most of the town walking to church, in headscarves and shiny suits and, on the young women, skirts just long enough to be respectable. We turned south and west toward Kolomyia: thirty-six kilometers of unpaved road. ("It's a terrible road," an old lady trying to hitch a ride assured us.) We passed a bus shelter accessorized with stylized wheat stalks and half a mock-Grecian urn. Across the road, someone had cut a ten-foot circular moat, creating a grass-covered artificial island. In the center of town (first mentioned in "the chronicles" in 1395, said a helpful sign), a concrete Jesus stood atop a socialist realist war memorial, flanked by platonically heroic soldiers.

"I'm gonna guess that Jesus wasn't part of the original design," said Maria.

A woman on the outskirts of Kolomyia wore a white tank top that read, mysteriously, "Bjorn Borg." Men in Speedos were taking advantage of the sun to drive their cars down into the river for a bath. Silver roofs of aluminum sheeting were hammered into patterns and gleamed alongside shaggy Cousin Itt haystacks. The Hutsuls have a skill for the decorative: wool-lined vests, every inch embroidered in every imaginable color; house facades completely tiled (or plastered, or carved, or clapboarded) in pastel and purple, or lined with hammered metal trim; iron gates with brass and silver filigree; felt rugs that hang heavy, like plywood or wet laundry; crossed lath, flowers, and glass over the bucket crank servicing dug household wells; and private shrines in which the Virgin Mary faces the road through a gilded glass fish tank. It's a self-conscious urge: as in many picturesque rural minority communities, there is a performative consciousness of regional color with an eye toward tourism.

Western Ukrainians plausibly blamed the potholes on the just-ousted government, run by Russophile men of the east who steered infrastructure spending away from the nationalist west. To the degree of driving difficulty we now added a long series of switchbacks as we ascended the Carpathians, through the kind of pine whose needles hang from branches like a medieval noble-woman's sleeve, past roadside sellers squatting behind baskets of dried mushrooms and mason jars of berries. The sheer mountains themselves were largely deforested, an impressive display of human ingenuity directed at living, herding, and farming at a forty-five degree—or greater—angle.

The Cheremosh River, which ties the region together like a tense ribbon, cut through not the regal canyon of a dignified international waterway like the Dniester but a squared-off notch chiseled, roughly but effectively, ten feet below the village floor-lines. The bridge into Verkhovyna had a new paint job, in both the blue and yellow of the Ukrainian flag and the red and black of the militant nationalists, and sported the patriotic slogan "Slava Ukraina, Slava Heroim" ("Glory to Ukraine, Glory to the Heroes") across its breadth. Maria's old friend Oksana had organized the repainting with a group of schoolchildren, not without local controversy. Notwithstanding the strong national feeling in the area—there is a large memorial in the town square to the

Heavenly Hundred, and a carful of Verkhovyntsi were on their way to Donetsk with food, guns, and cash—Oksana had been abused and threatened on the town's message board. She hadn't gone to the trouble of getting permission from the town council, the Ukrainian flag's colors were upside down, and the red and black were just too radical. She should be hung from the bridge, one commenter said.

A slim and boyish woman in her forties, forthright and motormouthed, Oksana was used to being a controversial figure in her village; being single and childless at her age was unusual enough. Born in Verkhovyna to a single mother, she had moved to Kyiv in her youth and lived the life of an urban hipster: music, art, parties. She had returned home to take care of her aging mother. When her mother died, just a few months before our visit, Oksana inherited a small enclosure and three buildings, two of which she had repurposed, built out, and decorated as a kind of bed and breakfast.

She was sitting on the porch when we arrived, wearing a bikini, flip-flops, and a baseball cap advertising Bitburger beer. She was cleaning potatoes with a knife. It was laundry day. Her close-cropped hair was dyed blonde and looked blonder against her sun-bronzed skin.

"These stairs are pretty steep," Maria said as we hauled a suitcase up a glorified ladder to the sun-baked second floor.

"Pff!" Oksana said dismissively. *"Americanskii protest!"*— what an American complaint.

Within her gates were a half-dozen cats, two goats, a small patch of grass for clover hay, a vegetable garden, countless flowers, raspberries, wild strawberries, broken glass and shards of pottery pressed decoratively into the cement walkways and exterior walls, a bench swing made from shellacked branches, a covered but wall-less teahouse, laundry drying on parallel lines.

Oksana had one tenant, a German in his ninth year of traveling the world. After a close friend died, he had quit his job and gone in search of spiritual contemplation. He had one set of loose-fitting, synthetic hiking clothes and wore those shoes with individual pockets for each toe. He fasts twice a year for thirty-five days at a time, he told us, and eats only once a day. When he feels hungry, he goes for a walk in the mountains. He has a twenty-five-year-old daughter but hasn't seen her in three years.

Oksana had her laptop out and was struggling with a dilemma: how to list her establishment on Airbnb in a way that wouldn't attract Russians. She's sick of dealing with Russians, she said. "They just want their *sto hram*"—100 grams of vodka—"and fried meat." In the end, she decided the solution was to run the listing in English.

She was a card-carrying member of the nationalist Svoboda party, and we asked how she felt about the recent presidential election, won by the billionaire businessman Petro Poroshenko.

She shrugged. "He's not so bad. Lyashko"—the radical nationalist member of Parliament who was in the middle of conducting a vigilante campaign in the eastern war zone at the head of a private militia—"would've been great, but Europe never would have accepted him. We need a manager, not a revolutionary."

Verkhovyna was clustered at the bottom of a wide river valley. Unlike American villages, where each house is separated by a buffer of trees, its houses were packed together as if they had slid down the valley walls and run up against each other. You could hear the cries of babies and shouts of fathers across the whole town. Dozens of roosters and hundreds of dogs sang in chorus over the square miles.

It was haying season, and whole families, including small children, pitched in. The yards and fields were left to grow tall, then scythed, left to dry in the sun, turned once a day with a rake or pitchfork, and eventually gathered, once the grass had browned, into one of the twenty-foot haystacks that each fell from their own central pole. Oksana's neighbors, Jehovah's Witnesses with five young children, had taken over their shared driveway to cut bark lath into kindling. The husband was shirtless and, though young, nearly toothless. He had a menagerie of bad tattoos: fantasy dragons fading across his back; a bust of Lenin over his left breast; and, in English Gothic capitals on the mound below his belly button, "Only Fur [*sic*] Lady," with an arrow pointing toward his crotch.

"He must have been in prison," I said. He had, it turned out: eleven years, for rape.

The high mountain lanes, rutted and exposed on the treeless slopes, were cut as deep as five feet below the ground level in the surrounding fields: the roads have followed the same paths, under more or less the same conditions, for a very long time. It's hard to credit the evidence that many motor vehicles use them, though I do see a dirt bike, an old Soviet army jeep, and a Lada with a jacked-up suspension pass by. One farmer tossed his drying hay with a preindustrial horse-drawn contraption whose two iron wheels turned rods that, as they rotated, waved four pitchfork ends up and down in pairs.

We were visiting a legendary local instrument maker, Tafiychuk, a squat old man with white hair and black eyebrows. He and his wife lived in the hills with their twelve-year-old granddaughter. Their daughter used to live there, too, but ran off last year with a drunk and left the child. Their house, like the bridge, was newly painted in patriotic blue and yellow. Maria asked him about the election.

"I'm a simple man," he said. "I don't think about these things." But he, like Oksana, had settled for Poroshenko.

We were buying instruments: a tsimbaly (hammered dulcimer), a selection of sopilky, and a duda—a bagpipe made from the skin of a whole goat. To keep the goat skin soft and supple, Tafiychuk said, toss fifty grams of vodka into the instrument every month or so. The tsimbaly had been built for another man, but he had been called up into the army. Maria could have it; the original owner had said: "If I come back, I can order another one."

We left and headed to Kosiv, where our friend Roman had set up an interview with a member of the Hutsuls, one of the region's first rock bands, begun in the 1960s. Lubko was a tired-eyed man in double denim and a khaki fishing vest, with one tooth in the middle of his upper gum like a Muppet. The Hutsuls' hit was a cover of Black Sabbath's "Paranoid" with lyrics rewritten in Ukrainian to refer to local topics. Their bearded singer, Slavko, could still be seen riding around town on his bike, playing trumpet at funerals and dances: "It's the rock and roll life," he said, "you want to play for people. Even dead people."

Roman was a photographer and a member of the local parliament ("the local mental hospital," Lubko added). "It gives me headaches and makes me enemies." He had arranged for the reunited Hutsuls to play the Maidan stage over the winter, though it had taken some convincing. "Why do I need to drive all the way to Maidan?" Slavko had asked Roman.

"Listen, Slavko," Roman told him. "You've been playing forty years in a jail. Even in free Ukraine, you're in a jail. Now you can come to Maidan and play in a *really* independent Ukraine."

It was time to start playing my own shows. I left Maria and Lesia in Ivano-Frankivs'k, in the hands of the mayor's wife, who was busy organizing fund-raising efforts for the army ("The boys need socks and thermal underwear"), and drove west to Kalush. "We call that road the chessboard," Roman said, "all patches of black and white"—i.e., potholed and patched. It was no small improvement on the mountain roads, though. In forty-five minutes I pulled up at a freestanding Irish pub incongruously plopped in the middle of a cluster of bedroom-community apartment towers.

"I am Max," said the schlubby, jovial proprietor, who wore a T-shirt that read "Music Is My Religion." "This is Maxwell Pub." The interior was hung with all manner of Irish knickknacks and "Proud to Be a Celt" football scarves. Max even had a clover tattoo. "I like Irish music, Irish football, Irish beer, Irish everything!"

He introduced me to his small crew of friends. Alex, from Odessa, wore a trendy but short haircut, a red-checked button-down, and black-rimmed glasses: a preppy hipster or a hip preppy. His greatest ambition, it turned out, was to live out a Carlos Castaneda fantasy and do peyote with a cult in Mexico. He loved Kalush, he said, though he couldn't explain why. He said it was an eco-disaster waiting to happen: a deep mining pit filled with chemical waste from a fabrication plant was just waiting to overflow.

The crusties from the festival had a week off, and I'd tried to get them to join this show. The game of telephone hadn't connected and it hadn't worked out, but another American showed up looking for them, a chatty hippie girl with a nine-month-old baby. She overheard me tell Alex that I didn't think you could just go to Mexico and get peyote these days. "Sure you can!" she interjected, and as she gave him the details, I slipped away.

I'd brought only my banjo on this tour. You can find an acoustic guitar anywhere, I figured, and if they could scrounge up an accordion too, so much the better. Max could. Not only that, he'd cooked a surprisingly credible falafel dinner. While eating dinner and scrolling through Twitter, I began to see unsettling reports that a civilian airliner had been shot down in eastern Ukraine. Early indications said that the Malaysia Airlines flight had been destroyed by the Russian-backed rebels. I excused myself to the patio and called Maria. "Did you hear what happened?"

She hadn't. She was scared. "Should we drive to the Polish border?"

"Let's give it a few days, see how it shakes out."

It seemed like a game-changer: hundreds of dead Europeans would surely be the spark that broadened this bloody, but so far regional, conflict. I returned to the bar and sat down next to Max. "Did you hear what happened?" I asked. He hadn't, and made a scornful noise when I told him.

"Donetsk and Luhansk, let them go," he said. "They are not Ukrainian. They think they are Russian, but if they join the Russian Federation, the Russians will call them Ukrainians. They are stupid and aggressive: drink, drank, drunk! In Soviet Union they had factory jobs, but in independent Ukraine the factory closed down. It is all criminal gangs."

Surely, I asked him, there are Ukrainian loyalists in the eastern regions?

"It is too bad," he agreed. "Maybe some percent of people there want to be in Ukraine, but their family is there. . . . Like the [Crimean] Tatars. But they have Turkey looking out for them, they will be OK."

Did you vote in the election?

"No. I have a friend who just came back from Slovyansk. He was in the army. He said it's all just a political game."

He dismissed my concerns about the plane and changed the subject. "You know Sasha Boole?" he asked, indicating a poster for the show. Sasha, from the border town of Chernivtsi, was the opening act. "Everyone thinks he looks just like you. We made up a myth that you were brothers, that you fell in love with a girl but she chose Sasha, and so you went to America."

When Sasha arrived, I saw what they meant—he did resemble a version of me from a few years earlier. He wore a handlebar moustache and a bowler hat and sported a tattoo of a skeleton playing a banjo. He had dark hair and light blue eyes, wore a sweater tied around his neck like a golf pro, and sang the kind of romanticized Americana that was increasingly popular in Eastern Europe: a bandolier of harmonicas, a stomp box, a version of "Down by the Riverside."

"I love gypsy music," he told me, and sang mock-theatrically to demonstrate. "In every song, a gypsy horse thief is falling in love with the daughter of the"—we debated the translation—"mob enforcer." Earlier in the year, he had done a forty-day tour in Moldova and Belarus. The former was harder, he said, because the number of permissions required to hold or advertise a show was prohibitive.

Unusually, Sasha mixed the unionist/progressive leftism common to most folk-punk Woody Guthrie fetishists with a radical militancy. "I played in Kyiv, at the Maidan," he said. "It was an honor. . . . [Maidan] was worth it not so much for the results but because it turned a tumbler in the minds of Ukrainians." He mimed a key turning beside his temple. "That we have to work together. The people from the medical school coming out under fire to help the injured. Like the American Communists, like Upton Sinclair—there is a history in America of organizing and popular uprising that we don't have."

I commented on the irony of a former Communist state looking to American communism—which had, after all, been even less successful in practical terms than the Soviet version—as a future for Ukraine. He made a gesture of acknowledgment. But pacifist, Occupy-style activism was too weak to force change, he said.

"People learned that the government only respects force. The first people in Maidan, they were doing art actions, flash mobs— the government came and beat them up. But the next time the government came, they were burning cars and setting fires, and the government said, 'OK, we will negotiate!' . . . I voted for Yarosh"—the leader of the Pravy (Right) Sektor, the militant nationalist faction. "Yarosh, in the election, they gave him money, he did other things like a regular politician, but . . ." He shrugged. "I think it will be better, whether you have strong arms from Europe saying, 'You have to do it this way,' or strong arms from the government. . . . I think there will be a second revolution, and it will be tougher, like Germany in the 1930s. You have these men coming back from the Russian war in the east, with guns, knowing how to kill people, saying to the government, 'What are you doing?' And there will be a leader, an Adolf Hitler type. Because the police are demoralized: one day [they] are fighting for the government, for the laws, and the next, you don't know. It will be a long process and a long struggle."

It was an all-too-plausible scenario, especially disturbing to hear from a member of the young cultural alternative (and echoing the appeal of Limonov's National Bolsheviks to the aimless counterculture of the Russian provinces). It was easy to see how the seductive power of revolution porn—the barricades, the Molotov cocktails, the "All Cops Are Bastards" rhetoric—could be co-opted by the rhetoric of militant populism, looking for a muscular defense against a powerful, aggressive, and unpredictable neighbor. At what point does the "castle doctrine"—that you have the right to protect what's yours—expand into dangerous aggression? Defending borders? Defending co-religionists, or, as Putin was arguing, co-linguists, regardless of nationality? At what phase of that expansion does "nationalism" shade from patriotism into something more menacing?

Sasha told me he had written a song about the separatists, specifically the Russian and Dagestani mercenaries crossing the border and "killing Ukrainian people and making money." Later, he sent me the recording, a duet with an accordionist from Kalush credited to "Sasha Boole & Zydeco Fam." It's "the first Ukrainian zydeco," they declare at the top of the track (though despite the accordion, the music has nothing to do with zydeco).

від і до ("Back and Forth")

якби хто запитав, що дорожче йому безтурботне життя чи валюта?

жив у горах собі, вівці пас на коні, піл віно, єл
  шашлик
тепер тута у камазі лежить
ну а між собі жить кілька діб—путь туда і обратно
  від і до—
це коли мертвих сєпарів у той самий камаз влазить
  більше, ніж живих

If you were to ask him: what is more important, a carefree
  life or cash?
He lived in the mountains, herded his sheep on a horse,
  drank wine, ate shashlik
Now he's here lying in a Kamaz car
He could have lived a few days—at least to there and
  back and forth—
This when that same Kamaz car can carry more dead
  separatists than those who are alive

He wrote me:

"*There was one battle when our army destroy a big group of
separatists. They were riding Kamazes* [the most popular car of
separatists at the beginning of the conflict]. *Just few days before
they was boasted, posting photoes of how they are riding Kamaz
with guns in their hand. And then there was a photoes of the same
cars, but full with the bodyes of separatists.*"

While Sasha began his set, I jotted down my notes from our conversation in the bathroom, the floor of which was constructed
from the sanded and finished sides of wooden wine crates. As I
returned to my table, the representative of a local television station approached me and asked if I would do an on-camera interview outside—give the perspective of an American on the events
of the day.

"I am on my own today," the reporter said, setting up his camera on a tripod and plugging in the microphone. "Everyone is busy with all the news." Did I have, he asked, any words of support for Ukraine in their time of crisis?

I paused, wanting to speak carefully. It's rare that one is called upon to speak as a representative of one's own country to one engaged in a high-stakes military and political struggle—with another country, Russia, known for its attention, and vitriolic response, to its critics. I had married into a Ukrainian family, I said, which makes my daughter part Ukrainian, so I have some kind of a stake in the game. But, simply, I would want for Ukraine what I would want for any country: rule of law, freedom from corruption, and self-determination and a dignified independence.

The club's cleaning lady, Pany Lesia, left a vase of fresh flowers at the front of the stage for my set: a blue vase, of course, with yellow blooms. Max and his friends were ready to get rowdy, and I ended my set a capella, atop the bar, clutching my banjo.

"Your folk singers," the bartender told Max, shaking his head. "They always want to get up on the bar."

But the locals weren't ready to let the show end. Sasha grabbed his guitar, and I my accordion, and we sat at the bar for another hour, hootenanny-style. They wanted to hear the iconic Johnny Cash bad-boy hits: "Folsom Prison Blues," "Cocaine Blues"—a vicarious thrill, like white Americans who love gangsta rap or *narcocorridos*. The hippie girl's baby was asleep on a bar table, sprawled on his back in pajamas printed with little monkeys. The war in the country's east had suddenly escalated, but there was *samohon* to drink and rebel songs to cheer, and what had the east to do with them? I understood: scary events in real time take time to process. On 9/11, I was on tour in Germany and tried to play the sympathy card to hit on a girl. (The next day I had to explain communism to our guitarist.) Stuff happens, but you can't let a big thing like history ruin your day.

Tempting as it may be, there's no point in lolling around in bed when you're hungover. You just end up obsessively cataloging and wallowing in the individual areas that hurt. Better just to jump up and start the hard work of recovery. Anyway, this wasn't one of the bad ones. When the problem was the liters of weak beer, not the *samohon* shots at the end of the night, I had at least, despite myself, done some preliminary hydration.

I took the train up to Chernivtsi—or down; it was almost due south, by the Romanian and Moldovan borders, on the route to Odessa. I have never been able to fully assimilate the idea that one can go south into mountains, any more than that rivers can run north to the sea. The filthy bathroom at the end of the train car was, despite the stench, the only place on the train to catch a gulp of fresh air. The old women, leery of the dreaded "draft," prohibited the opening of windows with fearful glares.

I was meeting a redheaded young man with the unlikely name of Artem Ketchup who—it was news to me—was the mastermind behind my Ukrainian shows, as well as Sasha Boole's Moldovan and Belarusian adventures. As it turned out, I'd met him once before: he was working at Kvartira Art Center in Dnipropetrovs'k when Maria and I played there two years (and about two hundred pages) ago. As a teenager in Chernivtsi, he opened a design studio, silkscreening bags and T-shirts. He first booked a show by a local band as a vehicle to sell some of his merchandise and found that he liked putting on shows more than making bags: "It's like a shitty tattoo—you get one, then you just want to get more."

So he became a booking agent, organizing tours for Ukrainian and foreign bands—a lot of Italian hardcore, for some reason ("I don't know why. I think they want to have sex with Ukrainian women"), not so much Romanian or Moldovan, despite their proximity. "They're all guys smoking weed and"—he mimed playing bongos. He routed several of his tours through Kvartira in Dnipropetrovs'k. He was impressed with their operation and e-mailed Olya asking for a job. She agreed. He got on the train the next day and stayed there for two years. Since returning to his hometown, he had been booking shows and working as a producer for the local TV station.

"Ketchup" was a relic from his teenage years as well. In middle school, like for Erden in Mongolia, English classes had been contracted out to missionaries (in this case, American Baptists) as a Trojan horse for religious after-school programs. Artem was assigned, or chose, the nickname "Ketchup" in a getting-to-know-you game at the Baptists' summer camp. Though the religious training didn't stick, he said, it was a good experience for him: "I thought it would be a joke, but that summer, all my friends got in trouble, and I got off to a good start."

We walked to the "Musico-Dramatic Theatre," a gorgeous opera house decorated with chandeliers, maroon velvet, and gold leaf, to film a segment for a local TV program he produced. Like many of the driven young men who are the engines of their local scenes, Artem propelled himself down the sidewalks with racehorse strides, twitchy with energy. I wanted to grab him by the shoulder and harness him to my slower pace.

Chernivtsi was a beautiful town in the Hapsburg style, but

unlike, say, Ruse, it was freshly repainted, on the occasion of its six-hundredth anniversary. And unlike L'viv, it wasn't overrun with tourists—just a few cars with Italian or Russian plates, the latter ostentatiously displaying Ukrainian flags. A trio of crew cuts in Adidas tracksuits glowered at an ATM. The language usage here was, Artem said, about evenly split between Ukrainian and Russian speakers ("and maybe twenty percent Romanian," he added). He himself was raised speaking Russian, but "I like speaking Ukrainian. You don't have here, like in L'viv or Ternopil, people saying, 'Oh man, why you speaking Russian?' It is more democratic, young people wanting to make art." He paused. "I hate borders."

Did he, I asked, think that this was a common sentiment, that there was a generation of young people who wanted to move past the bifurcations of the past?

He was unwilling to generalize or predict. All of his friends from Luhansk and Donetsk were in Kyiv now, which was good for the concentration of like-minded people (and causing a rent explosion in Kyiv) but not for the cultural future of the east. Poroshenko was, he said, "I don't know the word in English—not good, not bad." Far-right activist Dmytro Yarosh's Pravy Sektor?[5] "It's weird, two years ago the same people were just UPA"—the World War II–era western Ukrainian partisan guerrillas led by Stepan Bandera, whose legacy is revered in much of the west but extremely controversial—"nationalists, you know, not good, and now they are heroes because they made revolution."

5. In November 2015, Yarosh, who had been wounded in fighting in the east, resigned from Pravy Sektor leadership, claiming he was being shunted into a figurehead position.

Do you think it was all worth it, I asked—the chaos, the loss of Crimea, the war in the East—to overthrow the government and awaken the national consciousness?

"I don't know yet," he said. "It's like I'm reading a book of history, and I don't know how it ends."

The PA at the coffeehouse alternated between James Taylor covers and the Stooges, which was as good an introduction as any for my show. The crowd was made up of young Europeanized bohemians, who seemed rather affluent by Ukrainian standards: I counted at least a half-dozen iPad minis. One guy scrolled through the headlines, looked up, and said, "Today Verkhovna Rada [the Ukrainian parliament] banned Communist Party."

Plenty of technology, but not much reaction to my set. "That's just how Chernivtsi is," said Artem. I took the two a.m. train back to L'viv. It was too hot to sleep.

The show in L'viv was a last-minute affair in a crowded bar in a stone basement. Ljana, a journalist, put on shows "for a hobby. People say L'viv is the cultural center of Ukraine, but it's not true. There is no club to have loud music, like punk rock or grindcore like I want to put on. People only want cover bands that can play while they eat. So for now I am only doing acoustic shows." Anyway, she said, it was inappropriate to put on big shows with wounded soldiers coming back to L'viv hospital from the east. People would rather, she hoped, give blood and money to the war effort than pay for an expensive rock show.

Appropriately for a venue that looked like something out of Greenwich Village in the 1960s, the crowd consisted of hipsters in the beatnik sense, not the contemporary one: quiet, attentive, serious listeners. Maria, Lesia, and I caught the night train back to Kyiv: the Bulgaria Express, Sofia to Moscow. The usual shirt-less, potbellied drunk harassed the hallway, alternately grum-bling, belligerent, and supplicant.

Often when I tour a country for the first time, a person—almost always a young man—will come up to me and say, "Next time you come, let me organize the shows." Two years ago, in Kyiv, it had been the voluble, scruffy Sasha Grinevich, and I had indeed reached out to him this time around (though as it turned out he delegated most of the shows to Artem). We met up for lunch at Cult Ra. He was the picture of an Anglo scenester punk, in a Propagandhi T-shirt and pink Ray-Ban knockoffs; his friends play bike polo on Saturdays. He was from a circus family on his mother's side—a strongman, an illusionist—though, he conceded, "there are no pictures of them. They could have just been some alcoholics." He worked for a website run by Ukrainians but based in San Francisco (an "automated proofreader and personal grammar coach") and so had a much-coveted U.S. visa, though he hadn't made use of it. He booked a few shows a year for foreign bands—the Brooklyn-based group Obits, someone from Austria. Malaya Opera, where we played last time, had shut down shortly after our show, and the scene had moved to a big hangar, which also didn't last. Now it centered on a garage run by a small collective, who had recently put on a successful festival called "DIYstvo" (a pun on *dyjstvo*, or "happening").

"We have a pretty good scene here," Sasha said. In addition to Saturday bicycle polo, they had a soccer team: "We are terrible, true losers. We won one game in our league, the last game of the season. It was against the other team with no wins. Very dramatic."

The Kyiv punks perhaps were more social club than fount of artistry, and the kind of institutional memory and history that can be a foundation for creative breakthroughs was missing for a familiar reason: drugs, specifically heroin. "I have a friend, Timon, who is forty, and he is like the elder statesman. He was around in the late eighties, early nineties; he saw Sonic Youth play here to like twenty people, saw VV"—Vopli Vidopliassova, a seminal Ukrainian rock band led by singer/accordionist Oleg Skrypka—"when they were a punk band, before they decided to go for commercial success. There was a pretty good noise-punk scene here then. And then everyone got into drugs, and now Timon is the only one [older] than late thirties who comes to shows. It is too bad. The punks now think they are the first Ukrainian punks; but really, because of the Internet, it is just imitations of American punk.

"I like the scene in Greece. They have strong antifascist groups"—for good reason, it should be pointed out. The explicitly neofascist Golden Dawn party took nearly 10 percent of the vote in the 2014 elections, making it the third-largest party in Greece. "They even organized an MMA competition in Thessaloníki. Can you imagine!" Like the Bulgarians, he scoffed at the Greeks' economic woes. "Everyone is always saying, 'Greeks are so poor,' but all the kids in Greece had money to stay out all night drinking. They had cars. They weren't poor like us in Ukraine."

That day the Ukrainian parliamentary leadership, led by Prime Minister Arseniy Yatsenyuk, resigned. The international media reported this as a fatal breach in the governing coalition, but it had the feel of a choreographed and scripted maneuver—the fall of the coalition allowed the president to call early elections. The leadership of the government had changed after Yanukovych's flight, but the parliament hadn't: the revanchist Communists and Yanukovych's Party of Regions still held their seats. Yatsenyuk's resignation would trigger a new round of parliamentary elections in the fall, which it was hoped would wipe out the disgraced old guard and bring in a unified, reformist government. (A few days later, President Poroshenko refused to accept Yatsenyuk's resignation, allowing the latter to retain his position while the fall elections went forward.)

Sasha never spent a night on the Maidan, but he was part of groups that brought medicine and supplies. "I didn't agree one hundred percent with their goals, because I don't like the EU. I think we should be independent. But if the choice is EU or Russia, of course I choose Europe. I voted for Poroshenko. Usually my vote is for nobody," but under the circumstances, he felt, it was important to vote, and Poroshenko was the least worst option.

"Maybe," he said, echoing the consensus opinion, "he will be a good manager. Oligarch or not, I don't care. It is just money. Give any of those poor people on the square money and they would be the same."

I asked him what he thought about the rump occupation.

The people left on the Maidan, he said, "have nowhere else to go. They don't want to go to work. Eventually people will stop giving them money or food."

I mentioned that Sasha Boole had described the Maidan's effect on the Ukrainian psyche as an unlocking of a patriotic sentiment. "I never liked patriotism," said Grinevich, "but during the Maidan I felt patriotic. In Dnipropetrovs'k, it was a very Russian city—not as much as in the east, but very few people were speaking Ukrainian in the city center. Now it is one of the most patriotic cities. But it has gone too far. Everyone is painting"—he gestured to a low stone wall painted the Ukrainian flag's yellow and blue. "I think these are ugly colors, actually, but if you say that now, people say, 'Get out of here, you Russian!'"

I caught a sweltering bus by the McDonald's at the Kyiv train station, bound for Bila Tserkva (White Church), a small provincial city an hour and a half down the road toward Odessa. It's not always easy to figure out where to get off these buses—stops are often requested, rather than reliably made at obvious central stations—and I took a chance and lost. I managed to catch another local bus to the square where I hoped I'd find the Stare Misto (Old City) café.

I found a wide, sleepy commons, with grass growing between the asphalt tiles, and in the center a Mexican-looking enclosed plaza. There was something Graham Greene Mexican, or Hemingway Cuban, about the town in general: the overgrown and bedraggled square, depopulated buildings painted pastel blue and yellow, idling taxis, groups of young men and over-dressed women gathered around a motorcycle, a small café with plastic gingham tablecloths. On one end of the square was a low, wide, empty pedestal, obviously the former home of a Lenin statue, that now held only a rusting iron pipe and some crumbled cement. Beside the empty pedestal was a long banner memorializing the Maidan dead. Next to the banner were scattered, wilting flowers and a bottle of Nemiroff "Distinct" vodka. Well, not a bottle, that wouldn't have lasted—just the empty sleeve the bottle came in, with a floral wreath.

Turning back toward the white plaster compound in the center of the square, I ascended the wide staircase and passed through the arched outer doorway. To the left was Stare Misto: a restaurant with low, arched brick ceilings and rough, sturdy wooden tables. The short, barrel-ceiling stage was backed with generic classic-rock wallpaper images: Jim Morrison, Hendrix, Zeppelin. The café walls were painted in the earthy brown and red Trypillian tribal patterns familiar from Cult Ra, and a red-and-black nationalist flag hung over the sun-drenched back exit. I ducked under the flag and walked out onto the wide inner patio.

At the far end of this courtyard was an empty, festival-style outdoor stage. To my left were café tables. To my right was a crossbow range. A seven-year-old boy with a cocked crossbow in one hand was taking a cell phone call from his mother with his other.

Some local parents had organized archery lessons for the town's children, and young mothers corralled kids, from toddlers to ten-year-olds, while men in tank tops helped the older ones pull, aim, and shoot. At thirty yards stood two straw-stuffed targets— one circular, one a burlap-sack mock torso—mounted on sheets of plywood to protect the building's walls. On tables nearby lay a collection of homemade longbows and crossbows; wooden arrows, some with whittled points, some with dangerous-looking hand-filed steel heads; and eleven- by seventeen-inch color printouts—headshots of Putin and Yanukovych—which the event's leaders stapled to the targets. A balding man in sandals demonstrated an even more impressive piece of artillery, a chest-high stationary crossbow with a ratcheting windlass. It took two young boys to cock and aim it, and the arrow missed the target and sunk half an inch into the plywood. A man picked up a foot-long pair of pliers and wrestled it loose.

An elegant young woman named Dasha had opened Stare
Misto a year ago as not just a restaurant and music venue but as a
"local center for this kind of thinking"—promoting a muscular
Ukrainian patriotism for a young generation. The menu offered
buckwheat noodles and borscht. A burlap-bound copy of the poetry of the nineteenth-century national icon Taras Shevchenko
lay on every table. Light electronica pulsed from the DJ booth,
which also was painted in "native" Trypillian designs. They sold
local crafts—a great advance, Dasha said, for this "Soviet-style"
town. In addition to today's archery workshop, there was a "support our troops" event for kids the next morning: a drawing
class, with the results to be sent to soldiers on the front. (Next
week, Tim Burton movie night.) She also organized camping re-
treats to the Carpathians: rafting, hiking, music.

Dasha was slim, dark, and self-possessed, though shy about
her English. She had been working in logistics in Kyiv when
friends told her that this space in Bila Tserkva was available.
The similarities between this open-air building and those in
Latin America were no accident, she said: they were both Jesuit. This plaza was a Jesuit market, built some two hundred
years ago by a local Polish lord.[6] Under the Soviets, the building was a supply depot, then it passed into private hands under
the usual shady circumstances in the 1990s and became a haven
for drunks.

An elderly man with a Shevchenko walrus moustache and a

---

6. Bila Tserkva's place in Ukrainian history is twofold: as the site first of the 1651
treaty subordinating the Cossack host of Bohdan Khmelnytsky to the Polish-
Lithuanian Commonwealth, and second of the 1941 mass killing of the city's
Jews while under Nazi occupation. The city also has a footnote in American
Jewish show business as the home of the once-renowned cantor Yossele Rosen-
blatt and the father of clarinetist Benny Goodman.

shaved-head, Cossack-style topknot ordered a beer. Dasha introduced me to her friend Tanya, a friendly redhead in a loose green
dress with an earnest, uptalking lilt. Tanya had been an English
instructor in Indonesia and now worked as an online translator.
As we talked, she encouraged Dasha in a teacherly way to join in
and practice her English.

Tanya, in her own guileless and gregarious fashion, was a
fierce Ukrainian patriot. "I think Maidan should be no more,"
she said. "Maidan is in the heads of people now. Maybe the people there lost their jobs, or maybe they are from the east and have
nowhere to go, but the money and food that is going to them
should go to the soldiers now."

Does she, I asked, feel that the Maidan movement was a
success?

"There will be a second Maidan," she said firmly. "We didn't
achieve any of the aims."

It's a line I heard from several activist youth, who seem to
have willfully forgotten that the primary stated demand of the
Maidan protesters was the removal of Yanukovych. The final
government peace proposal came in late February and included
new presidential elections, but it was rejected by the protesters
on the grounds that Yanukovych must leave immediately. His
flight the next day was the cue that diffused the energy of the
protest. The belief that the first Maidan achieved nothing was an
attempt—like the men refusing to leave the square—to maintain
the emotional momentum of the movement, though without allowing anyone the satisfaction of achievement. The dispersal of
the Maidan, Larissa in Kyiv said later, put everything back to
normal without changing the corrupt system. Sasha Grinevich
agreed: "This is the second time we've done this," referring to the

2004 Orange Revolution. "I don't know when we will learn." The paradox is, if you won, there's nothing left to do—but if there's so much more to do, did you really win?

"Well, Yanukovych is gone," Tanya admitted. "But that is just one thing." Ukraine, she said, needed true independence. "There are people now who want to stop the war so it doesn't come to them, but they don't understand, Putin will just try to move the border closer. We have Russia as a neighbor," she said, and they can't just wish the Russians away.

I changed into my stage suit in their front office, which Dasha had leased out as a tattoo shop. Tattoos, she said, had become popular in the last year, especially tattoos of Ukrainian symbols. One of the café workers had both the trident and the line "Ukraine is not dead yet," from the national anthem. Dasha herself received the first tattoo on the new padded bench. It read "Wanderlust," though she hasn't traveled widely.

The tattoo shop was decorated in revolution chic: a glossy photo of silhouettes against burning barricades; gas masks and other vintage military paraphernalia hanging from the walls; an artist's jointed wooden hand arranged into an upraised middle finger; a poster-size propaganda calendar of "the patriotic year 2014" from the vodka brand Banderivska (a reference to the iconic nationalist leader Bandera), bearing the slogan "бандерібцька територія нескорених" ("Unbroken Banderist Territory"). On another poster, the scowling face of former president Yanukovych was drawn in the style of Shepard Fairey's André the Giant under the title "Lawful Dictatorship." With a series of captioned, black-on-red icons, it outlined the package of repressive laws the parliament had passed over the winter in a desperate attempt to create a legal framework for a crackdown on the Maidan ("Participation in peaceful gatherings in helmet, uniforms, with fire—up to 10 days"). And in one corner, confusingly, were paired a European Union flag and a Confederate banner—chosen, no doubt, as a generic signifier for "rebels." It was another disconcerting example of the resistance of symbols to cross-cultural translation. (Just to muddle the symbolism further, later in the summer, the pro-Russian separatists began to use a version of the Confederate flag as *their* "official banner." The designer, reported the *Moscow Times*, "stumbled on the flag online somewhere.")

It was Tanya and Dasha's friends who had pulled down Bila Tserkva's Lenin statue over the winter, with a truck-mounted crane, and then cut him up with a blowtorch for souvenirs.

Tanya said there was a difference between younger Ukrainians and "people forty to forty-five who grew up partly under Soviet Union. They think Donetsk, Luhansk, they are Russian, not really Ukrainian, let them go. Younger people, who grew up in independent Ukraine, believe" in the idea of a unified Ukraine and in its territorial integrity.

She made an interesting demographic point: in many ways, the conflict in Ukraine is generational. Stereotypically, societies troubled by violent unrest have a large proportion of young and unemployed men (see North Africa and the Middle East). The Russian and Ukrainian populations uniquely prone to manipulation by propaganda and populist appeal are likely the middle-aged, the lost generation trapped between the malaise of late communism and the betrayed post-Soviet promises of liberalism and privatization. Without a memory of the Soviet Union, and with the positive example of their peers in Poland, those under thirty are more resistant to Putin's pan-Slavic rhetoric.

"People around here are speaking *suzhik*," Tanya said, refer-ring to the hybrid Russian-Ukrainian pidgin common in the bi-lingual central regions of the country. "It's ugly. I didn't even know until I went to the west for school. I had roommates from L'viv and Ivano-Frankivs'k, and I learned to speak real Ukrai-nian." Her nationalism was inclusive, though: "I feel bad for the [Crimean] Tatars, because they have had such a hard history, and the last twenty years"—as a part of independent Ukraine—"have been very good for them. . . . I think Ukraine will accept them, because Ukrainians are very welcoming that way, and I think the government will help them. . . . It is harder to assimilate for the eastern [refugees]. They come and they say, 'My house is de-stroyed.' And women and children, OK, but men, you know, men from the *west* are going to fight . . ."

I wondered if she, like Sasha Boole, was sympathetic to the more radical fringes of Ukrainian politics, but like most of the pragmatic reformers, she had supported Poroshenko. "Porosh-enko was not the best option. But in fact there is no good op-tion. The three politicians who were on Maidan—Tyahnybok, Klitschko, and Yatsenyuk—people saw that they were not good enough. . . . Before last year, being a politician was a good job: you pressed a button and got money. Now it means real re-sponsibility, and people are dying, and no one wants to take responsibility."

Her torrent of opinion slowed. She sighed, afraid I was bored. (I wasn't.) "This time has been very stressful. I know many peo-ple who have become actually ill, from reading the news every day. So," she said, sitting up as if to physically change the subject, "I am hoping tonight we will just be having a good time."

We did. I slept at Dasha's sparse fifth-floor walkup. It was artist's quarters, furnished with three pallet beds and an air mattress on the painted concrete floor, no tables or chairs, a painter's easel by the window, and bathroom fixtures emerging like parasites through the chipped and gouged bare concrete wall.

Zhytomyr is north and west of Bila Tserkva, in the opposite direction from Kyiv, where Maria and Lesia had stayed. Unfortunately, there were no direct buses, so I first had to retrace my route to the Kyiv station, and then take another bus from Kyiv to Zhytomyr. The Kyiv station was down the hill in a parking lot below the train terminal. Bus drivers held signs listing their destinations, and some kept up a salesman's patter: *"Rivne, Rivne, ne cherepashka!"* ("Rivne, no turtle"—a fast bus.) One driver—white crew cut, polo shirt, Adidas track pants, leather purse tight over his shoulder and under his armpit—polished off a bottle of Stella Artois.

Yura met me in Zhytomyr. He was thin, heavy-browed, with a prominent Adam's apple and a penetrating, ironic look. He had cloudy light-blue eyes and dark Italianate hair. Like so many of the young people involved in the DIY scene, he did outsourced work for a foreign company—in this case, market research for an ad agency that had been founded by Americans and sold to Indians. He had been putting on shows in Zhytomyr for about five years, mostly foreign acts. "People don't want to see Ukrainian bands, they think they can't be any good. Phooey, who you will play with tomorrow, they are interesting noise rock. Most other Ukrainian bands are just trying to imitate European or American bands." Like Artem, he got a lot of Italian bands. He wasn't sure exactly why. And Belarusians: "They are not like Ukrainians—they are serious about the ideals. Belarusian and

Ukrainian punks have the same ideology, but in Belarus they are serious about it. . . . Now European bands are scared to come here. They don't know the war is nowhere near." As Sasha Grinevich had said, "If the shit hits the fan, the Russians are only five hours from [Kyiv], but for now . . ."

"We can't give Russia those regions," Yura said. "They will just come for more regions. They will want Kyiv.[7] But there won't be a second Maidan. The same people are in government as before, and the war is good for them, because they can go on stealing" while the country is distracted by the war. The fever, he agreed, broke with the flight of Yanukovych. "Maybe every ten years we will have a revolution."

Zhytomyr had a good punk scene, Yura said. Probably the best in Ukraine after Kyiv and Odessa. He had a band himself. "We are playing screamo."

What do you play?

A slight grin. "I am screaming."

We joined some friends at a restaurant for pizza. I tried to shake hands around the table. The sullen girl who was lending me her guitar wouldn't make eye contact. I moved on to her neighbor, a sly hippie.

"I have no name," he joked. "Do you smoke weed?"

I don't, I said.

He disapproved. "It opens the window. It is . . . flowers. Alcohol is poison."

You have your poison, I have mine, I said. Where do you get your weed?

---

7. The party line for influential ideologists of Russian nationalism is the reestablishment of Russian imperial borders, including the Baltic states, most of Ukraine, and parts of Central Asia.

"It is growing everywhere. I saw a patch of wild marijuana, twenty meters by ten meters, right in central Kyiv! I smoked ten meters from a cop, and he didn't do anything." He luxuriated in the memory. "How are you getting back to Kyiv?"

I told him there was a bus—maybe tonight, since the show is early.

He frowned again. "You should hitchhike. Hitchhiking makes you feel more alive!"

Despite my detour through Kyiv and the early showtime, we had some time to kill; along with some of the other members of Yura's band, we went on a walk. Zhytomyr is one of the oldest cities in Ukraine, dating to 884 in the Kievan Rus' period, but, Yura said, it "was destroyed in the war, so now it looks like any Soviet city." (It was also, briefly, the capital of a post–World War I independent Ukraine.) Like any self-respecting Soviet city, they had, until six months ago, "one of the biggest Lenins, bigger than Kyiv. It took them two hours to pull it down, with chains and a car." The empty plinth was now spray-painted "Heroes!" and, like Bila Tserkva's, held a banner with images of the Heavenly Hundred. The side of one office building was covered with a Ukrainian flag: "The biggest in the world," Yura claimed, substituting the new superlative for the old. "It is now in the Guinness book."

What is Zhytomyr known for? I asked.

A rocket scientist, he said. And socks. "You go around the country, and people say, 'Where are you from?' Zhytomyr. 'Oh, Zhytomyr socks!'" And a serial killer, "a maniac who killed fifty-three people" beginning in 1989. He gained the nickname "The Beast of Ukraine," and had died recently in the local prison. Yura had brought an Italian band over recently, and their first question was "Where's the maniac?"

Across from the venue was a lovely park with a huge stone commemorating the founding of the city. Tanned, half-feral drunks slumped on plaza benches. One washed his face in a sprinkler. Another swung, impassive like a metronome, in an otherwise empty playground. A group of tattooed kids sprawled on the grass, backpacks thrown on their scattered bikes. "Those are the anarchists of Zhytomyr and Kyiv," Yura said. "They held a lecture today on Makhno," the Ukrainian anarchist. "They don't do any direct action, just talking about their ideas."

We climbed a hill toward a weather-beaten column, a World War II memorial on the high ground overlooking a wooded canyon and a dam. Plastic beer bottles littered the overgrown stone tiles of the plaza. We opened our own and passed them around.

"It is a joke around here," said Yura, "any time there is a pause in the conversation, a cop is born."

One of the young men said the Nazis had called this river canyon "Ukrainian Switzerland."

He pointed. "Over there, that rock? That is the head of Chotsky." In local legend, a Cossack named Chotsky, galloping away from his enemies, came to the edge of the cliff and dove off rather than surrender. His horse kicked the rock on the way down and formed the profile.

"I'm having a feeling of déjà vu," I told them. I had done virtually this same thing in Krasnoyarsk, in Siberia, two years before, hiking to the dam and drinking beer with my hosts.

Yura laughed. "I think it is common," he said, "drinking by the dam and the monument." In the typical post-Soviet city, what else are you going to do?

I sang my songs in a neon-lit basement bar, under the gaze of pictures of David Bowie, Lou Reed, and David Lynch and in front of a pair of disembodied plaster hands clutching an American flag. Some of the crowd knew my song "This Is Not a Pipe" and sang along, filmed by a cameraman from a local TV station. In the rest of the country, violence was spreading: the house of the mayor of L'viv was hit by a rocket-propelled grenade, and the mayor of Kremenchuk, downriver from Kyiv, was shot dead. I caught the bus back to the capital, the sun still up, at the stop where the tank rested atop a stone pedestal.

We had all day to wander sweltering central Kyiv before my last show that night. Descending Andriyivsky Uzviz, the cobblestoned souvenir-stall district, we heard a crowd chanting. A revival, perhaps, of the dormant protest? A demonstration of Ukrainian patriotism in the face of foreign incursion?

No, it was a live taping of *MasterChef*, a television cooking contest. Behind barricades and a temporary stage holding a dozen or more full stove setups, an assistant producer urged a group of tired-looking chefs to shout into a camera: "MasterChef! MasterChef!"

We reached the bottom of the hill, approaching the student district. A loose stream of international flags processed toward a statue of a man on horseback, a Cossack named Hetman Petro Sahaidachny. I asked Maria what she knew about him.

"I guess he won some battles. Probably lost eventually, like all those guys."

The flags, we learned, belonged to expats—Europeans, yes, but also Indians, Sri Lankans, and Brazilians—marching "against terrorists." The small crowd was doubled by a swarm of scruffy cameramen and thin, pretty TV reporters, pressing the marchers for quotes. Someone struck up a set of bagpipes. A table of Sunday drunks heckled them: "Slava Ukraina!"

None of the cab drivers knew the address of that night's venue—because, it turned out, it wasn't a venue so much as a graffitied warren of self-storage units nestled in the hills. I trudged up the dirt road, past a napping stray dog, into the abandoned-looking alleys of locked gates. Up one alley, I found a band practicing; up another, an open fire and a makeshift plywood bar. In one unit a silver BMW sat on blocks next to a trash pile that crept toward the neighboring unit like a man-made landslide. The Kyiv punk scene was beginning to gather: tattooed young men in shorts and band shirts, canvas shoes and no socks, sat on stoops and drank beer; hip young women in nice dresses sipped wine (as usual, the women were dressed way up and the men ostentatiously down). Two shirtless older men, sarcastic and amused, washed the roof of their storage unit, lugging buckets and gas cans of water up a homemade wooden ladder; after pouring, they swept the excess water off the ledge with a straw broom. They were re-cementing the roof. Once it was clean, they started the mixer turning, poured water in its rotating mouth, and began carrying the cement up bucket by bucket, trowel by trowel, and spread it over the sheet metal and tarpaper roof while the young people milled around, drinking and smoking. A lone black dog roamed and lurked ingratiatingly. On the cliff on the other side of the valley sat the concrete hulk of an administrative building; behind a latched gate, another shirtless man in navy sweatpants scythed at weeds with the dull edge of a shovel.

The center of the scene was a steamy and nondescript storage space with a PA at one end. A couple of people from last night's show were already here, one with his young son, who rocked back and forth on a derelict office chair while one of the opening bands set up. Sasha bantered with the muscular soundman. "We were remembering the old days," he told me, "when people would come two hours early to shows and get drunk. That was before the Internet age." Now people are just off on Facebook and the Russian social network VKontakte? "It is more fun, I guess."

Sasha put a record on the PA—one of my old bands, World/Inferno Friendship Society, though a record from after I'd left. The soundman smoked a bowl with his girlfriend, a Louise Brooks manqué with oversize black-rimmed glasses, like a Berlin gallery intern. The owner of the space pulled up part of the floor and disappeared into a crawlspace beneath it. The venue had been open since February and had hosted just a few shows, including the "DIYstvo" festival, which had been organized like a street fair: bands in one unit, bar in the next, workshops down the street. We could have done the show at a bar, Sasha said—he had had Eugene Hutz's downtown Gogol BARdello in mind. "But at a club, you have to deal with the manager, they want to have a say [in] who are the opening bands. . . . Here, maybe I pay a little more—to rent the sp and the backline is maybe two-thirds of the budget— at least I know them, and I know this is how they make a liv- ing, and my friends who don't have any money can . Most bars around here don't want to book any show say it's punk rock. If you say it is a garage show, th 'Cool.' Or post-rock. Or even post-punk, they are into it. Anything 'post-' is cool."

So you do punk in a garage, split the difference.

"Ha, ha, yeah! When I came here on the tram, I saw an ad that you can rent out a tram car for weddings or parties. I think we should do an acoustic show there."

When the World/Inferno song ended, one of the older men fixing the roof next door asked Sasha, "Who is this band? Can you write down the name for me?"

We walked to the supermarket to pick up bread, cheese, warm beer, and wine for the bands. I tried to order a mushroom salad at the deli counter, but Sasha nudged me aside. He had a muttered exchange with the woman behind the cooler and shook his head. "Don't get these salads. These are things that are old and they can't sell."

On the way back, we ran into two women from Ai Laika, one of the opening acts: Nastia, thin, dark, in a cutoff Blink-182 shirt, wearing round black sunglasses and conveying a distant air; Lera, friendlier, in sandals and a yellow fanny pack, wearing anchor earrings. They would play first, followed by Phooey, the band Yura had recommended the night before.

"Phooey is the best Ukrainian band," Lera agreed.

"We are probably second-best," her bandmate added drily.

"Maloi is great too."

I played with them last time, I said.

"They are even better now." ("All of those guys are in like six or seven other bands," Yura had said of Maloi. "It makes them better, Odesak.")

Odesa, all the Ukrainian girls agree, had the best punk and hardcore scene in Ukraine. A festival had just happened there. "Also the kids

are younger. Here we have a good scene, but there are no younger
bands."

Why?

"Maybe they see they can't make a living at it."

Back at the venue, a folding table had appeared, strewn with a
few demo cassettes, zines, and a handful of vinyl for sale: Fucked
Up, Government Issue, a Hot Water Music seven-inch. I asked
Sasha what were appropriate prices for my merchandise.

"I don't know," he said. "Let me ask around. I haven't done
a show since the currency changed." He meant the post-crisis
inflation that devalued the hryvnia from about eight to eleven
against the U.S. dollar (the value would halve again by the end
of the year).

I went outside to do some people watching and greeted Constantine, whom I'd met at my last Kyiv show. He was earnest,
with a hardcore crew cut. He'd been in a band on the American
hardcore label React, and had recently been touring in Belarus.
"I really like Minsk—it is like Kyiv but easier. I don't like Moscow or Saint Petersburg because everyone is moving really fast
and pushing." He mimed throwing elbows.

Ai Laika began their set—upbeat, melodic pop punk, including a cover of Ace of Base's "All That She Wants." I asked
Constantine what he thought of current Ukrainian bands. He
mentioned Dakh Daughters and DakhaBrakha, a pair of female-
fronted acts centered around the Dakh Theatre in Kyiv, whose
Dresden Dolls–esque "freak cabaret" had made them viral video
sensations. DakhaBrakha "are doing really cool things. They did
a soundtrack for" Земля, a classic Ukrainian silent film. "I took
my dad because he liked this film, and he said, 'Get me all this
band's records.'"

His mother worked at the chocolate company Roshen, the centerpiece of the business empire of the new president.[8] "He is not really an oligarch like Akhmetov, who made all his billions at once in the nineties. [Poroshenko] made it as a businessman over twenty years." He also thought Poroshenko was a relatively straight dealer in a way uncommon, to say the least, at the highest level of Ukrainian business. Most companies, he said, paid their employees a different wage in cash than on paper, a tax-avoidance scheme. Roshen, at least in his mother's experience, paid aboveboard wages. "I voted for Poroshenko because I didn't want a [runoff]. We didn't have time as a country for more months and more tax money for more elections."

His mother had her own political awakening recently. A Russian from the Caucasus, she went to Crimea on vacation. "She saw all the houses, the architecture was Tatar, but there were no Tatars." (Under heavy pressure, thousands of Crimean Tatars have left the peninsula to become refugees in Ukraine.) "Before that she was a Russian nationalist; then she thought, this is not right."

Phooey set up. They were a shaggy trio with a 1990s-revival sensibility. The singer wore thick glasses and a Sonic Youth

---

8. Headline shorthand often referred to Poroshenko as a "chocolate king" or "the Willy Wonka of Ukraine," though his business portfolio was expansive: The Economist's satellite magazine Ukrainian Week listed "assets in the food-processing industry and agriculture (confectionery, sugar refineries, large agricultural enterprises, a starch plant, milk processing plants and their suppliers), machine building (the Bohdan corporation, the Leninska Kuznia shipbuilding plant and plants manufacturing car batteries and other spare parts), telecommunications, trucking business, a small bank, an insurance company, commercial real estate, a glass factory, resort centres and mass media outlets (the 5th Channel and a number of regional TV and radio companies in L'viv and Odessa oblasts)."

T-shirt, and they did sound like Sonic Youth, or Dinosaur Jr., or a noisier Smashing Pumpkins. I asked Constantine about the Kyiv punk scene's involvement in the Maidan protests.

"I am glad the punks got involved," he said. One Russian-language news site after another was parroting or succumbing under pressure to the Kremlin party line that the Maidan protesters and the new Ukrainian government were perpetrators of a neo-Nazi coup. "I woke up one morning, and overnight the first website I checked every day had been replaced with 'Crimea has always been Russian territory.'"

The Russian propaganda was confusing to some European punks and activists habituated to responding to calls for anti-fascist action. "Some Italian hardcore leftists wanted to do a tour of Novorossiya"—the separatist name for the southeastern regions—"because they thought it was all anarchists and communists" fomenting antifascist revolution. "Then they got there, and posted one photo on Facebook and nothing more, when they saw the crazy people that were there. . . . Many of the people I work with, their parents are in the east, and I hear them on the phone: 'We have a checkpoint fifty meters from the house. We haven't left the apartment in two weeks.'"

Sure, he said, there are right-wing elements in Ukraine. "There are two different kinds of right-wing: imperialists and anti-imperialists. All Ukrainians are anti-imperialists. There are even Russian nationalists who hate Putin, because all their tax money goes to the Caucasus," a region outside the ethnic Russian heartland. The lack of a distinction reflected a dangerously vague taxonomy both in the propaganda and the reporting surrounding the conflict, which blurred the differences on both the Russian and Ukrainian sides between legitimate fascists, Soviet imperial revanchists, ethnic purists, pan-Slavic utopianists, Trypillian neo-pagan primordialists, and simple patriots, lumping them all under the multiform adjective "nationalist."

"I don't see why anyone would care," said Vlad from Maloi. He wore a Hot Water Music T-shirt, rolled camouflage shorts, a backward baseball cap, and sockless slip-on shoes. "It's not like the poor rising up against the rich. It's just geopolitics." He had other priorities and asked if I could recommend a mixing engineer. "We have a new album recorded, and I want to get someone good to mix it. I was thinking to ask the guy from the Posies."

What do you want it to sound like? I asked.

"Kind of like the Posies."

Phooey finished their set, and I dropped my tuner and cables on the floor in front of the center mic. The singer, Nikita, approached me after packing up his guitar. He had, it seemed, an agenda and a message he wanted me to receive. "Do you need help setting up?" he asked. "Sorry, maybe that sounds condescending."

No, I said, my setup is pretty simple.

"No, to play acoustic is simple," he said. "They asked me about putting on your show last night in Zhytomyr, but you needed too many mics. I don't know anyone with that many mics, so I declined."

I use one vocal mic and lines for one, two, or three instruments.

"I think maybe there weren't too many people?" he continued, with a kind of deadpan smirk.

Actually, I said, there were a couple dozen. Not bad for me.

"Uh-huh, yes, shows are not as good there these days."

If that night was any indication, shows actually were quite

good in Kyiv these days. After the show, Nikita had some more opinions. "It was really great the way you combined humor with sadness and anger. I usually go outside. I am like an old person. I only like my own music. Maybe that sounds egotistical."

I had to agree, though only to myself—maybe it did.

"So, you're going to come have a drink?" Sasha asked after we'd cleaned up. Maria and Lesia were already in bed, so I said yes. "Then drop your accordion," he said, "and let's drink."

"This is a classic old Soviet bar," he said after a short walk. "Just beer and dried fish." It was a utilitarian, brightly lit room, a cross between a bodega and sports bar. It was prosaically named Podil, after the neighborhood (not that you would know from any signage). The proprietor was round and balding, with spectacles low on his nose. His shirt was unbuttoned and his chest hair was gray.

"No vodka, and there never will be!" advertised signs Sharpied on cardboard and posted throughout. An old propaganda poster showed a handsome man rejecting a shot of vodka: "Nyet!" While it looked like the owner had furnished and decorated the bar entirely with promotional items and branded miscellany from multinational beer companies, the handful of taps all poured local brews. TV screens on every wall played soccer highlights.

The real innovation—practically a sellout, Sasha's friends agreed—is that the bar had started selling chips.

"These chips, they are Soviet invention," said one, a long-haired hesher with a flat-brimmed Chicago Bears cap. "You can set them on fire. I have the right equipment." He demonstrated with a lighter. The paper-thin wafer indeed burned like a taper.

Sasha's cell phone sprang to life: Queen's "Flash." I raised my eyebrows at the melodramatic riff.

He shrugged, picking up the phone. "It's just . . . epic!"

The hesher had a tattoo of a boom box on his right bicep. "I heard you played with Leftover Crack," he said, referring to the infamous ska-punk band. I had, and told him a story about their singer, Stza (né Scott Sturgeon): The last time I'd seen him was at a punk festival in Blackpool, England, where he was supposed to play with his new touring band, the Star Fucking Hipsters. It was the first day of their UK tour, but the drummer hadn't got a visa and the guitarist had a court date in the States. When I ran into Sturgeon in the hallway, I hadn't seen him in years, but he picked up as if we'd been interrupted in the middle of a conversation.

"Yeah, man, our driver is gonna play drums," he said in his high-pitched rasp, like an ingratiating parrot. "Maybe you could do the lead guitar parts on your accordion? You remember those songs, right?"

The two songs I'd recorded on piano years before and never played again? Sure . . .

"Ah, don't worry about it. We just need to fill forty minutes to get our guarantee. So we'll play, like, five songs, and make 'em all like ten minutes long. Maybe you can play one of your songs!"

I don't know if your fans of cop-killing crust punk are going to be interested in my neo-cabaret stylings, I told him.

"Well, anyway, if we need to fill more time I'll just pick a fight with the crowd." All of these things came to pass, and they got paid in full.

"Some people, they just have trouble in their veins," the hesher said. "We have this friend, from Artemivsk in Donetsk Oblast— he's living in Moscow now." He asks one of the others to translate. "He is this thrash-metal guy," he explained. At one show "they formed a 'corridor of death,' the neo-Nazis and the Russian special ops with their batons, and he called the special ops faggots. They dragged him to their van, and said, 'Why did you say that? We will put this ammunition in your pocket, and take you down to the station.' And he said—there is this thrash band in Russia, they are called Corrosion of Metal, they are crazy, they have ugly naked girls on stage, and will fuck them; everybody knows their fans are crazy—he said, 'I am Corrosion of Metal fan.' And they said, 'Get the fuck out of here.'"[9]

He sensed that that the thrust of the story was perhaps deteriorating in translation. "I don't know," he said. "I have lots of stories, but you won't understand."

A man approached our outdoor table, recited a stanza of poetry, and got a round of applause for his troubles. Another tried to sell us an electric cigarette lighter: "It's Russian," he offered.

The abuse was instant and general.

"OK, OK," he said, backing away. "Slava Ukraina."

"I would have overthrown the crass fuckers too," as I had thought while at the tsarist vacation retreat Peterhof, outside Saint Petersburg. In the wake of Yanukovych's flight to Russia, his

---

9. Their thrash-metal friend, in addition to demonstrating that he was a crazy motherfucker, might have been signaling a common interest to the neo-Nazis. Corrosia Metalla, aka Corrosion of Metal, was active in the late 1980s. In a familiar story, the band's Wikipedia entry states, "In [sic] '90s, [singer] Pauk ("Spider") eventually fired all the original line-up and gradually shifted to right-wing ultranationalist lyrics. . . . The album 1.966 even featured a stylized version of a swastika on the cover and the song 'White Power.' During the promotional tour for Computer Hitler album, Corrosia even employed a Hitler impersonator for their live shows. Pauk indicated his interest in politics when [he] nominated himself for mayor of Moscow in 1993, and for mayor of Khimki in 2012."

compound, a palatial 350-acre private park on the banks of the Dnipro north of Kyiv called Mezhyhirya, was nationalized and opened to the public. Shuttle buses labeled "Mezhyhirya: Residence of the Citizen of Russia Yanukovych" left from Maidan.

"I don't need to see that shit," Sasha had said the night before, when I told him that Maria, Lesia, and I were going to visit Mezhyhirya. But I did: the shameless exploitation of a country for the benefit of a ruling cadre, it bears remembering, isn't a relic of a picturesque history.

The approach to the estate was through a suburb of McMansions and imported cars, and the road dead-ended in a lacquered gate. Yanukovych's neighbors constitute the cream—if that's not too positive a word—of the political and financial class. If their neighborhood, once an exclusive community of baronial privilege and access, had been transformed by a clutch of bike rentals and microwaved blintz, shashlik, and beer stalls, it was hard to feel sorry for them. Once they lived by the lion; now they lived by a zoo. Handmade plywood signs painted with the flag and slogans of national unity were tied to the fences around their properties. A few drunks in camouflage uniforms ate ice cream at a pop-up café, and two old vendor ladies with some ancient grudge abused each other: "Fuck your mother!" "My mother already met her truth, fuck *your* mother!"

Like Peterhof, Mezhyhirya was a wide, landscaped estate (Yanukovych had the tops of the trees shaved down to improve his river view) with a castle at its height, accented by faux Grecian ruins and an oversize statue of a horse. A buffet of fountains led down to the water. If you ignored the admittedly tacky monstrosities like the fake-gold-plated toilet brushes and pirate-galleon-*cum*-banquet-hall, most of the estate constituted a rather nice park of the sort that the Ukrainian public, who likely would have chosen to spend the millions used to create it on other priorities, might never otherwise enjoy.

But the anonymous protester who took a dump in the sentry box by the yacht dock expressed an efficient and eloquent rebuttal. The twenty-foot corrugated metal fences topped with electrified wire and security cameras (justifying the press references to Mezhyhirya as a "compound") reinforced that this was a pleasure dome for the head of a mafia state fearful of his security. The separate "Putin Building" underscored the identity of the real boss of bosses.

At the private petting zoo for exotic animals at the southern end, two baby ostriches (one month and two weeks old, respectively) roamed the sidewalk nipping at clover. A pair of reindeer languished in the dust and sun. There was an in-house dairy, a pig farm, and a greenhouse that was selling flowers, tomatoes, honey, and plants to raise money for upkeep. Hopefully it'll just be a short-term program, said the lady who sold us a small cactus. We dubbed it the Yanu-kaktus.

It was a sweltering summer day. We ran, yelping, through the lawn sprinklers, then took a tour of the two main residential buildings: the palatial wooden "hunting lodge" and, connected by an underground passage, the "health spa." The latter contained a virtually unused gym and boxing ring and room after room of massage chairs and tanning booths, indoor and outdoor tennis courts, alligator-skin couches, a salt-encrusted sauna, a life-sized stuffed lion.

Our guide was a Maidan protester from L'viv who had come to Kyiv in November. He and two others had appointed themselves in charge of maintaining the Mezhyhirya residence complex. He slept in the house, he said, but didn't use any of the facilities. He was meticulous about turning the lights off as we left each room. The government had retained the staff, and he was trying to get the workers to say what life had been like under the old president, but they were "still too scared to talk." He wore a traditional Hutsul vest and sandals and a red-and-black nationalist flag draped over his shoulders like a cape. "Get your damn feet off the bed!" he scolded one young man who had gotten too comfortable in the former president's bedroom. There was a framed $100 bill on the nightstand. The closets were empty—most of the clothes had been taken by the curious Ukrainians who flooded Mezhyhirya in the days after Yanukovych's flight. "I have a couple pairs of monogrammed underwear," said the guide. The hardwood-covered toilets had been helpfully accessorized with the Yanukovych-face toilet paper, which was captioned "I Feel Each One."

It was a sense-deadening menu of excess, in which only the most egregious ironies stood out: The scale model of the castle, in a gazebo-sized cage for hamsters. The infamous gold loaf of bread. In the foyer, the white limited edition "Imagine" Series Steinway, promoted as "like the songs of John Lennon . . . the perfect harmonization of music with creativity to achieve an end result that is much greater than the sum of its parts . . . modeled after the white Steinway grand piano John Lennon presented to Yoko Ono on her birthday in 1971," and decorated with a Lennon sketch. Speakers on the balcony blasted a Ukrainian hip-hop song about having a president who wasn't a crook; the literary icons Taras Shevchenko and Lesya Ukrainka got shout-outs in the breakdown, then a children's choir took over for the hook.

In the Mezhyhirya spa's guestbook are entries anonymously

labeled "Neighbor 1" and "Neighbor 2." One of them, the care-
takers suspected, was the former opposition politician and current prime minister Yatsenyuk, who lives five hundred meters
away. The battle cry of the rump Maidan, and the young activists who claimed that the Maidan had achieved none of its aims,
is "*Lustratsiya*"—lustration, or the removal of anyone associated
with the old regime from the new government. A spray-painted
banner to that effect hung from a statue on the Maidan when I
went to walk around the square one more time on our last day
in Ukraine.

Fight corruption, I thought, but be mindful of the American
experience with the lustration of Ba'athists in Iraq: it encour-
ages petty vengeance and creates a new class of disaffected un-
employables in opposition to the new government out of a caste
who, while perhaps dangerous in their banal way as agents of
intransigent corruption, are just as likely to be apolitical, ass-
covering bureaucrats. The process of nation-building is no less
messy and heterogeneous than the political life of the nations
built. The idea of a politically uniform, self-sacrificing polity of
parallel ideals is a communist one—the liberal-capitalist-social-
democratic idea requires jostling room for the pacifist left, the
militarist right, the pragmatist center, and the 99 percent who
just want to get on with their lives without unnecessary hassle
because everyday life is hard enough. The Ukrainians now had a
politically awakened populace aware of its strength. Few, if any,
nations have had two successful liberal revolutions in a decade.
That distinction also contains a criticism: they're getting good
at the revolutions, but not the follow-through—you don't need
a second revolution if the first one worked. And Ukrainian history (including its statuary) is on a battle footing, full of doomed

or pyrrhic characters (exemplified in the anthem's "Ukraine is not dead yet"). Many of the Ukrainian national heroes are men on horseback with a club, or up in the hills shooting all comers: valuable icons for revolution, but perhaps unhelpful in encouraging a stable, relaxed democracy.

But Ukrainians seem to be accepting pragmatism. The 2004 Orange Revolution elected the charismatic, populist savior-candidate Viktor Yushchenko, who failed to implement reforms. In 2014 the people elected Poroshenko, basically their Mitt Romney, with all the enthusiasm Americans mustered for the original article: "He's probably not a crook, and the alternatives are the laughable or the implausible." Now the new civic sensibility—as every good politician knows, war has its drawbacks, but there's nothing like it for uniting a country—stands in contrast to that of the cynical, stagnant Russians.

Unlike the nouveau bourgeois Russian protests of 2011–12, the Maidan movement engaged people across class lines. Begun by the usual Occupy demographic of college students and young hipsters, it spread to include the unemployed working class, yet brought to power a billionaire president. As our friend Larissa in Kyiv said, "It's like the war of independence that [Ukraine] never got to have. Because independence in 1991 came so easily, the country never had to make a positive decision, yes, we want to be independent. And now, people have to decide, do we really want to live in a different way?"

To zoom in on one minuscule demographic tranche, it pointed toward a role for the college-age punks and DIY activists in creating the future of Ukraine as a society in reform. Punk is largely a bourgeois phenomenon (some base-level security is a prerequisite for rebellion based on ideals) mostly staffed by students or people with mid-level creative-industry jobs, with decent English and Internet access. And there tend to be three kinds of punk politics—the "no borders, no war" pacifists, the revolution-porn radicals, and the generic center-left liberals—none of whom, for the most part, will be personally involved in the fighting, and all of whom want or assume, like most middle-class kids, the privileges of Western liberal society. But those sorts of assumptions have a kind of power too, in that they breed a powerful resentment when unfulfilled. And punk and DIY on the American model constitute training wheels for the kind of self-organizing civil society pundits long for in developing countries, taking the unused semi-public space the former communist world is lousy with and commandeering it for the common good. Or if not good, at least enjoyment. Or if not enjoyment, at least the feeling of doing something in common, with the idea that it might push the ball an inch toward a better society.

As an American and as a musician, I found something affirming in the opportunity to play for people for whom music and politics were meaningful in a concrete way, for whom the act of congregating and the investment of feeling in performing music were all serious business. It is a relief and an antidote to the prevailing sense in the West of the inherent valuelessness and disposability of both music and the people who make it. In her writing, Maria calls this "the privilege of political ambivalence"— in a context of economic stability and cultural freedom, people who make and consume art have the freedom to be apolitical. Before that zone of freedom is established, though, the mere act of gathering, independently, underground, in a condition of joy and fellow feeling, is inescapably a political act in itself.

There was a small noon rally in front of the now-empty festival stage in central Kyiv from which, at the height of the protests, the anthem was sung hourly. A "commander" in a beret and aviators took the wireless microphone and sang, tunelessly, a patriotic song to a mismatched and motley line of three dozen "soldiers" (and a handful of patriotic tourists) standing at semi-attention in camouflage, Hawaiian shorts, striped tank tops. The donation boxes mostly stood empty. A bearded young man wandered over to the upright piano, which was painted the flag's blue-and-yellow with an EU circle of stars, and picked out a tune. The cobblestones, ripped from the streets and sidewalks that winter for use as projectiles, were stacked neatly, and some workers had begun to replace them. Toward the center of the square, some cobblestones had been painted—yellow and blue, of course—and set out on the ground to spell out messages for some theoretical airborne viewer: "Patriotic Idea Maidan," "Stop Propaganda: Here Is Not Fascism!" and, simply, "Ukraine." Ten days after we left, the square was finally cleared by government forces.

I walked up Institutka, past the moldering barricades, stacks of rusting homemade shields, and flower-draped memorials to protesters shot by government snipers. At the top of the hill, a black-on-yellow mock street sign sat propped against a wall of tires. "Changing the country," it read. "We apologize for the inconvenience."

We boarded a plane to Istanbul that night, and woke at dawn to the contrapuntal tangle of the call to prayer, the muezzins like a hundred hands knitting from the same yarn. It was five years since I'd decided to stake my supper on songs. I took on the troubadour life as a single man in a windowless urban closet

the size of the loft bed I slept in. I wrote these words from the
second floor of my house in a village, a married man with a car
and a young daughter. I looked at my hands and at the instruments hanging on the wall. The thought of putting them on my
back again struck no spark: the restless impulse had once again
moved in me, now from the stage to the page. I had lived by the
maxim that I could stay one step ahead of myself but found that
the old itch would still be waiting for me when I finally arrived
at a home. As Socrates said to the man who complained that
travel had not improved him: "Not surprising. You took yourself
with you."

Bibliography

Ames, Mark, and Matt Taibbi. *The Exile: Sex, Drugs, and Libel in the New Russia*. New York: Grove Press, 2000.

Ames, Mark. "Free Edward Limonov." *The Exile*, March 7, 2001. http://exiledonline.com/old-exile/114/babylon.php.

Ames, Mark. "Who's Afraid of Edward Limonov?" *Freezerbox*, March 15, 2002. http://www.freezerbox.com/archive/article.php?id=189.

Anonymous. "Politician Eduard Limonov. Nationalist Calls for Ban on Foreign Merchandise." Gnostic Liberation Front. http://www.gnosticliberationfront.com/Russian%20National%20Bolshevists.htm.

Applebaum, Anne. *Gulag: A History*. New York: Anchor Books, 2003.

BBC News. "Russian Rock Star Makarevich Attacked for Ukraine Songs." August 19, 2014. http://www.bbc.com/news/world-europe-28855690.

Bennetts, Marc. "Eduard Limonov Interview: Political Rebel and Vladimir Putin's Worst Nightmare." *The Observer*, December 11, 2010. http://www.guardian.co.uk/world/2010/dec/12/eduard-limonov-interview-putin-nightmare.

Bennetts, Marc. "Deeper Than Oil: Yanka—The Tale of a Siberian Punk." *Ria Novosti*, August 11, 2010. http://en.rian.ru/columnists/20101108/161246237.html.

Bey, Hakim. *T.A.Z.: The Temporary Autonomous Zone, Ontological Anarchy, Poetic Terrorism*. New York: Autonomedia, 1985.

Brennan, Christopher. "Moscow Grants Rare Approval to Freedom-of-Assembly protest." *Moscow Times*, May 21, 2014. http://www.themoscowtimes.com/news/article/moscow-grants-rare-approval-to-freedom-of-assembly-protest/500637.html.

Boyer, Dominic, and Alexei Yurchak. "American Stiob: Or, What Late-Socialist Aesthetics Reveal About Contemporary Political Culture in The West." *Cultural Anthropology* 25, no. 2 (2012): 179–221.

Branigan, Tania. "Mongolian Neo-Nazis: Anti-Chinese Sentiment Fuels Rise of Ultra-nationalism." *The Guardian*, August 2, 2010.

Carrère, Emmanuel. *Limonov.* Translated by John Lambert. New York: Farrar, Straus and Giroux, 2014.

Chekhov, Anton. *A Journey to the End of the Russian Empire.* Translated by Rosamund Bartlett and Anthony Phillips. New York: Penguin Books, 2007. Selection from *A Life in Letters*. New York: Penguin Books, 2004.

Chekhov, Anton. *Plays.* Translated by Peter Carson. New York: Penguin Books, 2003.

Curtis, Adam. "The Years of Stagnation and the Poodles of Power." *Medium and the Message* (BBC blog), January 18, 2012. http://www.bbc.co.uk/blogs/adamcurtis/posts/the_years_of_stagnation_and_th.

Davison, Phil. "Yegor Letov: 'Father of Russian Punk.'" *The Independent*, February 26, 2008. http://www.independent.co.uk/news/obituaries/yegor-letov-father-of-russian-punk-787304.html.

Daughtry, J. Martin (2006). "Magnitizdat as Cultural Practice." Prepared for the conference "Samizdat and Underground Culture in Soviet Bloc Countries," University of Pennsylvania, April 6–7, 2006.

Davies, Norman. *Vanished Kingdoms: The Rise and Fall of States and Nations.* New York: Viking, 2011.

de Custine, the Marquis. *Empire of the Czar: A Journey Through Eternal Russia.* Translated by anonymous. With a foreword by Daniel Boorstein and an introduction by George Kennan. New York: Anchor Books, 1989.

de Tocqueville, Alexis. *Democracy in America.* Edited by J.P. Mayer and translated by George Lawrence. New York: HarperPerennial, 2006.

Dobson, William J. *The Dictator's Learning Curve: Inside the Global Battle For Democracy.* New York: Doubleday, 2012.

Dostoyevsky, Fyodor. *Crime and Punishment*, 3d ed. Translated by Jessie Coulson. New York: W.W. Norton & Company, 1989.

———. *The House of the Dead*. Translated by Constance Garnett. Mineola, NY: Dover, 2004.

Dunn, Kevin. "Never Mind the Bollocks: The Punk Rock Politics of Global Communication." *Review of International Studies* 34 (2008): 193–210.

The Economist. "The Rich, the Poor, and Bulgaria." December 16, 2010.

Eberstadt, Nicholas. "Drunken Nation: Russia's Depopulation Bomb." *World Affairs Journal*, Spring 2009.

Eremenko, Alexey. "Ukrainian Rebels Channel U.S. Confederates." *Moscow Times*, June 9, 2014. http://www.themoscowtimes.com/news/article/ukrainian-rebels-channel-us-confederates/501789.html.

Ferguson, Niall. "Start The Week" podcast. BBC; June 11, 2012.

Frazier, Ian. *Travels in Siberia*. New York: Picador, 2010.

Gabowitsch, Mischa. "Fascism as Stiob." *Kultura*, December 4, 2009.

Gessen, Keith. "Monumental Foolishness." *Slate*, February 20, 2003. http://www.slate.com/articles/arts/culturebox/2003/02/monumental_foolishness.single.html.

Gibbon, Edward. *The History of the Decline and Fall of the Roman Empire*. Edited by David Womersley. New York: Penguin, 1994.

Glenny, Misha. *The Balkans: Nationalism, War, and the Great Powers, 1804–1999*. New York: Penguin, 2001.

Gogol, Nikolai. *Dead Souls*. Translated by Andrew R. McAndrew. New York: Signet Classic, 1961.

Gomzikova, Svetlana. "Города и призраки: Иваново вместе с Венецией и Детройтом попал в «черный список»." Свободная Пресса, January 13, 2014. http://svpressa.ru/society/article/80458/.

Grow, Kory. "Cannabis and 'The Sound of Music': What Laibach Learned in North Korea." *Rolling Stone*, August 25, 2015.

Hebdige, Dick. *Subculture: The Meaning of Style*. New York: Routledge, 1979.

Herodotus. *The Histories*. Translated by Aubrey de Selincourt. New York: Penguin, 2003.

Hoffman, Eva. *Exit into History: A Journey Through The New Eastern Europe*. New York: Penguin, 1993.

Houellebecq, Michel, and Bernard-Henri Lévy. *Public Enemies: Dueling Writers Take On Each Other and the World*. Translated by Frank Wynne and Miriam Frendo. New York: Random House, 2011.

Hotham, Oliver. "Laibach Rocks N. Korea: Scenes from a Historic

Concert." *NK News*, November 24, 2015. http://www.nknews.org
   /2015/09/laibach-rocks-n-korea-scenes-from-a-historic-concert/.
Judah, Tim. "Ukraine: Inside the Deadlock." *New York Review of Books*,
   May 7, 2015.
Kanygin, Pavel. "The Donbass War: Assessing the Aftermath." *Meduza*,
   November 13, 2015. https://meduza.io/en/feature/2015/11/13/the
   -donbass-war-assessing-the-aftermath.
Kaplan, Robert D. *Balkan Ghosts: A Journey Through History*. New York:
   Picador, 2005.
Kasakow, Ewgeniy. "Models of 'Taboo Breaking' in Russian Rock Music:
   The Ambivalence of the 'Politically Incorrect.'" *Kultura*, December 4,
   2009.
Kennan, George. *Tent Life in Siberia*. CreateSpace, 2011.
King, John. *Human Punk*. New York: Vintage, 2001.
Kupfer, Matthew. "Ukraine Crisis Divides Russian Far Right." *Muftah*,
   September 15, 2014. http://muftah.org/ukraine-crisis-divides-russian
   -far-right/.
Limonov, Edward. *Memoirs of a Russian Punk*. Translated by Judson
   Rosengrant. New York: Grove Weidenfeld, 1990.
———. "Punk and National-Bolshevism." *The Exile*, December 11, 2012.
Malcomson, Scott L. *Empire's Edge: Travels in South-Eastern Europe,
   Turkey and Central Asia*. New York: Verso, 1995.
Mandelstam, Osip. *The Voronezh Notebooks: Poems 1935–1937*. Trans-
   lated by Richard and Elizabeth McKane. With an introduction by
   Victor Krivulin. Tarset: Bloodaxe, 1996.
McSmith, Andy. *Fear and the Muse Kept Watch: The Russian
   Masters—from Akhmatova and Pasternak to Shostakovich and
   Eisenstein—Under Stalin*. New York: The New Press, 2015.
Meier, Andrew. "Putin's Pariah." *New York Times Magazine*, March 2,
   2008. http://www.nytimes.com/2008/03/02/magazine/02limonov-t
   .html?pagewanted=all.
Mills, Laura. "Russian Conscripts Tell of Fears of Being Sent to
   Ukraine." Associated Press, February 21, 2015. http://bigstory.ap.org/
   article/269db5083bfe4c57a07701625b943952/russian-conscripts-tell
   -fears-being-sent-ukraine.
de Montaigne, Michel. *The Complete Essays*. Translated by M.A.
   Screech. New York: Penguin, 2003.
Nechepurenko, Ivan. "Public Spats over Ukraine Reflect Lack of Unity

in Russian Opposition." *Moscow Times,* August 21, 2014. http://www
.themoscowtimes.com/news/article/public-spats-over-ukraine-reflect
-lack-of-unity-in-russian-opposition/505640.html.

Oleksiyenko, Oles. "A Heavy Mace for Mr. Poroshenko." *Ukrainian
Week* (international edition); vol. 10, issue 76, July 2014.

Pasternak, Boris. *Doctor Zhivago.* Translated by Bernard Gilbert Guer-
ney. New York: Pantheon, 1958, 1986.

Pelevin, Viktor. *Babylon.* Translated by Andrew Bromfield. London:
Faber and Faber, 2001.

Pilkington, Hilary, Yulia Andreeva, and Elena Omelchenko. "Anti-fa
Youth Groups in Saint Petersburg Russia." *Groups and Environments,*
no. 2 (2010): 127–33.

Polonsky, Rachel. *Molotov's Magic Lantern: Uncovering Russia's Secret
History.* London: Faber and Faber, 2010.

———. "Russia: The Citizen Poet," review of *Living Souls,* by Dmitry
Bykov. *New York Review of Books,* November 8, 2012.

Pomerantsev, Peter. "Putin's Rasputin." *London Review of Books,* October 20, 2011.

Proust, Marcel. *Swann's Way.* Translated by Lydia Davis. New York:
Penguin, 2002.

———. *Remembrance of Things Past.* Translated by C.K. Scott Moncrieff.
New York: Random House, 1934.

Ramzy, Austin. "Hello, Pyongyang: Are. You. Ready. To. Rock." *New
York Times,* August 20, 2015.

Rayfield, Donald. "Osip Mandelstam: An Introduction." In Osip Mandelstam, *Selected Poems.* New York: Penguin, 1988.

Roberts, Julie. "Cultural Learning for the Benefit of All . . . *AEN Journal*
1, no. 2 (November 2006). http://www.aen.org.nz/journal/1/2/roberts
.html.

Saunders, Frances Stonor. *The Cultural Cold War: The CIA and the
World of Arts and Letters.* New York: The New Press, 1999.

Service, Robert. *The Penguin Modern History Of Russia: From Tsarism
to The Twenty-First Century.* New York: Penguin, 2009.

Simone, Alina. *You Must Go and Win.* New York: Faber and Faber,
2011.

Sorokin, Vladimir. *Day of the Oprichnik.* Translated by Jamey Gambrell.
New York: Farrar, Straus and Giroux, 2011.

Stanton, Geoff. "Soviet Punks and Pussy Riots 1980–2012." *From the*

Barrelhouse, August 18, 2012. http://fromthebarrelhouse.wordpress
    .com/2012/08/18/soviet-punks-and-pussy-riots-1980-2012/.
Steiner, Peter. "Introduction: On Samizdat, Tamizdat, Magnitizdat, and
    Other Strange Words That Are Difficult to Pronounce." *Poetics Today*
    29, no. 4 (Winter 2008).
Steinholt, Yngvar. "Punk Is Punk but by No Means Punk: Definition,
    Genre Evasion and the Quest for an Authentic Voice in Contempo-
    rary Russia." *Punk & Post Punk* 1, no. 3 (2012): 267–84.
———. "Siberian Punk Shall Emerge Here: Egor Letov and Grazhdans-
    kaia Oborona." *Popular Music* 31, no. 3 (2012): 401–15.
Taibbi, Matt. "Who Is 'Limonov'? Not Even His Biographer Really
    Knows." NPR Books, October 21, 2014. http://www.npr.org/2014
    /10/21/356988666/who-is-limonov-not-even-his-biographer-really
    -knows.
Theroux, Paul. *Ghost Train to the Eastern Star: On the Tracks of the
    Great Railway Bazaar*. Boston: Houghton Mifflin Harcourt, 2008.
———. *The Great Railway Bazaar: By Train Through Asia*. Boston: Mari-
    ner Books, 1975, 2006.
———. *Riding the Iron Rooster: By Train Through China*. New York: Ivy
    Books, 1988.
———. *The Tao of Travel*. Boston: Mariner Books, 2011.
Tolstoy, Leo. *Anna Karenina*. Translated by George Gibian. New York:
    W.W. Norton, 1995.
Trach, Nataliya. "EuroMaidan Turns into a Shady Place." *Kyiv Post*,
    July 19, 2014. http://www.kyivpost.com/content/kyiv/euromaidan
    -turns-into-a-shady-place-356891.html.
Trepper, Hartmute. "Fascism—With and Without Inverted Commas."
    Kultura, December 4, 2009.
Twain, Mark. *The Innocents Abroad, or, The New Pilgrim's Progress*. New
    York: Signet Classic, 1980.
United Nations. *State of the World's Cities 2012/2013: Prosperity of Cit-
    ies*. New York: UN-HABITAT/Routledge, 2013.
Verini, James. "Lost Exile: The Unlikely Life and Sudden Death of The
    Exile, Russia's Angriest Newspaper." *Vanity Fair*, February 23, 2010.
    http://www.vanityfair.com/culture/features/2010/02/exile-201002.
Wassterstrom, Jeffrey, and Jonathan Campbell. "Punk and Protest in
    China and Russia." *Los Angeles Review of Books*, August 25, 2012.

http://lareviewofbooks.org/interview/punk-and-protest-in-china-and
    -russia.

West, Rebecca. *Black Lamb and Grey Falcon.* New York: Penguin, 1982.

Winder, Simon. *Danubia: A Personal History of Hapsburg Europe.* New
    York: Farrar, Straus and Giroux, 2013.

Yurchak, Alexei. *Everything Was Forever, Until It Was No More: The Last
    Soviet Generation.* Princeton, NJ: Princeton University Press, 2006.

Žižek, Slavoj. "Why Are Laibach and NSK Not Fascists?" In *Primary
    Documents: A Sourcebook for Eastern and Central European Art Since
    the 1950s.* Edited by Laura Hoptman and Tomas Pospiszyl. Cam-
    bridge, MA: MIT Press, 2002.

Zhuk, Sergei. "Antipunk Campaigns, Antifascist Hysteria, and Hu-
    man Rights Problems, 1982–1984." Chap. 14 in *Rock and Roll in The
    Rocket City: The West, Identity, and Ideology in Soviet Dnipropetrovsk,
    1960–1985,* 265–79. Washington, DC: Woodrow Wilson Center
    Press, 2010.

Zülch, Tilman. "Stop the Propaganda for War Criminal Karadzic on the
    Munich Concert Stage!" Press release, January 24, 2009. http://www
    .gfbv.de/pressemit.php?id=1727&stayInsideTree=1&backlink=land
    .php?id=232&PHPSESSID=2f1dedafc4f649878d7fcef0c447395.

Playlist

Franz Nicolay, "This Is Not a Pipe"
Maloi, "Boys, You Gotta Slow Down"
Yanka Dyagileva, "Prodano"
Grazhdanskaya Oborona, "Все идет по плану" (Everything Is Going According to Plan)
Alexander Bashlachev, "Вемя колокольчиков" (The Time of Little Bells)
Niggers, "Ugly Russians"
The Wild Rover, "Russian Tragedy"
Namjilyn Norovbanzad, "Seruun Saihan Hangai"
Morning Glory, "Gang Control"
Koralli "феномен (Live at ArtPole 2011)"
Rail Yard Ghosts, "Shoplift from Tesco"
Mykola Ilyuk & Hutsuly Band, "Hutsulka"
The Hutsuls, "Paranoid"
Dakh Daughters, "Rozy/Donbass"
DakhaBrakha, "Vesna"
Sasha Boole & Zydeco Fam, "від і до" (Back & Forth)
Phooey, "Getting Better"
Ai Laika, "Whatever For"
Andrey Makarevich, "My Country Has Gone Crazy"

Itinerary

May 2012

May 21—Klub Place, Rijeka, Croatia

May 23—Izlog Ideja, Bačka Topola, Serbia

May 24—Youth Centre CK13, Novi Sad, Serbia

May 25—Tisza Virág Büfé, Szentes, Hungary

May 26—Rongy Kocsma, Szeged, Hungary

May 27—Acoustic Punk Picnic (afternoon show), Veszprém, Hungary

May 27—Szabad az Á (evening show), Budapest, Hungary

May 29—Meskalina, Poznan, Poland

May 30—Owoce i Warzywa, Łódź, Poland

June 2012

June 2—Malaya Opera, Kyiv, Ukraine

June 3—Kvartira Art Center, Dnipropetrovs'k, Ukraine

June 5—Gung'ю'6ass Bar, Donetsk, Ukraine

June 6—Nemata Perets Kolbasa Pub, Rostov-on-Don, Russia

June 8—Illusion Cultural Center, Voronezh, Russia

June 15—Copen Bar, Saint Petersburg, Russia

June 16—Big English Lunch, Moscow, Russia
June 20—Zdes, Samara, Russia
June 21—Vmeste Bar, Orenburg, Russia
June 22—Jimi Bar, Ufa, Russia
June 23—Custom House, Perm, Russia
June 24—New Bar, Ekaterinburg, Russia
June 26—Comedy Pub "Konets Frunze," Tomsk, Russia
June 27—Tass Bar, Baranaul, Russia
June 29—Abazhur Cafe, Krasnoyarsk, Russia

July 2012

July 1—Chicago Jazz Club, Irkutsk, Russia
July 2—Nikita's Guesthouse, Olkhon Island, Russia
July 13—Bojangles, Ulaanbaatar, Mongolia

March 2013

March 25—CK13, Novi Sad, Serbia
March 26—Tunel, Rijeka, Croatia
March 27—AKC Metelkova, Ljubljana, Slovenia
March 28—Klub Attack, Zagreb, Croatia
March 29—Inex Film, Belgrade, Serbia
March 30—Patent 46 Club, Budapest, Hungary
March 31—Gambrinus Pub, Cluj-Napoca, Romania

April 2013

April 1—Club Noir, Szeged, Hungary
April 3—Beriozka Bar, Plovdiv, Bulgaria
April 4—Studio Sounds Like, Sofia, Bulgaria
April 5—Elias Canetti Center, Ruse, Bulgaria
April 6—Atelier DIY, Timişoara, Romania

July 2014

    July 17—Maxwell Pub, Kalush, Ukraine
    July 22—Kanapa, Chernivtsi, Ukraine
    July 23—Medelin, L'viv, Ukraine
    July 25—Stare Misto, Bila Tserkva, Ukraine
    July 26—Lumiere Bar, Zhytomir, Ukraine
    July 27—Petrovskaya 34, Kyiv, Ukraine

Franz Nicolay is a musician who lives in New York. In addition to records under his own name, he was a member of the bands the Hold Steady, the World/Inferno Friendship Society, and Guignol; has performed and recorded with many more acts; and was a co-founder of the new-music collective Anti-Social Music. www.franznicolay.com